Erratum

The Southall Rail Accident Inquiry Report ISBN 0 7176 1757 2

Annex 09   Passengers & Staff believed to have sustained injury as a result of the accident

Include '**Stuttard, Janis, Mrs**   **Coach H**'

Delete ' **Stothart, Chloe Helen, Miss**   **Coach C**'

MISC 210

HSC
Health & Safety
Commission

The Southall Rail Accident Inquiry Report

Professor John Uff QC FREng

HSE BOOKS

LIST OF CONTENTS

Inquiry into Southall Railway Accident

Preface

Glossary

Report Summary

INQUIRY INTO SOUTHALL RAILWAY ACCIDENT

PREFACE

THIS Report follows an Inquiry held between September and December 1999 into the cause of a major rail accident which occurred on 19 September 1997 at Southall, 9 miles west of Paddington. The trains involved were the Great Western Trains (GWT) 10:32 Swansea to Paddington High Speed Train and a freight train operated by English Welsh and Scottish Railway (EWS), which was crossing the Up Main line to enter Southall Yard. Seven people died as a result of the accident and a further 139 people were injured, some severely. The Inquiry was set up within hours and directed to sit in public. The terms of reference are as follows :

The purpose of the Inquiry is to determine why the accident happened, and in particular to ascertain the cause or causes, to identify any lessons which have relevance for those with responsibilities for securing railway safety and to make recommendations.

The Inquiry proceedings began in December 1997 with a formal opening in February 1998. The driver was charged with manslaughter in April 1998, but no further progress could be made by the Inquiry pending decisions on criminal charges being considered against GWT. This was not resolved until December 1998 when manslaughter charges and charges under the Health and Safety at Work Act 1974 were brought against the driver and against the operating company. Criminal proceedings took their course and were not finally resolved until July 1999. The Inquiry proceedings then commenced at the earliest possible date. During the proceedings, a further tragic accident occurred at Ladbroke Grove which has led to the setting up of further Inquiries and to a review of the issues to be dealt with in the present Inquiry.

The Southall collision was the first major accident to occur within the British rail network since privatisation of the railway industry, which formally started with the transfer of the railway infrastructure to Railtrack on 1 April 1994. The public sale of Railtrack and letting of operating franchises followed. GWT had been set up as a separate operating division before privatisation. The company acquired its franchise on 1 February 1996 and had therefore been operating independently for some 19 months only, when the accident occurred. It would be wrong to see the Inquiry and this Report as an inquiry into privatisation. Nevertheless, the new structure of the industry has inevitably affected the events under consideration. At the same time it will be seen that the new industry is still heavily influenced by procedures and structures inherited from British Rail. It should be emphasised that the objective of this Report is to set down the facts and to draw appropriate conclusions in accordance with the Terms of Reference set by the Health and Safety Commission.

A large proportion of those who gave evidence at the Inquiry were railwaymen and women, all experts in their respective fields. Most of this Report deals with technical issues of varying complexity. While the Recommendations contained at the end of this Report are addressed to the railway industry, the Report itself is intended to be read by the travelling public who are entitled, through this Inquiry, to know how the railway operated and precisely what went wrong so as to cause such a tragic accident. The Inquiry heard witnesses and representations on behalf of a large number of parties including passenger groups and representatives, Trades Unions, rail operators, a rolling stock leasing company, an infrastructure maintenance company and Railtrack. Also represented were the emergency services including ambulance, fire and police services, and the Health and Safety Executive which includes HM Railway Inspectorate. A full list of parties and their representatives is at Annex 1. A full list of witnesses, including those whose statements were read to the Inquiry, is included at Annex 2. A list of terms and abbreviations follows this Preface.

I extend my gratitude to the skilled and experienced Inquiry team with which I was privileged to work. In order of their appointment, David Brewer took on the role of Inquiry Secretariat before my own appointment and has organised the efficient running of every aspect of the Inquiry throughout, including masterminding an information database which has been appreciated by all the parties who have appeared at the Inquiry. Major Anthony King OBE, himself a highly experienced Inspector of Railways and Chairman of many Inquiries, was appointed Technical Assessor. His tactful guidance on railway issues throughout the Inquiry has been invaluable. Counsel to the Inquiry was Ian Burnett QC, who appeared with Richard Wilkinson. Their capacity for mastering the huge volumes of documents generated by the Inquiry proved to be as prodigious as the task and their contribution has been appreciated by all. Last to be appointed to the team was Laurance O'Dea, Treasury Solicitor, who took on the task of collating the written evidence and organising the attendance of 107 witnesses who were heard in person, many of whom appeared on several different occasions. His success is measured by the fact that the Inquiry managed to achieve all of its timetable objectives, despite the intervention of the Ladbroke Grove crash. A list of Inquiry personnel is at Annex 3.

Finally, appreciation is due to David Brewer and to my secretary, Dorothy Dixson for producing the Report.

Keating Chambers
10 Essex Street
Outer Temple   John Uff QC FREng
London WC2R 3AA   31 January 2000

Glossary of Terms

Abbreviation/Term	Definition
ACEC	Suppliers of ATP equipment
AEA Technology	Technical Consultants
ALARP	As Low As Reasonably Practicable
Amey Rail	Maintenance contractors
ARS	Automatic Route Setting
ATC	Angel Train Contracts
ATOC	Association of Train Operating Companies
ATP	Automatic Train Protection
Audit	Procedural Check e.g. on Maintenance or Safety Provisions
AWS	Automatic Warning System
AWS test box	Equipment used to test AWS
BR	British Rail
BRB	British Rail Board
BRIMS	British Rail Incident Monitoring System
BTP	British Transport Police
CBA	Cost Benefit Analysis
Country end	Leading Power car on leaving Paddington
CPS	Crown Prosecution Service
CIRAS	Confidential Incident Reporting and Analysis System
CRUCC	Central Rail User's Consultative Committee
DRI	Driver Restructuring Initiative
Diagram	Driver's route card
DM	Driver Manager
DNV Technica	Technical Consultants
DOO	Driver Only Operation
DRA	Driver Reminder Appliance
DSM	Driver Standards Manager
DSD	Driver Safety Device
DVD	Driver Vigilance Device
EQE	Technical Consultants
EROS	Emergency Restriction of Speed
EWS	English Welsh and Scottish
FRAME	Fault Reporting And Monitoring of Equipment Computer System
Group Standard	Mandatory documents defining minimum requirements to ensure system safety and safe interworking on Railtrack's infrastructure.
GWR	Great Western Railway
GWT	Great Western Train Company
HEX	Heathrow Express
HMRI	Her Majesty's Railway Inspectorate
HSC	Health and Safety Commission
HSE	Health and Safety Executive
HST	High Speed Train
IECC	Integrated Electronic Control Centre

ISO	International Standards Organisation
Mark I	Older Type Rolling Stock
Mark III	Post 1974 Rolling Stock (in use at Southall)
London End	Leading Power Car on train entering Paddington
LMS	London Midland and Scottish Railway
LRM	Layout Risk Method
NRS	AWS maintenance contractors
OHL	Overhead Line
OPRAF	Office Of Passenger Rail Franchising
OOC	Old Oak Common maintenance depot
OTDR	On Train Data Recorders
POIS	Passenger Operations Information System
Railway Group	Group comprising Railtrack and duty holders of Railway Safety Cases accepted by Railtrack
Rail Regulator	Individual appointed to enforce Railway Group Standards and the Track Access Conditions.
R/A	Right Away system
RII	Rail Industry Inquiry
Right Side	Failure to a safe condition
RIO	Rail Incident Officer
ROSCO	Rolling Stock Company
RSC	Railway Safety Case
RT	Railtrack
S&SD	Safety and Standards Directorate (Railtrack)
S&T	Signalling and Telegraph Communications
Safety Case	Formal statement of competence
SAP	Safety Assessment Panel
Set Number	Train identified e.g. for maintenance exam
SN	Slough New signal number
SPAD	Signal Passed At Danger
SPADRAM	SPAD Reduction and Mitigation
SPT	Signal Post Telephone
SSI	Solid State Interlocking
SSR	Supervised Service Running
STP	Short Term Planning (Freight)
Track Access Conditions	Agreement for track use between RT and operator
TCI	ATP Project Management
TOC	Train Operating Company
TOPS	Total Operating Processing Systems
TPSG	Train Protection Steering Group
UMG	User Management Group
USSR	Unsupervised Service Running
VDU	Visual Display Unit
VSTP	Very Short Term Planning (Freight)
Wrong Side	Failure to an unsafe condition
WSA	WS Atkins Rail

1. A rail collision occurred at about 13:15 on 19 September 1997 at Southall East Junction, West London, between the 10:32 Swansea to Paddington HST operated by GWT and a freight train operated by EWS. The collision resulted in the   Para 1.10 death of seven passengers on the HST and many injuries.   Para 2.1 Extensive damage was caused to the power car and leading coaches of the HST and to the trailing freight wagons, with further damage being caused also to the track and to Overhead Line Equipment. Police, fire and ambulance   Para 1.2 services attended the site in accordance with the Major Incident Procedure. The accident site was taken into the   Para 2.7 control of BTP who regulated the following search and investigation operations. Technical investigations were   Para 2.9 subsequently carried out by HMRI, AEA Technology, Amey Railways and W S Atkins, under the control of BTP.   Para 2.18

2. At the time of the crash the Junction was protected by 3 signals, SN254 at red, SN270 at yellow and SN280 at double yellow. No relevant fault was found to exist in the track or in   Para 3.2 the signals leading up to the crash site, which were all adequately visible. The EWS freight train was proceeding   Para 3.12 across the Up and Down Main lines under the control of signals as the HST approached. The HST driver, Larry Harrison failed to heed either of the warning signals SN280 or 270. He braked on seeing signal SN254 at red, but the trains were still travelling at a relative speed in excess of 80mph when the collision occurred. The freight locomotive   Para 1.10 was not involved in the crash. The HST driver survived with

minor injuries.

3. The decision to route the freight train across the Up and Down main lines was taken by Signaller Forde at the Slough IECC. The decision was in accordance with current **Para 4.5** regulation rules. Driver Harrison had taken over the train at Cardiff. He was working within regulated working hours and had not driven for an excessive period at the time of the crash. The HST had travelled from Swansea with the AWS **Para 5.9** isolated. A fault with the AWS in the London-end power car had been reported on 18 September, but testing at the OOC Maintenance Depot overnight failed to reveal any fault and the train was passed for service. The AWS failed again at **Para 6.11** Paddington Station at 06:00 on 19 September 1997 where it was isolated by the driver, James Tunnock.

4. Driver Tunnock reported the problem both to the Operations Supervisor at Paddington and, by telephone, to GWT Control at Swindon. He did not, as the Rules required, report to the Signalman and Railtrack were unaware of the failure. **Para 6.16** Swindon Control overlooked or lost both this message and a further one sent by Driver Tunnock from Swansea. Fitters **Para 6.18** from the GWT Landore Depot attended the train at Swansea but did not attempt to repair the AWS. GWT took no action to withdraw the train from service. They could have turned **Para 6.20** the train so that the leading power car had an operational AWS, but failed to do so. **Para 6.24**

5. In addition, train 1A47 was rostered to run with ATP. The equipment, both at trackside and in the London-end power car was fully operational, but was not switched on because

neither Drivers Harrison nor Tunnock were currently qualified to drive with ATP and the operating rules did not allow ATP to be switched on in the course of a journey.   Para 6.27

6.   The primary cause of the accident was Driver Harrison's failure to respond to the two warning signals. Other causes of the accident were the failure of GWT's maintenance system to identify and repair the AWS fault, the failure of GWT to react to isolation of the AWS, the failure of Railtrack to put in place rules to prevent normal running of an HST with AWS isolated and the failure of GWT to manage the ATP Pilot Scheme such that the ATP equipment was switched on.   Para 7.19

7.   A Rail Industry Inquiry (RII) was set up within days of the accident and heard evidence in private over four days. A Report was produced on 20 March 1998 containing 16 Recommendations. During the period leading up to the start   Para 9.8 of the Public Inquiry, Railtrack and GWT took steps in accordance with the RII's Recommendations. In particular, Railtrack have revised the Rules governing AWS isolation but the revised rules do not mandate a withdrawal from service. Each TOC currently has a separate contingency plan covering AWS isolation.   Para 9.17

8.   The Public Inquiry set up after the accident by the HSC was delayed for two years by criminal proceedings brought against Larry Harrison and GWT. Hearings of the Public   Para 8.10 Inquiry finally took place between 20 September and 25 November 1999 with closing submissions on 20 December 1999. On 5 October 1999 a further major collision occurred

at Ladbroke Grove, London W11. As a result of setting up Para 10.1
further inquiries into railway issues, it was decided that the
present Inquiry would not consider wider questions of rail
safety systems nor general questions of safety procedure. Para 10.5

9. This Report considers wider questions of crashworthiness of
rail vehicles and means of escape in the event of accidents; Chapter 11
use of AWS equipment and procedures for its isolation; and Chapter 12
the history of the Great Western ATP Pilot Scheme up to the
date of the Southall crash and further developments
following the crash leading to full implementation of ATP
during 1999. Wider rail safety issues considered include Chapter 13
audits carried out on GWT, the general approach to safety
issues, and data collection by on-train data recorders, and the
Confidential Incident Reporting and Analysis System
(CIRAS). Chapter 14

10. It is concluded that Rules should mandate withdrawal from
service on the isolation of the AWS unless other adequate
protection is available. Since ATP is now virtually in full Para 15.11
operation, it is recommended that the system should be
retained on GWT services until replaced by an equally
effective train protection system. Recommendations are Para 15.14
made for the introduction of data recorders and the use of
CIRAS, for the review of issues of crashworthiness in Para 15.15
passenger vehicles, and for review of risk assessment Para 15.16
procedures. Audit procedures are recommended for review
elsewhere.

11. It is recommended that technical accident investigation
should in future be directed by HMRI with the ability to Para 15.23

require the assistance of outside experts; and that Rail
Industry Inquiry procedures should be reviewed to ensure
that all necessary rail safety issues are the subject of rapid   Para 15.25
action.

12.   Lessons to be learned from the Southall accident are   Chapter 16
reviewed and the report concludes with 93 specific   Chapter 17
Recommendations.

CHAPTER 1

HOW THE ACCIDENT HAPPENED

1.1   Since 1976 a high speed train (HST) service has operated between London
        Paddington and Swansea. In 1997 there were nearly 20 trains daily each way.
        The trains make a limited number of stops, generally at Reading, Swindon,
        Bristol Parkway, Newport, Cardiff Central and Bridgend. They operate at a
        maximum line speed of 125mph, taking around 3 hours to cover the 191 miles
        between London and Swansea. Since 1996, HSTs have been permitted to run
        at up to 125mph with a single driver. They operate with the familiar wedge-
        shaped power car at each end and can be driven from either cab.

The 10.32 Swansea to Paddington

1.2   On 19 September 1997, the 10:32 HST service left Swansea driven by James
        Tunnock. He had earlier driven the same train under headcode 1B08 as the
        07:00 Paddington to Swansea service. He now drove in reverse formation as
        1A47 to Cardiff Central, where he was to be relieved by Larry Harrison. The
        train comprised the two power cars and seven coaches, two first class at the
        London end (H and G) followed by a buffet coach (F) and four standard class
        coaches (E, C, B and A) at the rear. The lead power car travelling from
        Paddington was No. 43163. This formed the rear of the returning service
        1A47, where the lead power car was No. 43173. The leading and trailing
        power cars operate in conjunction, but are controlled exlusively from the front
        cab.

1.3   When the train had left Paddington at 07:00 driven by James Tunnock, he was
        aware of two faults. Who else knew of these faults became an issue of some
        substance in the Inquiry. The first fault, which was largely a matter of
        inconvenience, was that the driver/guard communication buzzer was not
        functioning correctly. In the rear London end power car, No. 43173, the

buzzer was sounding continuously, but in the lead power car, No. 43163, it was simply not operational. The result was that the guard could not, as is usual, give the driver two buzzes to signify that the train was ready to depart. Instead, the train had to proceed under the R/A (Right Away) system whereby platform staff either illuminate an indicator for the driver to depart or pass the guard's signal to the driver. This evidently came to the attention of staff on Reading station, the first stop, and a message was passed ahead so that all stations at which 1B08 (and subsequently 1A47) called were aware and could make the necessary arrangements to despatch the train.

AWS isolation

1.4   The second fault was more serious and had safety implications.   The Automatic Warning System (AWS) in power car 43173 was not operational. It had been "isolated" by Driver Tunnock at Paddington Station after he brought the set from the depot at Old Oak Common.   The AWS had operated normally during the short journey of 10 minutes from Old Oak Common. When he was in the station Driver Tunnock found that he could not cancel the AWS.   He therefore had to isolate the system in order to release the brakes. Driver Tunnock reported both faults to George Barnfield, the Operations Supervisor at Paddington.   Mr Barnfield's duties included passing drivers fit for duty, which he did both in respect of Driver Tunnock and a little later, Driver Harrison.   During the short time Driver Tunnock was in Mr Barnfield's office a phone call was made, the intention of which was to report the faults to the GWT Control office at Swindon. The result of this call is considered later.

1.5   AWS (which is described in more detail in Chapter 12) is a system, gradually introduced from about 1958 over the British Rail network, by which drivers are presented with an audible and visual warning in advance of every signal on the line being travelled.   In addition to equipment located in the power car, the track has a ramp containing magnets, located 183m (200 yards) in advance of

2

each signal. As the train passes over the ramp it receives a magnetic indication of the aspect of the signal, which activates warnings in the cab: for green aspect, a bell rings and a visual indicator registers black; any other signal aspect (whether a single or double yellow or a red) causes a horn to sound in the cab. An important part of the system is that the driver must acknowledge the horn, by pressing and releasing a reset button in the cab. This also has the effect of turning the visual indicator to a black and yellow "sunflower" pattern. The most significant part of the warning system is that a failure to acknowledge the horn results in the automatic application of the brakes.

1.6   The AWS in power car 43163, at the "country end", was working normally. Driver Tunnock thus had an indication at every signal passed between Paddington and Swansea. When the train was reversed at Swansea, Driver Tunnock left what was to become the rear power car on service 1A47 and drove the train back to Cardiff Central from power car 43173. While at Swansea station, fitters attended the train and succeeded in eliminating the buzzing by disconnecting the driver/guard communication device. They did not rectify the AWS fault in power car 43173. Driver Tunnock thus drove 1A47 back to Cardiff Central without an operational AWS. The train was still proceeding under the R/A system, as it had been since leaving Paddington. This was the state in which Driver Harrison took over the train. Driver Tunnock was concerned to impress on the driver who relieved him the non-availability of AWS. The fault repair book, which should be available in the cab of each power car, was full. Driver Tunnock therefore wrote out a note which he fixed prominently on the dashboard stating:

AWS ISOLATED REPAIR BOOK FULL

A facsimile of this note is at Annex 4.

1.7   Driver Harrison had not previously driven an HST without AWS operating. As considered in more detail later, little attention had been given to the consequences of driving with AWS isolated and neither Driver Harrison nor any other GWT driver had received any training or instruction on how to drive an HST without AWS. In 1997 there were different views within the railway industry as to whether AWS was merely an aid to driving, which should depend on the skill of the driver himself, or whether it should be regarded as an essential safety device. This issue is considered later. There is no doubt that both Drivers Tunnock and Harrison were able to drive without AWS and it is to be noted that both power cars had the Drivers' Safety Device (DSD), which required the foot pedal to be kept depressed and to operate as the "deadman's" pedal. The pedal was also fitted with the Driver's Vigilance Device (DVD). This emits a warbling sound approximately every minute, which has to be cancelled by the driver releasing and depressing the pedal within three seconds, in default of which there would be a brake application. The DVD was working in both power cars.

1.8   Driver Tunnock had no difficulty over the 50 minute journey via Bridgend to Cardiff Central. Driver Harrison similarly experienced no difficulty in taking the train on through Newport and Bristol Parkway. At Swindon, Tim Mayo got into the cab. He was an employee of Railtrack engaged in a signal sighting exercise. Mr Mayo had no driving experience and took cab rides infrequently. He travelled in the cab to the next stop at Reading. Mr Mayo noticed the hand-written note and remarked on it to Driver Harrison who responded with a shrug or other non-committal reaction. Mr Mayo's clear recollection was that Driver Harrison behaved normally, did not appear to be under stress and drove the train in a normal manner. Mr Mayo also recalled that a little rain fell between Swindon and Reading.

The accident

1.9   After leaving Reading on the Up Main line, 1A47 encountered a number of
       Emergency Speed Restrictions (ESR) of 100mph which had been temporarily
       imposed on account of the condition of the track.   Mr Harrison had been
       issued with a late notice showing the ESRs. There is no suggestion that these
       speed limits were exceeded.   After emerging from the last ESR West of
       Slough, Driver Harrison powered the train up to its designated line speed of
       125mph. The approach to Southall is initially on a rising gradient of 1 in 1640
       from West Drayton. Measurements along the Great West line run west from
       Paddington and are quoted here in miles with smaller distances in metres. The
       line becomes level from 10.71 miles, after which there is a falling gradient of
       1 in 1320 from 10.12 miles. This section of the track is on a left hand curve of
       varying radius.   The track straightens shortly after signal SN270.   Southall
       East Junction is located nominally at 8.75 miles, between Southall Station and
       Hanwell. The final approach to Southall on the Up Main line passes four
       signals, numbers SN298 at 11.38 miles, SN280 at 10.75 miles (1018m
       beyond), SN270 at 10.09 miles (1056m beyond) and finally, SN254 at 9.14
       miles (1530m beyond that) . This final signal was located just before the road
       bridge at Southall Station some 410 metres from the first point of contact,
       which was towards the western end of the crossing.   The line and signals are
       shown in sketch form in Annex 5.

1.10   As 1A47 approached, signal SN298 was at green but SN280 was set at double
       yellow and SN270 at single yellow, warning that the next signal SN254 was at
       red. Driver Harrison should have prepared to slow the train at signal SN280
       so that after passing SN270 he would be able to stop at SN254. He did not
       react when approaching and passing signal SN280, nor when approaching and
       passing SN270.   Driver Harrison saw SN254 at red, probably at the first
       moment that it came into view. At about the same time he saw directly ahead
       of him 6V17, a freight train operated by English, Welsh and Scottish Railway

(EWS) which was then coming from London on the Down Relief line and crossing Southall East Junction on its way into Southall Yard, south of the main lines. The freight train consisted of a class 59 diesel electric locomotive No. 59101 driven by Alan Bricker, together with twenty empty 8-wheeled bogie hopper wagons, used for carrying aggregate. When 1A47 came into sight, locomotive 59101 was already across the Up Main and the 20 hopper wagons were strung out across and immediately in front of Driver Harrison. A collision was inevitable. Calculations have been made as to the speed and distances involved. These depend on a number of assumptions and cannot be known with precision. For the Inquiry it was agreed between experts representing the parties that at the time of the first contact, which was 410m beyond signal SN254, the speed of the HST was probably in the range 60-80 mph. It was similarly agreed that the freight train was travelling between 21 and 25 mph in the opposite direction. The relative speed of the two trains was therefore the sum, which was in excess of 80 and probably in excess of 90 mph. These calculations were based on the times of occupation of the track circuits, which indicated that that the brake had been applied by Driver Harrison between 1100 and 1250m from signal SN254. Power car 43173 first came into glancing contact with the side of the seventh hopper wagon and then struck the eighth and successive wagons behind locomotive 59101. The collision occurred at 13:15, some 5 minutes before the scheduled time of arrival at Paddington.

1.11 The accident quickly came to the attention of Railtrack staff in the new Integrated Electronic Control Centre (IECC) at Slough known as Slough New (SN) signal box. Signaller Forde was using Automatic Route Setting (ARS) equipment to process the hundreds of trains passing daily along the lines controlled from Slough. The route for train 6V17 to cross from the Down Relief line to Southall Yard had been set manually. This had the effect of preventing any later route setting by the ARS and of setting all signals and points to permit the movement. Signal SN254 was therefore set to red and SN270 and 280 to single and double yellow respectively. As a matter of course, he observed the movement of some twelve trains within the area immediately under his control. Signaller Forde could see the movement of the trains, and estimate roughly their speed by the rate at which each train was recorded as occupying the track circuits as shown on the VDU within the signal box. Signaller Forde saw that 1A47 had not, as it should have done, slowed at signal SN280 nor, much more alarmingly, at signal SN270. Signal SN254 was set at red and Signaller Forde quickly became aware that the track circuits beyond had been occupied by 1A47 and that a collision was inevitable. Within seconds, the VDU registered other track circuits on both the Down Relief line and the Down Main as "occupied". They had been short-circuited by metallic objects across the lines or cables being cut, indicative of a crash. Signalman Forde reacted immediately as he was trained to do. He could have pressed an emergency button which would, within about 15 seconds, have returned all signals to red to prevent the possibility of further collisions. He decided instead that the job could be done more quickly by setting individual signals to red which also gave some control over where trains were stopped. This he did, bringing all trains in the vicinity of Southall to a halt.

1.12 Two direct witnesses to the crash were the drivers of the freight train and of the HST. Driver Bricker in 6V17 observed 1A47 approaching on the Up Main, expecting it to slow and stop. He became alarmed by its speed and saw dust coming from the wheels indicating hard braking. It quickly became apparent to him that there was going to be a collision. In a natural but hopeless attempt to avoid it, Driver Bricker tried to accelerate 6V17 out of the path of the HST, but to no avail. Power car 43173 initially made scraping contact with the trailing hopper wagons which quickly began to derail as the two trains passed, still at high speed. The derailment of the wagons rapidly severed the brake pipe, causing the hopper wagons to come to a halt as the brakes on the freight train were automatically applied. The momentum of the HST carried both the power car and the leading coaches forward. As they slowed, the leading coaches became separated and suffered different fates as they collided with the freight wagons and with each other, eventually coming to rest in the position shown in Annex 6. The damage suffered by power car 43173 consisted of impact and tearing damage to the right side of the cab and general damage to the body of the unit. The power car remained substantially upright, although derailed. Coach H, the first coach, became entirely detached, fell onto its left side and slid along the ballast, finally coming to rest after colliding with one of the overhead line supporting stanchions. Coach G also became detached but in the course of its rapid deceleration came into contact with the freight hoppers, lost a substantial part of the right side of the coach body and then suffered gross structural distortion. A reconstruction of the accident suggests that derailed hopper wagon No. 19891 collided with an overhead line stanchion at speed, rose upwards as the stanchion bent over and that the leading end of coach G was wedged under the wagon. The rear of coach G was almost immediately struck by the following coach F and forced into the "U" shape in which it finally came to rest. Derailed Coach F continued forward, finally colliding with hopper wagon No. 19819. It came to rest with some penetration damage but remained substantially upright. Coaches E and C were derailed but remained upright. Coaches B and A remained on the rails. An agreed account of the probable course of the accident, which is of relevance to the issues of crashworthiness (see Chapter 11), is contained in Annex 6. Photographs of the wreckage are contained in Annex 7. The shock of the collision was transmitted throughout the whole train such that Mr Abdul Khanghauri, the Senior Conductor in the guard's compartment of coach A was thrown about and fell to the floor, momentarily stunned by the force of the crash. Everyone on the train felt the terrible force of the impact.

Driver Harrison

1.13   The other direct witness to the crash was Driver Harrison. As related above, his driving had been independently observed as far as Reading. He had encountered signals with various aspects on the journey to Reading and had had no difficulty in complying with them. Driver Harrison and other drivers who gave evidence to the Inquiry recognised the importance of keeping a proper lookout, independently of the audible and visual warnings normally given by the AWS system. Despite this, Driver Harrison was to pass through two warning signals without reacting. In his oral evidence to the Inquiry, Driver Harrison was simply unable to account for his actions. The only recollections he could now call to mind were *"whizzing through Hayes"* after passing signal SN298 at green. He then recalled some action involving his bag, which included putting away paperwork. This would have been a copy of his job diagram, a notice giving changes to track layouts etc, and the "late notice" sent out to drivers by fax notifying any ESRs. Driver Harrison must have had this documentation in front of him while driving. Some of it was subsequently found in the bag and returned to Driver Harrison, providing corroboration of his recollection. However, he estimated that putting this material into the bag would have occupied only five seconds or so.

1.14   Driver Harrison's next recollection, apart from putting material into his bag, was seeing signal SN254 ahead of him at danger (red). At this point the train was still rounding a left hand bend. As the tracks straightened ahead of him Driver Harrison saw the Class 59 locomotive "at a funny angle" and realised that it was crossing the Up Main. To his horror, Driver Harrison realised there was going to be a collision. The freight train was then about 1600m (1 mile) ahead, the HST was travelling at about 125mph and would need approximately 1.3 miles to stop under full braking. Driver Harrison said in various statements that his first reaction was that the signal had "gone back" on him, i.e. that the signalman had changed the signal aspect. There is some corroboration for this recollection also, in that Driver Harrison's oral evidence was that he applied the full service brake *not* the emergency brake. Had Driver Harrison realised that he had gone through two earlier warning signals he must surely have applied the emergency brake. Evidence of the state of the cab after the accident suggested that the emergency brake had in fact been applied but this could have been a subsequent reaction. The difference between the two modes of application is not great but the full service brake application is marginally less abrupt. The emergency brake would have reached full braking force slightly earlier by perhaps one or two tenths of a second. Once the brake is fully applied, the braking force is the same, and the questions whether and when the emergency brake was applied would not have affected the course of the accident in any material degree.

1.15 When Driver Harrison realised that a collision was imminent and there was nothing further he could do, he left the driving seat and went back through the bulkhead door into a narrow passage to the left of the engine (facing the direction of travel) where he remained during the collision. Fortunately, the substantial damage to the power car occurred on the other side and the vehicle remained upright. Apart from cuts and bruises, Driver Harrison was able to emerge, severely shaken and shocked, but otherwise substantially uninjured.

1.16 Much expert evidence and speculation has been offered on precisely what occurred during the period when Driver Harrison was approaching and passing signals SN280 and SN270. He stated in oral evidence that he saw signal SN254 at danger not when he looked up but when it first came into view. Driver Harrison did not say that he was unable to see either of the signals SN280 or 270 despite keeping a lookout. It was, however, suggested on his behalf that these signals were not adequately visible. Particularly, signal

SN270 was misaligned and both were located above the optimum recommended height. These issues are considered in detail in Chapter 3 where it is concluded that both signals were adequately visible. Significantly, no complaint has ever been received about visibility of these signals from any of the drivers who regularly pass through them. It was further suggested that sunlight might have interfered with the driver's vision. Some corroboration for this was provided by the sun visor in the cab being found in the "down" position after the crash. Expert evidence as to weather conditions was given by Mike Walley of the Meteorological Office, Bracknell. This established that there was general cloud cover over the area in the middle of the day on 19 September 1997 and no possibility of sun which would, in any event, have been coming from the right, just behind a line perpendicular to the direction of travel. There was, therefore, no reason why signals SN280 and 270 would not have been easily sighted and acted upon. Whether or not Driver Harrison was keeping a proper lookout, it is necessary to consider how he behaved at the critical time in more detail.

1.17   Simple calculation shows that at the line speed of 125mph the distance between signals SN280 and SN270 would be covered in just over 18 seconds. Driver Harrison must have been inattentive for the 7 seconds during which signal SN280 would have been in view and for a further period of about 10 seconds during which signal SN270 would have been in view. Were there two periods of inattention, separated by not more than about 8 seconds between the two signals, or was there one continuous period in which Driver Harrison was inattentive for at least 25 seconds (7 plus 18) and possibly more? Other calculations have shown that the period might have been as long as 40 or 45 seconds. The chance of two periods of inattention falling within the precise timing necessary to have missed both signals would seem to make this unlikely. Rail experts (Roy Bell and Peter Rayner) and a psychologist (Dr Deborah Lucas) considered it more likely that Driver Harrison had been separately inattentive before each signal, Mr Rayner on the basis that he did not think it possible for a driver to look away for as long as 25 seconds. Others considered it more likely that there was one single period of inattention.

1.18 As noted earlier, the DVD, which emits a warbling sound and requires the driver's foot pedal to be released and depressed approximately once a minute, was working. The DVD in power car 43173 was subsequently found to have a period of 55 seconds, and Driver Harrison must have been alert to react to the device. The period between the warnings is, however, not inconsistent with the longer period of inattention considered above. Driver Harrison might simply have dozed off between the successive warnings from the DVD, long enough to have missed the two signals and have looked up only in time to see signal SN254 at red when it came into sight.

The driver's bag

1.19 An alternative possibility must also be considered, as to which the evidence remains sparse. Its importance is such, however, that this report would be incomplete without considering it. The possibility was explored by British Transport Police (BTP) that Driver Harrison might have been misusing the train controls so as to allow him to break off from normal vigilance. The suggestion is centred on Driver Harrison's bag. He chose to use a sports type holdall in lieu of the smaller railway issue. The driver's bag is needed to carry particular items of equipment including a Bardic lamp, various items of refreshment, a high-visibility vest for use on the track, and various keys and security devices for operating the train controls, carriage doors, etc. Driver Harrison's bag was found to contain two cans of fizzy drink and a railway issue metal vacuum flask, together with a jar of tea bags. His preference was for decaffeinated tea. Why, then, did the bag also contain soft drinks? Driver Harrison explained that he occasionally preferred this when he wanted a long drink. The explanation seems plausible enough. Those investigating the incident considered, however, that the possibility existed that he had deliberately weighted his bag in order to be able to use it to hold down the DSD pedal, which has to be kept depressed.

1.20   The proposition was, thus, that Driver Harrison might have used his bag to depress the pedal leaving him around 55 seconds between pulses of the DVD, during which he could stand up, stretch and carry out other activities inconsistent with keeping a proper lookout. The bag, as recovered from Driver Harrison by the police was not, in fact, heavy enough to depress the pedal, nor even to hold it down. It was confirmed, however, that the bag could have been used at least to hold the pedal down after being depressed manually if it had contained some additional weight. If this is the case, then what happened to the additional weight?

1.21   The circumstances in which the bag was recovered were the subject of a considerable amount of evidence. Shortly after the collision Driver Harrison had emerged from the engine compartment and left the train taking with him a red flag and his job diagram. His first duty was to report the collision to the signal box, and he would need to be sure of the Train Number (he had driven more than one train that day). After one unsuccessful attempt to call the Slough IECC from signal No. SN251, he made a second call, this time successfully, at about the time that PC Vipas first appeared on the scene. PC Vipas took over the end of the call. A transcript of the call is at Annex 8. PC Vipas subsequently noted down Driver Harrison's statement concerning putting things away in his bag. Perhaps this triggered Driver Harrison's memory, because he then became anxious to recover his bag, such that PC Vipas thought that Driver Harrison would have to be restrained. Instead, he was allowed to go back to the power car to retrieve his bag. There was conflicting evidence about the exact position of the bag in the cab. However, this was partly resolved by the clear recollection of PC Vipas that Driver

Harrison, without looking in, went straight to the right hand side of the cab, which had been partly demolished by the collision, and "reached in" to pick up the bag. Driver Harrison seemed to know where the bag was. Was it resting on the driver's pedal?

The feet-up allegation

1.22 These suggestions would seem incredible given the serious and responsible way in which Driver Harrison conducted himself at the Inquiry. His demeanour as a witness contrasted sharply, however, with contemporary descriptions by several witnesses who said that they saw him drive 1A47 at very slow speed into Bristol Parkway with both feet up on the front console and subsequently into Swindon Station with one foot up. There was much speculation as to what witnesses meant by this and whether one or both feet were substantially away from the floor while the train was still in motion at Bristol. Driver Harrison initially denied that he had driven the train in this manner, but subseqently accepted he might have had one foot up. GWT also accepted that a driver might have one foot up without objection. In my view, the recollection of those on the station was so consistent and compelling that, given other significant events that Driver Harrison could not now remember, there is no ground to reject this evidence. Furthermore, there was technical evidence to the effect that the train could coast at very slow speed (1-3 mph) without the driver's pedal needing to be depressed, which could be the explanation for what was observed at Bristol Parkway.

1.23 In addition to their recollection of Driver Harrison having his feet up, witnesses were alarmed at his apparently casual manner. It was impressed on me that Driver Harrison had an excellent record and was rated in the lowest category of SPAD risk. He did, however, have two blemishes on his record going back to the 1970s, each relating to signals passed at danger, although these both involved relatively low speed travel. More significant, an event occurred in December 1996 which was not formally reported as a driving offence, but a record was made. On this occasion, Driver Harrison is recorded as having started a train without the proper signal from the guard shortly after an incident when Driver Harrison's bag was misplaced. He was said to be flustered. Did the bag hold more significance than its contents might suggest? At least, this event showed that criticism of Driver Harrison's conduct should not be lightly disregarded.

Human behaviour evidence

1.24   On behalf of ASLEF and Larry Harrison, two experts, originally part of the defence team in the criminal proceedings, were called to give evidence about the likely behaviour of a driver in the situation that existed immediately before the collision. Professor John Groeger, a Chartered Psychologist, expressed the view that, given many years of reliance on warnings from the AWS, the likelihood of a driver looking away at inappropriate times, when driving without AWS, was very high. Professor Neville Moray, a Human Factors Consultant, was also of the opinion that, given the large number of visual tasks which drivers had, the absence of AWS inevitably increased the probability that the driver would, at sometime, fail to see a signal. Dr Deborah Lucas, Principal Psychologist at HSE and formerly with BR, stated that lowered alertness resulting from fatigue could lead to periods of inattention of 5 to 15 seconds referred to as "microsleeps". However, it did not appear that Driver Harrison was suffering from fatigue at the time. Professor Moray pointed out that fatigue was not a necessary condition of microsleeps, which could occur even in stimulating circumstances. Messrs Livingston and Porter, consultants to W S Atkins, commented on the evidence of Professors Groeger and Moray, concluding that it overestimated the degree to which drivers were reliant on AWS as a cue.

1.25   Having heard the witnesses' oral evidence I believe that it would be unsafe to apply behavioural theory in the absence of firm evidence as to the actual pattern of drivers' behaviour in the cab, which is substantially lacking. Recent developments, including data recorders and confidential information reporting (considered in Chapter 14) may begin to provide such evidence. The possibility of significant periods of inattention through involuntary "microsleep" is, however, very real and could account for the tragic events which occurred. It is not possible to conclude, on the evidence gathered, that Driver Harrison was deliberately misusing the train controls. The most likely explanation is that he was involuntarily inattentive either for two periods of 7 and 10 seconds or for one longer period, sufficient to pass signals SN280 and 270. It is possible that he was lulled into inattention between the regular pulses of the DVD and therefore forgetful of the mortal danger created by the absence of an effective AWS.

CHAPTER 2

THE EMERGENCY RESPONSE

2.1   There were some 214 people on the train. A number travelling towards the rear were unscathed and left the scene of the accident as soon as arrangements were made for evacuation. A total of 139 persons were injured in varying degrees of severity. Seven people died as a result of the accident. A list of those killed and seriously injured is contained in Annex 9. In coach G, which had suffered gross structural distortion, four people died in the collision: David Eustace, Marcus Olander, Anthony Petch and Gerard Traynor. All of the remaining ten passengers in coach G were severely injured including Peter Allen, who died in Charing Cross Hospital six days later from his injuries. The survivors in coach G included Derek Thompson, Alan Lockyear and Alan Napier who had been travelling with Gerard Traynor; and Mrs Janet Allen, who had been travelling with her husband.

The rescue operation

2.2   In coach H there were twelve passengers, including two who were killed: Clive Brain, who had travelled in coach H and Peter Kavanagh who had been in coach G but may have walked through just before the accident. All the survivors suffered injuries but five of these managed to extricate themselves from the wreckage. Mrs Anne Varney climbed out through a shattered window in what was now the roof of the coach as it lay on its side, and then managed to slither to the ground, helped by the first rescuers on the scene. Tim Banfield found that it was possible to exit through a shattered window in what had become the floor, where there was a gap between the lower part of the carriage and the ballast beneath. He helped Mrs Janice Stuttard and Dr Michael Hellier to escape in this way, as he did himself, followed by Dr John Boddy. They had been unable to reach the end of the coach as the sliding door (now operating vertically) was jammed shut.

2.3   Many passengers expressed concern that the fires which they could see burning might lead to further disaster (as was the case in the accident at Ladbroke Grove two years later). Fortunately, the fires did not spread and were extinguished relatively quickly when the Fire Brigade arrived. When the Emergency Services were able to assess the severity of the accident, it was initially thought that there were many more fatalities than was in fact the case. Some 16 persons remained injured and trapped in the wreckage. After the rescue operation, thirty persons in all were admitted to hospital. These included the survivors of coaches G and H, some of whom suffered severe injuries requiring long periods of medical treatment.

2.4   Many on the train remembered the crash being followed by eerie silence, broken only by the sound of the injured and expressions of reaction from those still within the coaches, many of whom were surprised to find themselves still alive. Some were on the edge of panic, feeling trapped and threatened by further disaster. But in coaches F and those further to the rear, which all remained substantially upright, a number of individuals made it their job to encourage a calm and orderly response so that the injured could be given assistance. In coach F, GWT staff located in the buffet area, some of whom were themselves injured, quickly organised help for passengers. Glynn Williams, Mary Shuttleworth, Nicholas Wilson and Marcia Patterson all deserve mention for their exemplary actions. Also in coach F Richard George, then Managing Director of GWT, played a valuable role in establishing calm. In coach C Richard Middleton, a director of Railtrack, who was also a passenger, helped to establish calm. Passengers remembered also the service given by Abdul Khanghauri, the conductor on the train, who made calming announcements and subsequently organised and assisted in the disembarkation of many passengers from the rear coach.

2.5   The first thing that many passengers noticed outside the train was Mr Khanghauri, who had alighted and taken it on himself to warn passengers of the danger posed by the overhead electric wires which had been brought down by the crash. At the same time, local residents appeared on the trackside, again warning passengers of the danger from the fallen wires. Many people remembered the care and kindness of the inhabitants of Southall, who came back to the scene to provide the injured and the rescued with much needed comfort. Blankets, tea and drinks were provided, together with help for those who had suddenly found themselves in such an appalling situation. A plan of the location of the crash site is contained in Annex 10.

2.6 Many people contacted the rescue services within minutes of the crash. They had already been contacted from the Slough IECC and within a short time the civil authorities were aware of the need for a major emergency response. First on the scene were PCs Vipas and Churchill who were travelling in a police car along Park Avenue shortly after the accident occurred. They reported back to Southall Police Station and then made their way onto the railway where they gave assistance, including dealing with Driver Harrison. PC Vipas participated in Driver Harrison's call to Slough IECC and then took down a statement. Driver Harrison was subsequently taken to Southall Police Station where further statements were given and tests organised for alcohol and drugs, which proved negative. Detective Inspector Connell of BTP then arrested Driver Harrison.

2.7 Within a short time the police and other emergency services had put into effect the Major Incident Procedure, well known to the emergency services. The procedure is contained in a manual, last revised in March 1997, and agreed between the London Fire Brigade, Metropolitan Police, London Ambulance Service, City of London Police and British Transport Police. The combined command structure was to be organised under three levels of authority known as Gold (strategy), Silver (co-ordination at site) and Bronze (individual functions as required). Each of the services in question rapidly organised appointments at each level and liaison between those at equivalent levels.

2.8 For the Metropolitan Police, Gold control was assumed by Superintendent Smythe at New Scotland Yard, while Chief Inspector Morris, acting Superintendent at Southall Police Station, went to the site to act as Silver

Control. There, he appointed Bronze commanders to deal with matters such as establishment of cordons and traffic control. A meeting point for emergency services was established at 81 Park Avenue, close to the site, through the public-spirited actions of the owners, Mr and Mrs Dawell. From this base, Chief Inspector Morris was able to liaise with Silver commanders from the fire and ambulance services, who each directed their own Bronze commanders at the scene. For the Fire Service, Station Commander Staynings had just returned to the Southall Fire Station and heard the crash. The Southall pumps were then attending another fire, so he went straight to the site himself and assumed Silver command. Pumps soon arrived, first from Ealing Station followed by those from Northholt, Heston, Hayes and then Southall.

2.9   Although the Metropolitan Police were first on the scene, the accident occurred within the jurisdiction of the British Transport Police. Chief Superintendent Edwards was the Area Commander for the London North Area. He arrived at the site at 14:30 and assumed the role of BTP Incident Commander, equivalent to Silver command. Detective Superintendent Satchwell was appointed as the BTP Senior Investigating Officer. He arrived at the site at 15:45 and took control of the inner cordon with Detective Inspector Morrissey as his deputy. The Metropolitan force retained control of other cordons in accordance with the Major Incident Procedure.

2.10   For the Ambulance Service, the first vehicle, which happened to be in the vicinity, arrived at the site at 13:24 and itself declared a major incident, activating the Ambulance Service Major Incident plan. An early decision was made to mobilise staff and instructors from the Paramedic Training Centre to assist at the site. Their presence offered additional benefits in the triage of patients and freed up ambulances for transporting patients to hospitals. Ten ambulances were initially mobilised, subsequently increased to 15, together with an Emergency Control Vehicle. Six doctors attended the site from where the injured were sent to West Middlesex, Central Middlesex, Hillingdon and Charing Cross hospitals. A helicopter ambulance was also mobilised which evacuated Mr Thompson to the Royal London Hospital. Dr Hellier, himself a

Consultant Gastroenterologist at the Prince of Wales Hospital, Swindon, spoke warmly of the skill of paramedic staff who had accurately investigated priority injuries. Mercifully, it transpired that major injuries were fewer than had initially been predicted. The medical services were well able to cope with those needing treatment. The rescue operation continued into the evening. There was some uncertainty as to exactly when the last body was removed from the wreckage. It was most probably at 10:30 p.m.

2.11 Commanders appointed by the emergency services changed throughout the day as circumstances and availability dictated. The system operated, as was intended, in a flexible manner. By general consent, the rescue operation was a notable success, aided as it was by local inhabitants. One of the few expressions of concern about the operation was that some passengers, in the course of their evacuation, were led past the bodies of crash victims. This will be considered in the recommendations to be made. One of the additional facilities which Chief Inspector Morris was able to establish was the use of the nearby Villiers High School where, by kind permission of the Headmistress (Ms Juliet Strang), victims were taken initially. Here they were given tea and other necessary comforts, largely by the pupils, whose care and concern for the victims is to be commended.

Rail industry response

2.12 The rail industry had their own emergency management procedures based on Group Standard GWP/P7/04 (revised October 1996). This involved the setting up of a similar command structure to that of the emergency services, with the equivalent of Silver Command, designated Rail Incident Officer (RIO), to be provided by Railtrack. They received very early notification of the incident through Slough IECC. Swindon Railtrack Control then made prompt contact with the Metropolitan Police and HMRI as well as informing the Area Production Manager and the Contract Management Team at Reading. Railtrack's interest in the infrastructure included securing and earthing the overhead electric conductors which had been brought down by the collision.

2.13 GWT, then located at the same control centre as Railtrack in Swindon, put into operation their own incident room, using procedures set out in their Major Incident Handbook. GWT were able to assemble the necessary emergency staff rapidly and the performance of the incident room in managing the huge disruption to services within the region resulting from the crash was noted as a considerable success. The procedures included arranging alternative routes via Waterloo for commuters who needed to reach Reading. Re-programming work continued during the three and a half days that the lines at Southall were out of action. It is reported that other TOCs have noted the success of GWT's incident room and procedures, which appear to have performed all that was required of them.

2.14 GWT's Accident Plan involved setting up rescue services for stranded passengers, particularly those from the crashed train who were physically able to continue travelling. For this purpose, GWT mobilised Mr Tim Buxton, a Business Group Manager, then at Paddington. He rapidly mobilised a team and set off to the site of the accident, maintaining contact with Swindon Control. Thames Trains were the "lead operator" for the relevant geographical area, but GWT's interest was obviously paramount and they arranged to take over responsibility. Mr Buxton arrived at the site and began to put in place arrangements for the transfer of passengers from Southall, as well as repatriation of other passengers stranded by the accident. His work included despatching GWT representatives to hospitals to make arrangements for those who were being discharged after treatment. These arrangements were not wholly successful. A number of passengers considered that the arrangements were insensitive, for example, putting crash victims back onto trains. Some passengers had uncomfortable and prolonged journeys which added to their distress, for which GWT were criticised. Some of this was well founded, but I do not discount the fact that Mr Buxton's team, and many others as well, were attempting to restore order where there was potential chaos and it would not be right to expect that this could be achieved without some mishap.

2.15   Railtrack's Site Emergency Procedures were contained in their own standard document   based on, but separate from, the Emergency Services Manual. Alan Kelleher (Mobile Operations Manager based at Hayes) together with Mark Gordon, and Mike Moodie (Area Operations Manager, Reading) were despatched to the Southall site, but were delayed due to congestion on the M4. Martin Twibill, Acting Signalling Manager, who was in Slough at the time of the accident was also directed to the site, arriving at 13:35.   He made arrangements for movement of the stranded trains. Alan Kelleher arrived at 13:49, supervised an emergency electrical isolation and made arrangements for earthing the overhead wires, which were still not known to be safe (although evacuation of passengers was then well under way).   Earthing was not finally completed until 15:08.   Mr Kelleher formally assumed the role of Rail Incident Officer (RIO).   Mr Moodie, who was senior to Mr Kelleher, did not arrive until about 14:45, having been delayed by an accident on the M4. He decided not to take over as RIO since Mr Kelleher appeared to be coping with the job in hand. It should be said that neither of them had experience of an accident on such a scale, but Mr Kelleher had at least one hour's experience to his credit. What then happened was characterised by BTP as a failure to perform effectively,   since neither Mr Kelleher nor Mr Moodie managed to attend a Silver Meeting organised at 3:00 p.m. at 81 Park Avenue, or a later meeting at a different venue. I do not believe that such criticism of Railtrack staff was justified.   They performed under the extremely difficult circumstances, being vastly outnumbered by the police and other emergency services.   What emerged was the need for a more structured procedure for liaison between Railtrack and the emergency services and also the need for the RIO to act in a more assertive manner.   This is the subject of a recommendation at the end of this Report.

2.16   As soon as the site was secured by the Metropolitan Police and subsequently handed over to BTP it was, according to convention, treated as a scene of crime. This resulted in all non-police personnel being restricted in gaining access to the site and to the crashed vehicles, while the BTP carried out a thorough search to locate and secure evidence. Thus, when Dave Smart of GWT (Senior Operating Assessment Manager) arrived at the site with Brian Clark at 15:18, they were allowed only to note the damage to the lead power car and the position of controls. They were able to inspect the crossover points and the rear power car, which was undamaged. Mr Smart was allowed to return to the inner cordon at 17:35 with John Hellicar of HMRI and Brett Cornock of GWTs Fleet Department, where a more detailed inspection was made, including checking the status of the ATP and AWS. Messrs Kelleher and Moodie, who were still on the site, developed strained relations with BTP when the latter decided to suspend the search operation for the night, at 18:30, notwithstanding the provision of mobile lights by Railtrack. Mr Moodie expressed concern that perishable evidence may have been lost as a result.

Technical investigation

2.17   HMRI had received early notification of the accident and sent a technical team to the site which included Amanda Rudd, Stanley Hart, Roger Short and John Hellicar, who arrived between 15:00 and 16:00, and Dr Derek Hill and Andrew Harvey who arrived a little later. Mr Short went to Slough IECC, Ms Rudd staying at the crash site to record the position of points and of controls in the locomotives. Mr Hart inspected the track and signals on the approach to the crash site and secured all relevant equipment with the aid of BTP. Mr Harvey took over responsibility for co-ordinating the HMRI investigation. He spoke by telephone to Roger Short, then at Slough IECC, where he had reviewed the recorded information. The tapes from Slough IECC were taken into the possession of BTP and subsequently analysed in the presence of Mr Short.

2.18   Railtrack had standing arrangements with AEA Technology and with W S Atkins to provide technical expertise in connection with rail accidents. They also had in place maintenance contracts with Amey Rail Ltd which provided for emergency action. Pursuant to these arrangements Mick Barradell, Principal Derailment Investigator at AEA, visited the Southall site during the evening of 19 September 1997. He called in another AEA expert, Robert Wood, and they attended the site again on Saturday, 20 September. Mr Barradell inspected the vehicles, including bogies and bogie components, as the debris was being removed. He also inspected coach G and made notes on the extensive structural damage suffered. Representatives of Amey Rail attended the site on Saturday 20 and Sunday 21 September. Peter Day, together with others, carried out testing on signalling and on AWS and ATP track equipment. They returned on 23 September to remove for testing, and to replace, parts of the signalling equipment. On Sunday 21 September, John Martin and Mark Waring of Amey undertook a locomotive cab ride from Reading through to Southall to check signal aspects, sighting and signal post telephones and AWS response at all signals through to SN254 on the Up Main line (all were found to be working correctly).

2.19   While other investigations were being conducted, BTP continued their search of the site, which went on until the evening of Saturday 20 September 1997, with items of equipment being removed and secured for later testing. Railtrack were given access during the latter part of Saturday, 20 September. Assuming that all relevant evidence had been removed, Railtrack began the removal of wreckage and making preparations for re-laying the tracks, including re-positioning the ballast. In the course of this work, on Monday 22 September, evidence that subsequently turned out to be vital and which had been overlooked in the BTP search, was found partly bulldozed into the ballast. This included the ATP Controller containing the Master Byte Card. The equipment was collected up by Mr Paul Ardiff of GWT who returned to the site the following day to find the AWS Receiver, also partly submerged in the ballast. Mr Ardiff wrote a letter on 28 September to Richard George which is at Annex 11. There had plainly been a breakdown of communication and lack of effective briefing by BTP when the crash site was handed back to Railtrack as to whether any further searches were required and as to the limitations on the investigation that had been carried out up to that point.

2.20 AEA Technology, Amey Rail and W S Atkins each operated under standing contracts with Railtrack and attended the site in that capacity. However, having commenced their investigations, the BTP required that the data and reports produced be submitted to them. Subsequently, a formal arrangement was made by which the contracts were effectively "taken over", apparently without reference to specific powers, by BTP. An arrangement was made to divide the costs between BTP and HMRI. Such an arrangement inevitably gave rise to commercial difficulties, given that the original contracts with Railtrack remained in place. BTP emphasised the potential conflict between the roles of the rail companies in the investigation and their roles as potential defendants to criminal proceedings. While this is a factor to be taken into consideration, the arrangements for investigating the Southall collision were far from satisfactory.

2.21 Subsequent to the investigations on site, W S Atkins Rail (WSA) were instructed to carry out a series of tests on equipment from power car 43173 and on other equipment removed from the site. In each case, they prepared suites of reports comprising Part A: Findings of fact and established information; Part B: Professional discussion and findings; and Part C: Urgent safety-related observations. This arrangement was devised by BTP in their role as technical co-ordinator. Parts A and B were retained as prosecution evidence and therefore treated as being confidential. Part C was to be disclosed to Railtrack or GWT to allow them to attend to urgent safety matters. The success of this system is considered later in the Report. WSA prepared such reports on the following:

- operation of the trackside signalling equipment;
- operation of Solid State Interlocking;
- the data and audio tapes from Slough IECC;
- the speed of the HST;
- position, alignment, sighting and spacing of the relevant signals;
- HST train-borne AWS equipment;
- HST driver's safety/vigilance device;

- HST braking system.

Further on-site testing of the signals was carried out on 25/26 October by Amey/WSA. Additional laboratory testing was carried out on the AWS equipment on 1 December 1997 at the request of Halcrow Transmark on behalf of GWT.

2.22 For the criminal investigation led by Superintendent Satchwell, an Incident Room at St Pancras Station was established on 20 September 1997 and continued in use up to the start of the Inquiry. In the course of their investigation, BTP collected 1208 statements, 2606 documents and 993 exhibits. The BTP investigation team liaised with the Crown Prosecution Service and with HM Coroner, Dr John Burton. The BTP material was progressively made available to the Inquiry but could not be released to the parties until after disposal of the criminal proceedings on 27 July 1999. This included the bulk of the expert reports which had been submitted to BTP and which had not been seen previously by Railtrack or GWT.

The aftermath

2.23 Evidence was given about the gathering and release of information on casualties. Those trying to ring various emergency numbers which had been announced found that they did not receive a satisfactory response. In the case of relatives of the deceased, the uncertainty added greatly to their distress. Families who had good grounds to fear that their loved ones would be among the deceased had to wait through agonising hours while the process of official notification ran its slow course. Meanwhile, information about some of the deceased became public and even appeared on teletext/ceefax. At the same time, the emergency numbers were being swamped by calls about people who were not on the train. Plainly, no system can work perfectly in such a situation, but material improvements should be achievable. Superintendent Satchwell of BTP accepted that:

- Better provision was needed for answering telephone calls, such as switching to other stations.

- The Metropolitan Police Casualty Bureau closed too early.

- The release of information by teletext was to be avoided.

2.24 The foregoing matters were, in fact, within the control of the Metropolitan Police Force who put in a written submission in response to the evidence of Superintendent Satchwell. They pointed out that the Metropolitan Police Force was one of the few police forces within the UK which retained a dedicated casualty bureau, in this case at New Scotland Yard. The bureau had 20 telephone positions and 30 incoming lines, which had since been increased to 52 positions and 60 incoming lines. Facilities exist for linking to other police forces to increase the capacity of the bureau. Once a decision is made to open the bureau, trained staff are called in. Facilities include appointment of a "next of kin" officer to supervise the arrangements for transmitting news of a fatality. This is, as a matter of policy, delivered in person by the local force as it is considered wholly inappropriate to pass on such information by telephone. The Casualty Bureau had been opened within 26 minutes of the crash. The aim of using teletext to circulate information was to reduce the number of calls and this had been substantially successful. No information on victims was knowingly placed on teletext until next of kin had been informed. It is clear that these procedures are complex and must work in conditions of great strain and sensitivity. Lapses are to be regretted. These should be investigated and a full explanation provided to next of kin, which did not happen in the case of Mr Gerard Traynor. In general, the work of the Casualty Bureau is to be commended, but a review of procedures, in the light of the Southall crash, is appropriate.

2.25 Railtrack held a review of procedures in the light of the Southall crash on 24 September 1997 which led to a series of recommendations for revision and improvement of procedures. A further independent report was commissioned from Roger Miles. He concluded that, while problems of management and liaison in large incidents had been identified, the rail industry's approach to emergency planning was basically sound, and particularly that Railtrack and the TOCs had co-operated in jointly addressing emergency planning matters. A de-briefing took place between members of the emergency services, including the police forces on 15 December 1997. The rail industry, however, were not invited to attend, nor were the emergency services asked to contribute to the Railtrack review. Post-accident de-briefing should be conducted in such a manner as to cover all relevant interfaces.

2.26 Concerns had been expressed by a number of parties, notably Railtrack, but others as well, about the conduct of the immediate accident investigation. This was seen as giving rise to two areas of criticism: first, lack of technical co-ordination leading to duplication and to omissions; and secondly, restrictions on the technical investigation as a result of the accident being treated as a scene of crime. The investigation of rail accidents is provided for, as between BTP and HMRI, in a jointly issued document (March 1996) which recognises that a number of investigations may be held. These include an internal railway investigation, a coroner's inquest, a criminal investigation by BTP and investigation by HMRI using powers under Health and Safety legislation. The effect of the document is that BTP lead the investigation in the case of a suspected serious offence involving deliberate intent or gross recklessness. In matters of error or carelessness, HMRI lead the investigation. The interests of Railtrack are dealt with in the BTP Major Incidents Manual by which rail staff may seek access to evidence via the RIO who will deal with the Police Incident Officer. All evidence must be kept secure by the police.

2.27 The foregoing events and procedures clearly created a number of actual or potential conflicts:

- As between BTP and HMRI, the decision to treat the incident as involving potentially serious charges with the investigation then being taken over by BTP was made implicitly by BTP themselves without consultation with

HMRI. There was an assumption that the interests of enforcing the criminal law should take precedence over the needs of safety, although BTP were conscious of the need to pass on any safety-critical information coming to light.

- The release of information, particularly that which was relevant to ongoing rail safety, raised conflict between the need for confidentiality in the context of criminal proceedings and the wider public interest in rail safety. Under their agreed procedure, BTP made available to HMRI copies of all statements relating to the accident. HMRI could not, however, release these to other persons without the authority of an Assistant Chief Constable.

- Statements and information received by HMRI were not passed on to Railtrack or GWT with the exception of the W S Atkins' Part C reports, and in the result Railtrack considered that potential safety-critical information was withheld. Particularly, information was not available during the hearings or deliberations of the Rail Industry Inquiry (see Chapter 9) upon which recommendations and actions were taken which affected the future safety of the railways during 1998, 1999 and beyond.

2.28 Since the Southall accident and its aftermath, these issues have continued to be the subject of discussion between interested parties. They are said to have resulted in improved search procedures aimed at ensuring that no evidence is lost. A formal agreement has been made between BTP and Railtrack for sharing information on the basis that the safety of the public must come first. Sharing of information is, however, subject to consultation with the CPS. The effectiveness of these measures remains to be seen, particularly in the context of the collision at Ladbroke Grove.

CHAPTER 3

THE TRACK AND SIGNALS

3.1   The track and signalling equipment form part of the "infrastructure" owned and maintained by Railtrack. The stretch of line at Southall was used by GWT and by Thames Trains, who was the lead operator, as well as by freight companies including EWS. The track at Southall has not been called into question as a contributory cause of the accident. Its state at the time of the crash will be considered briefly.

3.2   The signals played a more prominent role and will be considered in more detail. For the purpose of the Inquiry, it was accepted by all parties that at the time of the accident, the signal equipment was operating correctly. Analysis of the SSI tapes from the Slough IECC provided positive evidence that the signals at the relevant time were set as described in Chapter 1, namely, signal SN298 at green (as recalled by Driver Harrison), SN 280 at double yellow and SN270 at single yellow.   SN254 was set to red, as also confirmed by Driver Harrison. The issues raised in the Inquiry and in the investigations following the accident concerned the visibility of the signals, particularly SN280 and SN270, including their alignment and positioning. These were affected by the Heathrow Express (HEX) overhead electric lines. The weather conditions at the time of the crash are dealt with in Chapter 1. For the purpose of these issues, the weather conditions are to be taken as overcast and dull, but dry.

The track

3.3   The track in the area of the accident was relatively new, having been installed from Southall West Junction in 1984 with a life expectancy of 30 years. The Southall East Junction crossover was installed in 1988 and enhanced in 1994 with additional fittings on the relief lines. . The permitted maximum speed over the crossover was 70mph to the Down Main and 15mph into the Yard.

31

There is no record of a maintenance problem concerning the immediate area of the accident. The track leading up to Southall West junction was installed in 1965 and is nearing the end of its working life, but was not, in 1997 overdue for renewal. Railtrack accepted that the quality of the ride on the Up Main approaching Southall did not provide as smooth a ride as other areas of track. Track quality was monitored routinely by a track recording coach. Recorded deficiencies were normally to be dealt with within 10 working days. Early on the morning of 17 September 1997 a track circuit failure west of Southall led to the identification of a broken rail on the Up Main line between signals SN270 and SN254. A temporary repair was carried out within two hours and the relevant section of rail was replaced during the night of 17/18 September. At the time of the accident, therefore, the track was in a properly maintained condition and within its specified working limits.

The signals

3.4   The relevant signals were installed as part of Phase II of HEX in 1994 and taken into use in March 1995. They were maintained by Amey, who kept computerised records of faults on a database known as FRAME (Fault Reporting and Monitoring System). Records revealed that there was a total of seven reported faults for the three signals SN280, 270 and 254 over the period of one year before the accident. Of these, five were first filament failures in bulbs. On such a failure, the auxiliary filament comes into operation so that the signal aspect is unaltered but the intensity reduced. The failure is then detected by the SSI system and the bulbs replaced in the normal course of maintenance, as would have happened in this case. The other recorded faults related to a report from a driver that a signal post identity plate was obscured (this was corrected) and a fault reported on the SSI system, which was subsequently found to be caused by a "collar", i.e. a restriction applied to the signal (this was not a fault). As regards their operation, the signals were apparently operative and adequately maintained. The Maintenance Contract (known as RT1A) required Amey to check the general serviceability of the signals every three months.

32

Maintenance

3.5 The maintenance of the line, including track and signals, was contracted out to Amey Rail Limited (Amey) under a Standard Form Railtrack Infrastructure Maintenance contract (RT1A). Amey's duties under the RT1A contract included both regular maintenance and the provision of a rapid response facility designed to ensure that faults affecting railway safety were remedied promptly. The contract also included investigation and testing work in the case of accidents. The performance of Amey under RT1A was subject to extensive performance monitoring. This involved an annual plan submitted to Railtrack containing a programme of maintenance and other work to be carried out within the year. Amey provided a report every four weeks recording progress, which was reviewed at regular management meetings, with local meetings being held to discuss individual work or projects.

3.6 Railtrack conducted an audit of Amey's performance annually for sections of the system, including compliance with Railway Group Standards and the effectiveness of their management. The most recent audit before the Southall accident was carried out for the Oxford area. The audit carried out in 1998 covered part of the West Ealing area. Amey's maintenance work involved regular patrols and inspections to comply with Amey's own Railway Safety Case and Railway Group Standards. This involved a weekly track inspection by a leading trackman patroller, whose walks alternated between the Up and Down line, looking for any track defects. The track was also walked and visibly checked at 4-weekly intervals by a track chargeman; and at 8-weekly intervals by a Permanent Way Section Manager or assistant. Once every two years the track was to be walked by a Permanent Way Maintenance Engineer and visibly checked. For Railtrack, the acting track Engineer at the time of the accident was Geoffrey South, whose responsibility was to ensure that Amey performed their functions under the maintenance contract.

On-site testing

3.7 No tests were carried out on the track since its condition had not been called into question and considerable damage had been caused to the track within the area of the crash. In relation to the signals, however, even though Driver Harrison appeared to have accepted immediately after the crash that he had gone through warning signals, immediate steps were taken to verify that the signals were operating correctly and were adequately visible. For this purpose, a very large amount of evidence was collected following a number of on-site inspections. The first of these was carried out for Railtrack on 20, 21 and 23 September by a team from Amey Rail led by Peter Day. They carried out functional testing on signals SN254, 270 and 280 in conjunction with BTP (who were in control of the site on 20 September) and the Railtrack representative (RIO). Amey were not requested to carry out a full Signal Failure Investigation, since there had been no suggestion of such failure. Mr Day subsequently prepared a report on these investigations. On Sunday 21 September a cab ride was conducted from Reading through to the Southall crash site by a party including John Martin of Amey, which recorded that, for the three signals in question, their sighting was generally good. For this purpose, no distinction was drawn between signals SN280 and SN270. On-site testing of the signals was carried out by W S Atkins, accompanied by Amey on 25/26 October 1997. Detailed signal sighting tests were carried out by W S Atkins for BTP and HMRI on 19, 21 and 23 November 1997, the report being prepared by Steve Wilkins of WSA. The tests included sighting of the signals using a periscope device, with position measurements being taken along the rails. Sighting tests were repeated on 28 November by WSA for the benefit of Symon Murrant of Railtrack and Roy Bell, an expert instructed on behalf of Larry Harrison. Roy Bell and Steve Wilkins were conducted on a cab ride on 11 December 1997. Finally, AMEC Rail conducted signal sighting tests for Railtrack using periscope equipment on 17 and 24 May 1998, details of which are contained in the Expert report prepared by David Weedon.

3.8   For the purpose of signal sighting, the relevant Group Standard is GK/RT0037, first issued in October 1994.   The signals in question were designed and installed under previous BR standards, but the Group Standard which applied at the time the signals were taken into use, was very little different.   For the Inquiry, reference was made to Issue 3 of the Group Standard, which came into force in December 1997.   This laid down the following provisions for signal sighting:

> Paragraph 4.1.2
>
> Signals shall normally be positioned to give drivers an approach view for a minimum of 7 seconds and an uninterrupted view for at least 4 seconds.......
>
> Note: Interruptions of very short duration (e.g. caused by overhead line equipment) may be ignored when determining the uninterrupted sighting distance.
>
> Paragraph 4.3.4
>
> The signal shall generally be directed so that the centre of the beam is aligned towards a point 3 metres (10'0") above the left hand running rail at a distance of 183 metres (200 yards) from the signal.

Additionally, Issue 3 of GK/RT0037, made provision for the "normal" height of the most restrictive aspect (red) of the signal, which was to be (in the case of a straight post signal) 3.35 metres above rail level or (in the case of a gantry-mounted signal) 5.03 metres above rail level.   There was no provision as to height in the earlier versions of the Standard, or in the rules applicable at the time the signals were designed and installed.

3.9   In report No. 98801A, April 1998, W S Atkins recorded that all three signals were at a height above normal in accordance with Issue 3 of the Group Standard, that signal SN270 was incorrectly aligned as a result of the sighting device incorporated in the body of the signal being itself misaligned, and that signal SN280 was also misaligned, but to a lesser extent. In report No. 98801B WSA concluded that all three signals were readable at 125mph and that the sighting distances all exceeded the minimum requirements of the Group Standard. Report 98801C did not record any urgent safety-related observations. It will be recalled that the Part C report was disclosed to Railtrack at the time of its production, but Parts A and B were not – see para. 2.21 above. AMEC Rail also concluded that the three signals in question presented acceptable sighting for an approaching driver. On behalf of Larry Harrison, however, Roy Bell contended that the misalignment of signal SN270, which was effectively pointing downwards from its intended position, meant that the driver would be "in the beam" for less than two seconds and that the effect of the signal outside the area of "focus" would be to produce only a "dull glow" (he subsequently said that this was incorrect). It was pointed out that the horizontal filament of the signal lamp produced a horizontally elongated area of maximum illumination, which made vertical focusing the more critical. There was some dispute as to the shape of the area of illumination, which was also described as a flattened cone. I accept that it is elongated, but in terms of visibility, a more helpful analogy is of a torch beam which can be pointed "at" an object to illuminate it, but is still visible as a light to an observer outside the beam.

3.10 The relevant experts together with representatives of all parties at the Inquiry met in order to agree the appropriate figures for each of the signals in question. The result of such agreement was as follows:

- Height of red aspect: SN280 and SN254 were respectively 470mm (18in) and 720mm (28in) above normal height. Both were gantry-mounted. SN270 was 1580mm (62in) above the normal height for a straight post signal. It was, however, slightly lower than the normal gantry height by 90mm (4in).

- Alignment of centre of beam in advance of signal : SN280 was somewhat misaligned downwards at 153 metres; SN270 was grossly misaligned at 60 metres; and SN254 was, within the limits of accuracy, correctly aligned at 180 metres before the signal, in each case relating to a point 3m above the LH rail.

- Time for which signal could be seen at 125mph : the signals were timed at averages of : SN280 - 6.7 seconds; SN270 - 9.6 seconds; and SN254 - 13.2 seconds.

3.11   In judging the adequacy of visibility of signals it is to be noted that the 7 second approach view at 125mph commences 391 metres in advance of the signal, and the 4 second uninterrupted view 223 metres in advance. Thus, the correct alignment of the signal should put the driver's eye in the centre of the beam approximately 3½ seconds before reaching the signal, but it is nevertheless anticipated as being in "view" well before this. Where drivers consider signals to be ineffective or inadequate, they should fill in a fault report form, RT3185. No such forms or other complaints were recorded for any of the signals in question, including SN270. Indeed, as regards the day of the crash, evidence was taken from three drivers whose trains preceded 1A47 on the Up Main : Brian Smith who drove the 10:55 Cheltenham to Paddington, William Sleep who drove the 11:02 Penzance to Paddington and John Dillon who drove a Thames Train which was the last through Southall junction before the collision. Each of these drivers saw all the signals in question (at green) and did not report any fault or difficulty.

3.12   In the light of this evidence and the above considerations, it appears to be the case that signal SN270, while incorrectly aligned, was adequately visible on the day of the crash. The height of the three signals in question exceeded normal recommendations, but this was done in order to achieve the best compromise in the light of the potential sighting problems arising from overhead electrification equipment and in the circumstances had no material impact on visibility. The recommendations were not in force at the date of the accident. It must be concluded that the signals were adequately visible to a driver keeping a proper lookout.

Remedial action to SN270

3.13   The misalignment of signal SN270 gave rise to further issues. As noted above, W S Atkins were brought in to carry out testing under a term contract with Railtrack. Their services were requisitioned, together with AEA Technology, by BTP and shared with HMRI. In October 1997, before WSA had commenced their work, the parties sought to come to an arrangement whereby WSA would conduct investigations on behalf of BTP and HMRI and that WSA would pass on any safety-critical information to Railtrack. A meeting was held on 16 October 1997 and was followed by correspondence, but no agreement was reached. Consequently, BTP imposed the arrangement referred to at para 2.21, by which separate reports would be prepared for disclosure to Railtrack. On 27 October 1997 HMRI informed Railtrack that they still wished to carry out further investigatory work into alignment and sighting of signals and that Railtrack should resume normal maintenance provided that signal focusing, alignment and height of signals SN280, 270 and 254 were not altered. After the signal tests had been carried out by WSA, and in the absence of further correspondence, Richard Spencer of Railtrack wrote to HMRI on 19 February 1998 asking for confirmation that remaining restrictions could be lifted. By this date WSA were aware of the misalignment of signal SN270, even though their formal reports were not issued until April. Mr Spencer sent a chaser and on 17 March 1998 HMRI stated that, so far as they were aware there was no non-compliance with Group Standards, nor significant safety-related findings identified as a result of W S Atkins' work. The result was that Railtrack took no action and the misalignment of signal SN270 remained unattended to for six months after the crash. More delay was to follow, however.

3.14   Railtrack had obtained an initial report from Amey which stated that signal alignments were satisfactory. Railtrack commissioned a further report from AMEC Rail which involved further signal sighting checks carried out in May 1998. The report did not address the question whether the signals had been altered since the crash, but must have assumed that they had not. The alignment of signal SN270 was checked through the alignment device on the signal, and found to be in order. Direct measurements from the line, carried out by Scientifics Limited, revealed a wide spread of figures between the three signals, and did identify that SN270 was aligned much too close to the signal. The report, however, identified only that the signal was "slightly low and could be improved". Railtrack did not commission any adjustment as a result of the AMEC report. Railtrack finally received the full WSA reports Parts A and B in August 1999 as part of the Inquiry core bundles.

3.15   A separate dispute arose as to whether Railtrack had in fact become aware of the misalignment. Railtrack accepted that in February 1998 Steve Wilkins, after obtaining permission from BTP, had supplied part of his notes to Martin Govas of Railtrack. The notes referred to a defective "peep-site" (sic) but there was doubt as to whether the meaning of this had been grasped by Railtrack. In the light of the further actions of Railtrack including the commissioning of a report from AMEC Rail, it seems clear that Railtrack remained unaware of the defective sighting device until August 1999.

3.16   During the course of the Inquiry itself, it became apparent that signal SN270 had still not been realigned. This work was rapidly put in hand during November 1999 and a further dispute arose between Railtrack and Amey as to whose duty it was to check the alignment of signals. By letter dated 16 November 1999 (Annex 12) the Inquiry invited Railtrack and Amey to address this issue further. Railtrack submitted that the duty was placed squarely on Amey Rail by virtue of their RT1A maintenance contract. Amey disputed this and contended that they had a justified and *bona fide* belief that they were under no such obligation. They pointed out that the obligation to ensure that signals were correctly aligned was placed on Railtrack by the Group Standard. Railtrack, however, entertained the *bona fide* belief that they had contracted with Amey to take on such responsibility. It is not the task of this Inquiry to resolve contractual differences but the following conclusions are apposite:

- No check can have been made to ensure the accuracy of the sighting device at the time the signal was installed;

- No check can have been made on the actual alignment of the signal when installed;

- No maintenance checks on the actual alignment of the signal was made by either party;

- No steps were taken by either party to ensure that the other was in fact carrying out alignment checks.

All the foregoing matters call for appropriate remedial action to avoid reoccurrence.

Stopping distance

3.17 Assuming adequate visibility of the signals, Group Standard GK/RT0034 requires adequate stopping distances to be provided between the signals. The section of line through SN280 and SN270 is substantially level, but falls from a point close to SN270, at a gradient of 1 in 1320 through SN254 and Southall East junction. The standard requires the provision of braking distances from an initial speed of 125mph of 2054 metres for a level track and 2245 metres for a track falling at 1 in 200. W S Atkins have calculated the average gradient between the signals as 1 in 1573 falling, and an interpolated braking distance appropriate to such a gradient of 2100 metres. The parties agreed upon the following distances between the signals:

> SN254 – SN270   1530 metres
> SN270 – SN280   1056 metres

The agreed distance between signals SN254 and SN280 was therefore 2586 metres, which exceeds the Group Standard requirement by 23%. Assuming adequate visibility and driver response, there was no reason why 1A47 should not have stopped or slowed adequately before signal SN254.

CHAPTER 4

WHY WAS THE FREIGHT TRAIN CROSSING?

4.1   Early reports of the Southall accident in the press suggested that EWS train 6V17 consisted only of empty wagons, which were being shunted across the main line into Southall yard. True it was that the wagons were empty. They comprised, however, a fully operational freight service which had been timetabled to travel from Allington, Kent, departing at 09:58 and due to arrive at Southall yard at 12:31, forty-four minutes before the collision. This was a regular service which had to cross from Acton Yard to Southall Yard daily. There were some 12 similar movements of freight trains each day. HSTs to and from Bristol and elsewhere passed regularly on the main lines and other trains on the relief lines. There were, therefore, inevitable conflicts which occurred many times daily which were controlled by the signalling system briefly described below. The question remains, however, why the freight train was permitted to cross in front of the HST, where popular expectation, expressed in the press reports, was that the freight should have given precedence to the faster passenger train, such that this accident should never have been possible.

Regulation and the Signaller's decision

4.2   In the past, regulation policy applied by signallers comprised a rigid system of priority depending on the classes of the trains involved. There are currently ten classes, HSTs being Class 1 and fully braked freight trains Class 6. On this basis, the HST should always have priority. In past years, freight trains were forced to wait sometimes hours for routes, while express and other passenger services were allowed priority on congested lines. This system was already changing well before privatisation, led by the new generation of faster freight trains and new route setting signalling equipment, which were introduced during the 1980s. In 1996, following a change to the Track Access Conditions (which govern the use of the track by operators) the priority system was formally abandoned and replaced by a system of regulation based on minimum overall delay. This was necessarily driven, to an extent, by privatisation and the perceived need for commercial equality in the face of the penalty payment system, also contained in Track Access Conditions. The way in which the new system was brought into operation proved to be controversial at the Inquiry and is considered below.

4.3   Before the new regulation system was formally introduced, however, the section of line in question underwent complete re-signalling as part of the Heathrow Express (HEX) Scheme, in the course of which control of signalling was taken over by the newly installed Slough Integrated Electronic Control Centre (IECC) which incorporated Automatic Route Setting (ARS). The basic signalling system in use throughout the network involves interlocking of points and signals, so that it is impossible to set conflicting routes. In addition, the ARS takes over most of the work (estimated at 95%) by automatically setting routes for trains as they approach. The ARS system has access to substantial volumes of data, including timetables, and is regularly updated. The processor calculates the expected time of every train at every signal on its route and passes this information to the ARS which maintains 2 green signals ahead of each train. The system is programmed to regulate train movements on the basis of minimising overall delay similar to the new regulation policy. But in doing so, the system automatically applies a degree of weighting (or precedence) to different train classes, the highest weighting being applied to HSTs.

4.4   On 19 September 1997 the route for the EWS freight train 6V17 was not set by the ARS because Southall Yard, its destination, was outside the system. It was therefore necessary for Signaller Forde at the Slough IECC to set the route. In doing so, he had to make a rapid decision as to the point at which 6V17 was to be taken from Acton Yard across both the relief and main lines. He could have crossed 6V17 from Acton yard directly to the Down Main before crossing into Southall Yard. Signaller Forde decided, however, that delay would be reduced by 6V17 running on the Down Relief as far as signal

43

SN243, because this would give more time to make the decision, and then crossing both the Up and Down Main lines into Southall Yard. Having routed the freight train from Acton yard to SN243, Signaller Forde telephoned Southall yard where the shunter confirmed that the freight train could be received and pressed an acceptance plunger which permitted the signaller to route 6V17 across into the yard. This routing decision prevented the ARS setting any conflicting route and set the protecting signals on the Up and Down Main lines, so that 1A47 should have slowed at signals SN280 and 270 and come to a stand (if necessary) at SN254. Different calculations indicated some uncertainty as to whether it would, in fact, have been necessary for 1A47 to stop completely.

4.5   In addition to trains 1A47 and 6V17, there were 10 other trains identified from the ARS printout which could have affected the Signaller's decision. Paul Balmer, a former employee of Amey Rail, now Independent Expert, performed a large number of calculations on different possible train regulation decisions using the basic data contained in the SSI tapes recovered from the Slough IECC. He calculated the overall delay for each of 30 possible regulating decisions. This suggested that Signaller Forde's decision involved least delay overall with one exception, which consisted of routing 6V17 across to the Down Main at Acton ahead of, but without delaying 1A47 and the preceding 1A46, and resulting in delay only to a train on the Up Relief line. There was plainly no opportunity or time for Signaller Forde to make any calculation. His decision was a matter of instinct and experience and Mr Balmer's calculations suggest that he was substantially right. These caclulations were challenged by ASLEF, but this had the effect of casting further doubt on what the "correct" decision was, to minimise overall delay. Had 1A47 been allowed to pass in front of 6V17, the freight train would necessarily have been delayed and been in conflict with other trains. There remained, however, the issue whether the regulation policy applied by the ARS system and as applied by Signaller Forde was the appropriate policy. This involved additional consideration of risk assessment at junctions. The question was also raised whether signallers, following the 1996 policy, were influenced by pressure to avoid incurring penalty payments and, therefore, whether regulating decisions were being made on commercial rather than safety grounds.

Change of regulation policy

4.6 Regulation policy based on the class of a train began to change during the 1970s. No risk assessments were carried out, but there had been significant changes in operation, for example, as a result of improved braking systems, particularly for freight wagons. When automatic route setting came into use in the 1980s, the criteria on which the computer calculated routes had to be fixed. This was determined to be the minimising of overall delay, but applying a weighting system to different classes so that the result incorporated some features of the old system. The regulation policy introduced in 1996 applied only to those decisions of the signaller outside the ARS system and this was determined to be on the basis of minimum overall delay as estimated (not calculated) by the signaller. A draft policy was circulated in May 1995. GWT (before privatisation at this stage) raised the only objection to the new policy by their letter of 22 May 1995. Richard George accepted that this was not on the grounds of safety or risk, but because GWT considered that the policy was wrong, and ought to minimise the number of passengers delayed and keep time-sensitive goods moving, in accordance with GWT's draft proposals. After a hearing on 4 June 1996, the objections were overruled by the Timetabling Sub-Committee. The absence of a risk assessment of the new policy was highlighted by several parties at the inquiry.

4.7 Prior to introduction of the new regulation policy, briefing documents were sent to Railtrack zonal production managers in April 1996. Local meetings were arranged to discuss issues with local Railtrack and TOC staff. For the GW zone, a meeting was held at Reading Town Hall on 22 July 1996. The change was not considered controversial at the time and the new policy was implemented without serious disapproval. The policy was introduced into the

Summer 1996 Timetable and fully implemented by the following Winter Timetable, with a further meeting being held at Reading Town Hall in October 1996. From a performance viewpoint, the regulation policy change was said to work well and there were no serious problems on GW zone.

4.8 Anthony Walker, Railtrack Project Delivery Manager gave evidence about the penalty and compensation system built into the Track Access agreements. There were three parts to the system:

- Charter Agreement – this may involve payment of compensation to passengers and may also involve the levying of a fine by the Rail Regulator for persistent failure to run services to time.

- Consistent Delivery – involves penalty payments between Railtrack and the TOC. In the case of GWT this was on the basis of achieving 83% of services arriving within 5 minutes of their scheduled time, calculated by aggregating delays above 3 minutes on a rolling 3 month basis.

- Assured Delivery – involves payment of specific penalties between Railtrack and the TOC where individual trains are delayed for more than fixed periods (20 minutes, 30 minutes etc.) or are unable to call at a particular station.

4.9 These were the immediate commercial pressures on Railtrack and GWT to run to timetable. Railtrack had similar arrangements with other TOCs and freight carriers such that, in addition to calculating the delay resulting from any particular train movement, it would be possible in theory to calculate the financial consequences, or at least (in the case of aggregated penalties) the possible contribution of an individual delay to the eventual payment of a penalty. Although precise calculations could not realistically have been carried out, Railtrack were naturally aware of the effect of regulating decisions on their commercial position overall. Mr Walker confirmed that Railtrack did organise Track Access Awareness sessions for their staff including signallers in 1996. He explained, however, that signallers would not understand the detail of penalty payments other than to appreciate the general regulation policy. He also pointed out that signallers would not know the reason for a train having been delayed before reaching the regulating point, i.e. whether further delay imposed by a signalling decision would be adding to Railtrack's liability or reducing that of the TOC. These are theoretical considerations. The practical question is whether the present regulation policy has an adverse effect on safety in terms of the decisions made by signallers. The separate issues of theoretical safety are considered further below.

4.10   The Rail Regulator became involved in regulation policy in 1995 at a time when Railtrack had taken over as Infrastructure Controller, but was still under public ownership. Under the Railways Act 1993, the Rail Regulator has a duty by section 4(3)(a) "to take into account the need to protect all persons from dangers arising from the operation of the railways, taking into account in particular any advice given to him in that behalf by the HSE". In January 1995 the then Rail Regulator introduced a change in the Track Access Conditions, adding a new Condition H11, which was to lead to the new regulation policy. Condition H11.1 provided that the train regulation objective was to be the striking of a fair and reasonable balance between:

(a)   minimising overall delay to train movements (including ancillary movements);

(b)   minimising overall delay to passengers travelling or intending to travel by railway and the movement of time-sensitive goods, both in respect of the aggregate delay to any one of them and the aggregate numbers of passengers and goods delayed;

(c)   maintaining connections between railway passenger services;

(d)   avoiding undue discrimination between any person and any other person;

(e)   protecting the commercial interests of Railtrack and each affected train operator;

(f)   the interests of safety and security.

4.11   Condition H11.2 required Railtrack to establish a Train Regulation Statement in accordance with the above requirements for each part of the network, with a process of consultation and provision for representations and objections. Train Regulation statements set out guidance to signallers which apply at three levels :

- Level 1 – Policy statement applicable to the whole network
- Level 2 – Policy for particular areas, operators or specific types of trains
- Level 3 – Specific policy for busy or complex locations.

Level 2 and 3 policies were to take precedence over Level 1. Mr Walker confirmed that he had seen copies of such policy statements posted up in signal boxes. For the Southall area no level 2 or 3 policy statements existed on 19 September 1997. The Level 1 statement is reproduced at Annex 13. As noted above, no risk assessment of the new policy was carried out at the time. The internal Rail Industry Inquiry following the Southall crash recommended (para 4.1) a risk assessment of regulation policy, for which Railtrack commissioned Arthur D Little. In addition, the wider issue of whether a regulation objective should include protecting commercial interests was raised by a number of parties at the Inquiry.

Risks involved in regulation

4.12   The risk assessment of regulation policy was carried out by David Maidment (who gave evidence to the Inquiry) and Anthony Pickett. During the course of their investigation, interviews were conducted at a number of signal boxes including IECCs similar to (but not including) Slough. This revealed that signallers generally believed that delaying Class I trains (including HSTs) incurred a higher penalty than delaying a freight train. This would militate against the regulating decision made by Signaller Forde, given that it was inevitable that the freight movement would involve a potential conflict with Class I trains. The conclusions of the Pickett-Maidment report were that there was no adverse impact on risk on SPADs (Signals Passed at Danger) and, specifically, little evidence of increased signal checks to Class I passenger trains. The report was criticised as insufficiently rigorous and particularly for not having taken into account the need to avoid potential conflict or "collision opportunities". This was the subject of a major theoretical study which is considered below.

4.13   The data gathered and reported by Messrs Picket and Maidment established that signallers generally appreciated the potential danger of slowing a HST as well as the commercial consequences. Interviews with Signallers provided no evidence of putting commercial considerations ahead of safety, or of being encouraged, or of feeling under pressure to do so.   Mr Tom Winsor, the present Rail Regulator, gave evidence to the Inquiry. He expressed general concern with the new Condition H11.1(e), in relation to which he stated:

> "I believe that that consideration is potentially dangerous to the interests of safety and security. It was put in in January 1995, against my advice as legal advisor, and I do not believe that the review which I have initiated in relation to train regulation and Condition H of the track access conditions…will leave that untouched. It's a matter on which we're out to consultation in the industry, and before making a change to this I should like to have the benefit of the conclusions of this Inquiry.
>
> However, I should add that the signallers are obliged…to comply with safety obligations first.   Therefore they have an essential and overriding objective of running a safe railway.   Insofar as these matters, the commercial interests of the companies, conflict with safety, then, in my opinion the safety considerations should always be paramount. If there are arrangements in the industry which prejudice those, then they are arrangements that I would like to change."

4.14   The theoretical study referred to above is contained in a report prepared by Dr Ian Murphy of the University of Glasgow, supported by his book "Risk Assessment of Railway Junction Layouts". This area of research originated following the report into the railway accident at Newton in July 1991 when the Inspector, Mr David Eves, recommended that BR should develop and adapt a system of risk analysis combining engineering and operating factors to be applied to proposed layout schemes.   The accident at Newton and the Inspector's recommendation, related to single-track working. Following this recommendation, BR commissioned Arthur D Little to undertake development of a Layout Risk Method (LRM) for junction layouts. As the analysis continued, it was extended to cover multiple tracks and layouts. It proved much more complex and cumbersome than had been anticipated. Initial (and subsequent) attempts to apply LRM to particular junctions typically led to numerical risk assessments which were orders of magnitude (in excess of 10) above actual risk figures to be assessed from real data. The method independently employed by Dr Murphy was to analyse two trains passing through a junction on all the possible routes in order to identify "collision opportunities", necessarily involving one train passing a signal at danger. The measure of risk associated with a particular layout and timetable is taken as the total collision opportunities for a period (1 week) which may then be compared to other layouts or other timetables.

4.15   Dr Murphy, in his evidence, criticised the ARS system because it did not look beyond the signal in question, did not assess risk and did not take into account the length/speed/time involved in completing a manoeuvre. The ARS thus acted as a very unimaginative signaller. Dr Murphy analysed the particular circumstances of the Southall crash and concluded that the "vital interval" during which one train was in the path of another was excessively long (64 seconds) and could have been reduced by calling the route of 6V17 as late as possible. The ARS could have operated in a safer manner by taking into account the speed and length of the trains involved. Dr Murphy also proposed that more green signals should be set for fast trains. Such a requirement would, however, make the system less flexible for other trains operating on ARS and would reduce track capacity. Dr Murphy's analysis assumed that there was to be a SPAD, while Railtrack contended that the only basis for regulation policy was that red signals would be obeyed – a view which HMRI shared. Dr Murphy did not contend that the old regulation policy based on priority was necessarily safer than the new policy, but considered the system of priority to have in-built safety factors.

4.16   The debate as to whether the new regulation policy was less safe than the previously applied policy remained inconclusive. HMRI stated that there was no safety reason why passenger trains should be given priority and remained unconvinced by Dr Murphy's analysis. The question whether the new policy of minimising overall delay involved fewer rather than more SPADs was also inconclusive. David Maidment pointed out that figures for SPADs during the period of change in Regulation Policy, 1995 –1997, showed no change except in the case of freight where there was a slight increase in SPADs for 1996/97, which is contrary to expectation if freight services were encountering fewer red signals. These figures are necessarily influenced by many factors and no firm conclusion is to be drawn, other than that the incidence of SPADs does not suggest any increase in risk. Railtrack have, however, agreed to consider Dr Murphy's work.

Volume of traffic

4.17   Finally, it is appropriate to recall the huge numbers of services passing through the lines in the vicinity of Southall and the necessary complexity of the regulating operations needed. The total number of passenger services, Monday to Saturday, in 1997 was estimated in the following figures:

- Passenger services, on main lines – 2130

- Passenger services, on relief lines - 1345

- Freight services, all on relief lines – 186

This produces a daily total of "through" trains of 610 to which an estimated 12 trains using the crossovers is to be added. These figures exclude empty stock trains and additional short-term (STP) or very short-term planning (VSTP) freight trains outside the timetable, which were said to represent 60% of total freight. In terms of regulation as between passenger and freight services, it is also relevant to note that EWS, the operator of 6V17, stated that they intended to run freight trains hauled by Class 67 locomotives at up to 125mph. The present regulated intervals between trains will come under review in the future when new train protection systems are brought into operation. It is important that regulation policy, still in its relative infancy, should keep pace with all relevant safety and operational developments.

CHAPTER 5

DRIVER COMPETENCE AND TRAINING

5.1   The driver is, by tradition, the most important person in the train crew. In the days of steam, he was the individual who oversaw and operated the essential mechanics of the locomotive, aided by his fireman, and working in the open environment of "the footplate". In the transition to electric and diesel traction, the driving environment changed totally, becoming enclosed and with the exhilaration of the footplate turning into the routine of an enclosed cab. The fireman maintained a brief appearance as the "second man" now virtually gone, leaving the driver in sole charge of a train weighing up to 2000 tons or more.   The transition to single-man operation occurred much earlier and with far less attention on the Southern Railway and on other suburban routes where electric traction has been in widespread use since the 1920s. The way in which single manning on High Speed Trains was introduced on GWT requires separate consideration.

Management and training

5.2   GWT employed drivers at six depots, namely Paddington, Swansea, Bristol, Exeter, Plymouth and Penzance. In September 1997 the total number of drivers employed was 242. They were managed by 12 Driver Standards Managers (DSMs) including Lester Watts and Dave Hockey, referred to elsewhere in this Report. Supervision was carried out by two Driver Managers (DMs) including Tony Cardall, referred to elsewhere. DMs reported directly to Alison Forster, Operations and Safety Manager, subsequently promoted to Director in 1998. In parallel with this system, Dave Smart was the Senior Operating Assessment Manager who, *inter alia,* provided advice to DMs and DSMs on technical matters. He reported to Clare Kitcher, the Safety and Standards Manager who herself reported to Alison Forster.

5.3   Driver competence and training, which is largely centred on safety issues, is the subject of Group Standard GO/RT3151: Safety Requirement for Train Drivers. Training covers rules and regulations applicable to driving, traction and train operating knowledge, route knowledge and practical driving skills. Drivers must undergo regular medical checks and new applicants must undertake a psychological assessment. Drivers are assessed by DSMs during and on completion of training and during the first two years following qualification. They are then subject to periodic assessments of competence, including retention of route knowledge, throughout their career and in a bi-annual Rules examination. Each driver must hold a certificate of competence and must always carry personal identification. Drivers are issued with documents and personal equipment on a controlled and recorded basis and must be provided regularly with essential safety and operating information. Drivers are monitored when booking on, and at other times, to ensure their fitness and competence.

5.4   Driver training is carried out by individual TOCs, subject to the requirements of the Group Standard. In the case of GWT the basic training course lasts 36 weeks, followed by a period of route learning and supervised driving. The total length of training for a driver employed at Bristol or Paddington is 67 weeks approximately. The cost of training a driver was put at some £60,000. Drivers can move freely between TOCs. No evidence was received as to comparative salaries or inducements, but records indicated that, since 1994, GWT had trained only eight drivers. During the same period, they had recruited 48 qualified drivers from other TOCs, although they required some degree of training.

5.5   Evidence also indicated that while some TOCs were scrupulous in maintaining and passing on driver records, the practice was not universal. It was not ascertained whether drivers were able, through these means, to rid themselves of past misdemeanours, but the possibility clearly exists. Although driving skills will vary considerably between TOCs, not least because of different forms of traction, it is surprising that no centralised core training programme exists, nor any unified system of record keeping and transmission of driver records between train operators. A recommendation for ensuring consistency between drivers working for different TOCs was made in the Watford Inquiry Report (Recommendation 8) but it was not clear what action (if any) had been taken. This is an area which is recommended for further consideration by Railtrack in conjunction with ATOC.

5.6   A particular issue raised at the Inquiry was the status of ATP training in 1997. It was not at that time part of GWT's Driver Competence Assessment, so that a driver who had no or no current ATP training was still competent to drive. Particular issue was taken over one of GWT's Driver Standards Managers, Dave Hockey, who was not himself trained in ATP. Tony Cardall, his Driver Manager, was aware of his lack of training but thought it sufficient that two other DSMs were ATP competent. Despite GWT's explanation, this was a surprising omission, and one that was entirely consistent with a lack of commitment to ATP demonstrated elsewhere. It is also to be noted that Annette Driver, a GWT administration Manager, gave evidence as to the lack of any system for matching ATP competent drivers with ATP designated services. This was undoubtedly a major factor in GWT's inability to run services with ATP, as was the fact that no (or virtually no) basic training and little refresher training (as accepted by GWT), was provided to its drivers between the date of GWT acquiring its franchise (February 1996) and the date of the Southall collision. The consequences of these failures as regards ATP training are considered further in Chapter 13. While they constitute significant omissions by GWT management, they are not to be seen as impacting on general driver training which continued, during the same period, in accordance with established standards.

5.7   Since 1994, GWT had operated an "at risk" driver competence system whereby drivers were listed as Category A (highest risk), B or C (lowest risk). This operates on a points system (similar to motoring) in which, for example, the witnessing of a suicide counts as 2 points, a technical SPAD as 7 points and excess speed as 3-18 points. Drivers are then categorised as follows:

- Category C (lowest risk) 3 to 8 points
- Category B (intermediate risk) 9 to 14 points
- Category A (highest risk) 15 or more points.

Drivers are entitled to be re-categorised following a successful reassessment. Driver Harrison first qualified as a driver in 1975 and was passed competent to drive HSTs in 1981. He remained competent apart from a temporary re-assessment in 1994 which took account of much earlier blemishes on his record. He was, however, passed as competent in July 1995 and re-categorised as C (low risk) in December 1995 after which he remained Category C following successive annual assessments, despite the event in December 1996 (see para 1.23 above). Driver Harrison underwent all the requisite tests for knowledge of the rules and achieved all applicable performance criteria. He was medically examined at required intervals. At the time of the Southall crash, he was 50 years of age and had been medically examined on 9 September 1996. He did not require a further examination until the age of 55. Driver Harrison had received ATP training and refreshment in 1995 but was overdue for further refreshment (see para 6.26). In addition to the blemishes on Driver Harrison's record, it should be noted that he was complimented for exemplary behaviour during a train derailment in November 1995 when, travelling as a passenger, he took over from an injured train driver.

Hours of work

5.8   Limits on working hours for drivers had not been reviewed post-privatisation and had remained the same as those recommended by Mr Anthony Hidden QC in his report on the Clapham Junction crash for safety-critical railway workers. In accordance with these recommendations, drivers' working hours are restricted to

- No more than 12 hours in any day
- No less than 12 consecutive hours rest in any 24 hour period

- No more than 72 hours per week

- No more than 13 shifts in 14 days

Rostered turns of over 12 hours are only permitted to cover engineering work diversions on a Sunday and other occasional work loads. Despite these figures, the average weekly rostered duty of drivers is 37 hours (excluding Sunday) although varying amounts of overtime may be worked in addition to the 37 hours because of delays etc. Drivers are limited to four hours continuous driving Mondays to Saturdays and four and a half hours on Sundays, with reasonable breaks provided within route diagrams.

5.9   There was no evidence suggesting that any of the drivers or staff involved in the Southall crash had worked excessive hours or were subject to potential fatigue. On 19 September 1997, Driver Harrison was rostered to work a shift of 6 hours 19 minutes with 1 hour 55 minutes maximum continuous driving. Before taking over 1A47 at Cardiff, he had had a break of 1 hour 10 minutes. He was therefore well within the maximum permitted working periods. Given the actual weekly hours of drivers, it is difficult to see what justification exists for allowing even the possibility of a 72 hour week, given the progressive increase of speed, technology and general pressure on drivers in the last decade. The effect of research into human behaviour may also dictate a review of working conditions generally. It will be recommended that the permitted working hours for drivers should be the subject of further review on an industry-wide basis, which will also be necessary as a result of the EU Working Time Directive.

Drivers' Safety Response

5.10   It was impressed on the Inquiry that, while drivers were encouraged to avoid delay and to keep to timetable, they were not subject to any penalty or loss of bonus in the event of lateness of a service. Delays were investigated by DSMs but no disciplinary action was provided for. The question was also raised when and in what circumstances drivers were entitled to refuse to work on safety grounds. In regard to non-operational AWS, the provisions of the Rule Book and Standards are considered in Chapter 12, including the question of who should take the decision to take a train out of service. Drivers in common with other workers also have a general right to refuse to work in situations where there is danger, either to themselves or to others who might be affected. This was covered by the GWT Railway Safety Case (section 6.19). Any complaints are usually verbal and settled by a supervisor but there is also a written procedure by which the matter is to be reported to a supervisor who investigates. In the event of disagreement, the matter is to be referred to the manager who may consult safety technical experts if required.

5.11   The written procedure did not form part of the documentation handed to drivers and was not necessarily available to them. However, it was established that drivers were in fact briefed on the procedure, and there is no doubt that they were aware of its existence and of their right to refuse to work. Examples where the right could be invoked by drivers were the breaking of a windscreen or failure of the cab air conditioning, which could lead to temperatures in excess of 100°F.

Restructuring Initiative

5.12   In 1996, shortly after GWT acquired their franchise and at about the same time as the fleet maintenance reorganisation (see para 6.7), GWT embarked on the reorganisation of drivers in a package which became known as the Driver Restructuring Initiative (DRI). This involved changes to working hours, reduction in the working week, improvements to pay and other benefits and, most significant, abolition of double manning of HSTs. An agreement reached between BR and ASLEF in 1988 had allowed single manning up to 110mph but HSTs, with a maximum permitted speed of 125mph, continued to be double-manned up to and beyond privatisation. The introduction of single-manning up to 125mph clearly represented a material cost saving to GWT in that the number of drivers was to be substantially reduced.

5.13 GWT had, before privatisation, commissioned a risk assessment for single manning of HSTs from EQE International. Their report, delivered in October 1995, was based on a risk matrix assessment, and concluded that at speeds above 110mph, a second driver in the cab marginally increased the single driver risk potential, with or without ATP. ATP was, however, noted to be a more effective protection than a second driver in preventing accidents where the driver was at fault. Conversely, there was no clear evidence that double manning led to a reduction in the overall risk. In July 1996, the privatised GWT commissioned a further risk assessment by DNV Technica in respect of the whole DRI. Their report concluded that there were a number of possible benefits and dis-benefits associated with removal of the second driver and that GWT should closely monitor long turns and turns involving drivers at risk. It was further concluded that the combined effect of all the proposals was "not expected, based on available evidence and scientific principles, to adversely affect risks".

5.14 Following the DNV risk assessment, GWT issued a paper for Safety Case approval in August 1996 on the full range of driver restructuring proposals, including single manning. The paper concluded that duties and responsibilities of the drivers would not change with the removal of the second driver. It was stated that current double manning appeared to be based on historical agreements rather than any quantified or scientific basis, and that the change would be subject to frequent monitoring. The proposed changes to the GWT Safety Case were accepted by Railtrack in August 1996. HMRI considered that single manning would not involve any worsening of performance and possibly a marginal improvement. In evidence, examples of accidents caused by the driver being distracted by a second man were cited. Other evidence forming part of the SPADRAM project suggested that 1.3% of SPADs were attributable to distraction by the second driver (generally at speeds in excess of 110mph).

5.15 The negotiated package was put to ASELF members at the same time as a similar package negotiated with GNER, which was the only other operator at speeds over 110mph. The Executive supported the GWT package but opposed that in respect of GNER. Both were passed by conference and came into effect on 29 September 1996. Since that date driving HST's on GWT and all other lines has been single manned.

5.16 The DNV Risk Assessment did not take into account running with safety equipment isolated. Alison Forster, for GWT, accepted in evidence that the DNV report had been equivocal but stated that regular monitoring of single manning had been carried out and reported to team meetings every 4 to 8 weeks with no report of adverse consequences. The crash would probably not have occurred had there been two men in the cab, but it would not be right to conclude that the adoption of single manning above 110mph was itself a contributory cause of the accident. No expert listed single manning as a cause of the accident. The virtually unanimous view was that 1A47 should not have been running with its safety systems isolated. The AWS, if operating, would have provided the necessary warning to the driver.

CHAPTER 6

WHY WERE THE SAFETY SYSTEMS NOT WORKING?

6.1   Shortly after the crash, and following intensive speculation and questioning in the media, it was revealed that 1A47 was, at the time of the accident, running without the Automatic Train Protection (ATP) system operative and with AWS isolated. Subsequent investigations revealed that the AWS system had been subject to a comparatively simple component malfunction which had led to its isolation. As regards the ATP, however, both the trackside and the train-borne equipment were operational. The system had not been switched on. This chapter considers why the train was being driven in this condition. The AWS is considered first.

Failures of the AWS

6.2   In para 1. 4 above, it was noted that the AWS in power car No. 43173 had been isolated by Driver Tunnock at Paddington Station after he brought the set from the depot at Old Oak Common (OOC). This was by no means a simple "one off" failure. It raises questions as to the adequacy of maintenance and fault-reporting systems. Furthermore, as already noted, Driver Tunnock had attempted to report the fault, and it is necessary to consider in some detail the events during the evening of 18 September and the morning of 19 September 1997, which might have led to some action being taken to rectify the fault in power car No. 43173.

6.3   The AWS system involves a number of mechanical and electrical components which, although essentially robust and tested by many years of experience, occasionally fail or malfunction. Power car No. 43173 had no recent history of AWS faults. The last recorded failure was in December 1996 and there was nothing to link this to the malfunction in September 1997. On Thursday 18 September 1997, the set which was subsequently to be driven on the following day by Messrs Tunnock and Harrison, was taken out of Paddington as the 18:02 service to Oxford, as train 1D62. Allan Taylor was the driver and he recalled driving without the driver/guard communication system working, so that station staff had to use the R/A system. After a pause outside Oxford Station, Driver Taylor got out of the country end power car and entered the London end power car No. 43173, to drive the train as 1A85, the 19:47 service, back to Paddington. On being given signal clearance, Driver Taylor took the train across onto the Up line and into Oxford Station where the departure signal was red. As the lead power car passed the AWS ramp, the warning horn sounded and Driver Taylor found that the AWS would not cancel. Consequently the brakes came on automatically with the train halfway into the platform. He therefore took the only action open to him, of going into the engine room and isolating the AWS.

6.4   Appendix 8 of the Rule Book, which Driver Taylor was bound to follow, provided in the case of AWS isolation that the signaller must be informed at the first convenient opportunity, and that the signaller must inform operations control. The driver was required to record the details in the repair book. He was also required to fill in fault report form RT3185, and to complete a GWT Incident Report form. Other requirements of the Rule Book and Group Standards are reviewed in Chapter 12.

6.5   Mr Taylor could not recall whether the AWS was then sealed (as it should have been). After isolating the AWS he went back into the cab where the station supervisor was waiting by the door. Mr Taylor told him what had happened, asked him to obtain permission to draw the train up to the signal and observed this being passed on by radio to Oxford signal box. Richard Parker, who was the signalman on duty in the box recalled being informed that the train had come to a stand due the brakes "going on" and that the driver had reset the brakes. He did not recall any mention of the AWS, however, and did not record the incident in his Occurrence Sheets. Consequently, Signaller Parker did not pass on any information to Operations Control. Permission was given for the train to pull up to the signal. Driver Taylor made an entry in the Defects Repair Book stating "AWS ISOLATED UNABLE TO CANCEL". He subsequently drove the train to Paddington without incident. After the passengers had disembarked, Driver Taylor went back to the country end and took the train to OOC for overnight servicing. He omitted to complete either a Defect Report form or to fill in an Incident Report form. Either of these should have resulted in the fault being recorded on the RAVERS computer system. A report to the signaller (or direct to GWT Control) would similarly have led to the fault being logged on RAVERS. As will be seen in Chapter 12, Driver Taylor was not alone in failing to follow the rules. Mr Taylor thought he had mentioned the fault verbally to Mr Francis, but I discount this: as will be seen, Mr Francis had no knowledge until the entry in the defect book was found. Driver Taylor did fill in an Incident Report form some days after the accident.

Overnight servicing of the train

6.6   Old Oak Common is one of four service depots in which GW train "sets" are serviced, either overnight in the case of routine servicing or for longer periods where heavier servicing is required. Under the relevant Group Standard GM/RT2004 the set delivered by Mr Taylor, designated set PM24 for the purpose of maintenance, required an A Examination which is to be carried out every 3-4 days. A daily S Examination is carried out and heavier maintenance, designated as B through to G, is required at periods ranging from 25 days up to 12 years. The vehicles in question had all received appropriate servicing at the designated periods. The details of servicing are not an issue. On the evening of 18/19 September, the Maintenance Supervisor at OOC was Oliver Francis. The team which worked on PM24 was David McKenzie, Austin Thomas and Greg De Souza. One of the fitters was off sick so that Mr Francis also worked with the team himself. The Production Manager in charge of OOC was Frank Gronow. The Depot Group Manager was Andy Cope and the Director in charge of Fleet was Ian Cusworth.

6.7   It is relevant at this point to consider serious criticism, advanced on behalf of the Passenger Groups, and receiving some support from the documents, that the workforce at OOC were overstretched, disorganised and inadequately trained. The Fleet Maintenance Depots were undergoing a re-structuring of the workforce which involved trials which were still ongoing at OOC in September 1997. Mr Cusworth explained in evidence that the objective was to do away with job demarcation and to increase efficiency. In his view, there was plenty of capacity at OOC. Re-structuring was subject to a risk assessment carried out by DNV Technica in May 1997 and an internal risk management exercise carried out by GWT in June 1997 which recommended monitoring. While numbers of staff had been reduced and hours increased at other depots, there was no substantial change in working hours or in the overall numbers employed at OOC as a result of re-structuring. There were, however, changes to particular trades, such that there was a reduction in technical staff, reflected in the size of teams. This necessarily led to some increase in workload consistent with GWT's view that the depot had spare capacity. The effect of this on 18/19 September was that the men were working under more pressure, and cannot have been motivated to spend more time than the minimum necessary to carry out the required tasks. GWT pointed out that the re-structuring had gone ahead, successfully, at other depots before OOC. They also noted that re-structuring had been supported both by managers and by the workforce. None of these factors can reduce the need for careful monitoring of the effects on performance which, at OOC, should have revealed shortcomings.

6.8   As regards training, while the individuals employed in maintenance work were qualified in their particular trades, training and competency assessment for the specialised tasks involved in vehicle maintenance were organised on an *ad hoc* basis. Staff were trained in some tasks and not others, and the keeping of training records was inadequate. The ATP self-test, which should be carried out as part of the A-Exam, became a particular example. Neither Mr McKenzie nor Mr Thomas knew that the test should be carried out as part of the A Examination. Evidence produced later in the Inquiry by GWT showed that some of those working on A-Exams did perform the test and others did not. There was no systematic training and no records kept. Nor did documentation for the A-Exam include the ATP self-test. As will be seen, failure to perform the self-test can contribute materially to the incidence of faults and therefore lack of availability of ATP.

6.9   At the same time as GWT were involved in their maintenance reorganisation, Railtrack commissioned the special investigation into GWT rolling stock incidents, following nine incidents related to component failure on HSTs between June and November 1996. The audit, carried out by David Parkes, an independent safety auditor, was highly critical of some areas of fleet maintenance and of performance monitoring. Particularly, it was noted that repair sheets checked in the course of the investigation had not been completed in accordance with the quality system. The report also questioned whether adequate human resources were available to undertake key safety work (see also para 14.11). In response, GWT undertook the provision of additional resources, proposed corrective action and commissioned Halcrow Transmark to assist in updating maintenance and overhaul policy, to ensure compliance with the Safety Case and Group Standards. Thus, GWT were, on 18/19 September 1997, in the course of improving their maintenance procedures, subject to the restructuring which had been carried out.

6.10   As the Maintenance Supervisor, Mr Francis received by fax from Swindon, information about the sets to be serviced. Defects should be recorded in a Defect Book, kept in the cab of each power car, and in a further comprehensive list maintained on the RAVERS computer system, to which the depot had access. For PM24, the RAVERS system recorded an intermittent AWS fault on power car No. 43163. Mr Francis and Mr McKenzie attended to this. No additional faults were logged on RAVERS for power car No. 43173. Towards the end of the work on PM24, Mr Thomas examined the Defect Book in power car No.43173 and found there Mr Taylor's note of the AWS defect. Mr Thomas, therefore, requested help and he and Mr McKenzie attended to the AWS in power car No. 43173. Unknown to the maintenance staff and revealed only by tests carried out after the crash, the AWS reset switch had contamination on its electrical contact surfaces which rendered its performance intermittent.

Testing the AWS

6.11   In each power car, investigation of the AWS fault consisted of conducting a magnet test, by which one of the fitters (Mr McKenzie) went under the power car with a magnet to simulate the service conditions for both a clear signal and a restrictive aspect, while the other operated the reset button to cancel the horn and checked the bell. Each test was performed three times. In all cases, the tests revealed that the system was working normally with no faults. Both Mr Francis and Mr McKenzie confirmed their understanding that if, when such a test was performed, the horn sounded and the reset button functioned correctly, then there was assumed to be no fault. Mr McKenzie was aware of the existence of a "test box" which could be used to investigate reported faults which could not be replicated on test. This would have taken half an hour to carry out. The procedure was not attempted. Mr McKenzie thought that the test box at OOC was not calibrated and therefore could not be used. Further investigation during the course of the Inquiry revealed that the test box, even if calibrated, could not have replicated the particular fault on the reset switch, since the box was capable only of checking that electrical circuits were complete and not measuring electrical resistance.   The subsequent development of an alternative type of test box is referred to in para 9.22.

6.12   Further evidence and documents were produced during the course of the Inquiry as to repair procedures introduced by BR in respect of AWS faults. In the case of a "right-side" failure (i.e. failure to a safe condition) where the magnet test (as carried out by Messrs Thomas and McKenzie) failed to reveal any fault, BR Specification MT/169, issued in 1980 provided that the vehicle should be returned to traffic. A later Specification TEE/CM/89/M/200, issued in 1989 required, after a successful magnet test, that all items of the system should be examined and a test set (test box) used. Only after such examination had verified the equipment to be fully functional could the vehicle be returned to traffic. It was unclear whether the later Specification should be taken to override the earlier. Andy Cope, in a supplemental witness statement, stated that the intended incorporation of these two documents never took place. By 1996, GWT had drawn up its own technical procedure, FLT/2042 for the AWS test, which required an examination of all items of the system, and included the following:

"3.2.5 Perform a full AWS test on vehicle using either (sic) the AWS test set as specified in MT169 (vehicles fitted with separate bell, horn and indicator)."

"3.2.8 After any repairs or replacement of parts then re-test carrying out 3.2.5 to verify the system is operational. Once 3.2.5 has been carried out satisfactorily, even if no equipment has been found defective, the vehicle may be returned to traffic."

6.13 Given the uncertainty as to precisely which rules applied and the combination of ambiguous and obscure drafting, it is not a matter of criticism that Mr Francis and his team acted as they did. Even if they had interpreted the Rules as requiring the use of the test box, as noted above, it would not have assisted in identifying the faulty component. Without the aid of the more sophisticated test box subsequently developed (see Chapter 9) it was a matter of chance whether any test procedure could have diagnosed the faulty reset switch.

6.14 PM24 was therefore passed for service. The AWS in power car 43163 had not been isolated and no further action by the fitters was required. The system in power car 43173 had been isolated by Mr Taylor. After returning the handle to the normal position, the fitters should have applied a seal, but failed to do so. There was some confusion as to whether lead seals were, in fact, available at OOC. Although the fitters thought they were not available, spare lead seals were found within the engine compartment of power car 43173 after the collision. In any event, plastic seals were available. Neither were used. Additionally, the procedure required completion of a "Work Arising" sheet from which the Supervisor, Mr Francis, should have filled out the maintenance log. This was not done in regard to the work to the AWS in power car 43173. Further, although the Repair Book in power car 43173 was full, it was not replaced; and although the fitters had attended to the AWS fault recorded in the Repair Book in power car 43163, they failed to sign off the counterfoil, as they should have done. This small collection of errors and omissions may be seen as indicative of a general lack of care or, contrary to the views of Messrs Cusworth and Cope, as indicative of being overworked. For this purpose it is necessary to look a little further at the evidence.

6.15   It appears from the evidence of Mr Francis that, at the end of the shift, at 06:00 on 19 September 1997, he was still working on another train, while others had completed their tasks and were ready to clock off. This may be why Mr Francis was not able to complete the paperwork or to check that all necessary procedures had been completed. On the night in question, Mr Francis' maintenance team consisted of four fitters, as opposed to the six which had been employed prior to the re-organisation in 1996. Mr Francis, as a result of working with the fitters, had difficulty in carrying out his supervisory duties as well as completing the paperwork. There is no reason to conclude that such events occurred only on the evening in question. Other records revealed a similar picture during the days preceding the Southall accident in regard to other maintenance work on power car 43173. Documents revealed that recurrent faults had been reported in respect of the horn and the driver/guard buzzer which had not been adequately dealt with, nor had all the appropriate paperwork been completed. It was confirmed that the RAVERS system had no provision to record whether defects were recurrent. It must be concluded that the maintenance procedures at OOC were far from robust. Whatever the effect of the re-organisation of 1996 and the on-going team trials, there was, in September 1997, a lack of attention to details, some of which were safety-critical.

Driver Tunnock collects the train

6.16   After completion of maintenance and repair work by the fitters at OOC, set PM24 was collected by Driver Tunnock at around 4:40 am on 19 September 1997. In accordance with established procedures, he made a visual external examination along one side of the train. He then entered one power car, examined the engine room, checked the parking brake and started the engine, which automatically started that at the other end. He then alighted and checked the other side of the train. On reaching the other power car, he again inspected the engine room. A brake test was conducted, with the co-operation of the shunter. He checked the headlights, took off the parking brake and went back to the other power car to conduct identical checks. He did not, as he should have, check the seal on the AWS isolating lever in power car 43173. At the front of the train he was given a "Driver Only Operating" (DOO) slip which authorised him to drive away. Driver Tunnock then took PM24 out of OOC towards Paddington. He passed an AWS test ramp on leaving the depot which operated the AWS horn. He would have passed other signals on the 10 minute journey, at least one of which would have been displaying a restrictive aspect. The AWS functioned normally. He arrived at Paddington, platform 3 just after 06:00, shut the engine down and went to the country end power car No. 43163. Here he found that the guard/driver buzzer was not working. It had not been working on the previous day when Driver Taylor drove to and from Oxford. Driver Tunnock went back to the London end power car No. 43173 and put in the key to activate the system. It was at this point that he found he could not cancel the AWS.

Driver Tunnock reports two faults

6.17   As noted in Chapter 1, Driver Tunnock proceeded to Mr Barnfield's office where he reported the two problems on his train (Mr Barnfield remembered only one of them specifically, the AWS). Mr Barnfield recalled asking if

Driver Tunnock required the station fitter and attempted to contact him by phone, without result. Accordingly, Mr Barnfield rang what he thought was GWT Control at Swindon. He did this by pressing the top automatic dial button on his telephone and then handing the telephone to Driver Tunnock who spoke to a person whom he recalled as a male voice who identified himself as Swindon Control. The result of the telephone conversation, as recalled by Mr Barnfield, was Driver Tunnock stating that he would have to take the train to Swansea and sort the problem out there. Apart from the use of the R/A procedure, there was no "problem" at the country end power car No. 43163, which had an operational AWS. However, there was no question of Driver Tunnock being unconcerned about the AWS because someone else was to drive the train back to Paddington. On the contrary, I am satisfied that Driver Tunnock took a responsible attitude to a problem which was not of his making. All those concerned must have been aware that the proper procedure was for the AWS fault to be reported to a signalman, who would in turn, report it to Swindon Control. On the day before, Driver Taylor had thought (mistakenly) that the signalman had been informed. Now, on 19 September, Driver Tunnock was short circuiting the system, as he thought, by reporting direct to Swindon Control and asking for fitters to attend at Swansea.

6.18　For the Inquiry hearing, GWT called evidence from members of the night shift at Swindon Control (22:00 to 07:00), each of whom stated that no call was received from Driver Tunnock. Swindon Control involves three separate functions, namely Service Control, Fleet Maintenance Control and Information Control. On the night shift in question, there were two Service Controllers, Andrew Kirwan and Tony Hart with Gordon Vinnicombe as Fleet Maintenance Controller. In addition, owing to staff shortage, Andrew Kirwan acted as Information Controller. Michael Ford had been the Service Delivery Manager since June 1997. He started work early at about 06:45 on 19 September and could have been present at the time of Driver Tunnock's call. Andrew Glover, who controlled the POIS/TOPS computer systems started work at 06:00. None of these gentlemen recalled receiving a message. Had they done so, they considered that they would have taken appropriate details and made a record. No record has been found. Evidence was introduced purporting to establish that no telephone call was made to Swindon Control at the relevant time; but other records showed calls being received at 06:12 and 06:31 on 19 September 1997, the origin being unknown.

6.19 As already noted in Chapter 1, on arrival at Swansea, Driver Tunnock, believing that Swindon Control had been duly notified, expected fitters to be in attendance to deal with both the driver/guard communcation and the AWS fault. They were not there. Driver Tunnock went to the platform office where he telephoned GWT Swindon Control. The call went through to the desk of the Fleet Maintenance Controller, John Harris (who had taken over from Gordon Vinnicomb at 07:00). John Harris was not at his desk and the call was taken by Sandra Hallett, Information Controller. A former GWT stewardess, she had been working at control for some 3 weeks, following 4 weeks training. She was not yet familiar with "railway jargon" and acronyms, and recalled only that a driver at Swansea had called regarding "isolating something". Mrs Hallett stated that she made a note of the message which got destroyed at the end of the shift. She believed that she passed the note either to Philip Malyon, who had taken over as Service Controller at 07:00 or, more likely, to John Harris. Both denied receiving such a message. Mrs Hallet subsequently confirmed that, contrary to her earlier belief, no papers were thrown away at the end of her shift and consequently it appears that no note was in fact made of Driver Tunnock's call.

6.20 Evidence was also called from Michael Ford, Service Delivery Manager at Swindon Control and Nigel Fulford, Planning and Performance Manager, who had overall responsibility for control. There was initial uncertainty as to what documentation was maintained at Swindon Control. Mr Ford was able to confirm that the Master Rule Book was available but it was subsequently accepted on behalf of GWT that no copy of Group Standard GO/OT0013 was available. The effect of the Rule Book and of the Group Standard is considered in detail in Chapter 12. It is sufficient to note that the Rule Book required, in the case of AWS isolation, that the train must be taken out of service "at the first suitable location without causing delay or cancellation". The Group Standard stood as advice to those making decisions, but did not change the rule. Driver Tunnock had his own copy of the Drivers' Rule Book (but not the Group Standard). There was a degree of ambiguity between different versions of the Rule Book as to whether a decision to take a train out of service was to be made by the driver or by control (and some uncertainty as to what was meant by "control"). These were not live issues on 19 September 1997 since it was clear that Driver Tunnock had made successive attempts to pass the relevant information to GWT Control at Swindon and no one on the day suggested that, for an AWS fault, it was Driver Tunnock's duty himself to withdraw the train from service. There was much debate on whether drivers in fact had the right to refuse to work in such circumstances. This has been considered in Chapter 5. It is sufficient to say that this issue was not present in anyone's mind at the relevant time.

Why nothing was done

6.21 Driver Tunnock was therefore left on Swansea Station with no assistance. He next tried the Station Services Manager, William Palmer, who telephoned the GWT Landore Depot, only 10 minutes away, to request assistance. The call was taken by Raymond Lloyd, Acting Team Leader, who promptly despatched Andy Arnold and Ken Bass to Swansea to deal with the problem. Again, there was confusion as to who had said what. Driver Tunnock believed that the fitters had been informed about the AWS and had tried to repair it. Mr Palmer was clear that he had not got involved in the nature of the problems. Mr Lloyd and the fitters seemed to be aware only of the driver/guard communication problem and that was certainly all that was attended to. Time was against Driver Tunnock as the fitters arrived at 10:15 and his scheduled departure was 10:32. Mr Lloyd was adamant that had he been told about the AWS, he would have reported to control (as Driver Tunnock had attempted to do, repeatedly). No note was subsequently found containing any reference to AWS, even though a number of records were made of the fitters' work.

6.22   According to Mr Lloyd, the fitters returned at 10:45 and he then phoned Swindon Control to report to someone called "Graham". In fact, the call was taken by John Harris and logged at 11:55, at which time 1A47 was already on its way from Cardiff driven by Driver Harrison. According to Mr Harris, Mr Lloyd's call was in response to an earlier request from Swindon Control to carry out work to another train. During the call to confirm the work done, Mr Lloyd mentioned isolation of the driver/guard communcation system on 1A47 but not the AWS. Mr Harris accordingly informed the Service Controller, Philip Malyon, who put out a wire to alert the platform staff of the need to use the R/A procedure.

6.23   These were some of the reasons why 1A47 was travelling towards London with the AWS isolated. Only Drivers Tunnock and Harrison were aware of it. In fact, although numerous officials could have taken the decision to withdraw 1A47 from service, or to have insisted on the train being turned, the Rule Book did not then make such action imperative. Nor in my view, would any such action have been taken had Swindon Control been fully aware of the situation. Had any of Driver Tunnock's messages regarding the AWS been received by a person in authority, it would not have been possible to repair the AWS before the return journey to London. No work could have been done to power car No.43173 without the use of a pit and this would have required the train being taken out of service. In the light of these conclusions, the question of what happened to Driver Tunnock's successive messages is of secondary importance. The condition of the train at Paddington was caused directly by the failure of the maintenance team at OOC to diagnose and rectify the fault noted in the repair book by Mr Taylor on 18 September.

6.24   A further reason why 1A47 was running from Swansea to Paddington without an operational AWS in power car 43173 was that no steps had been taken to turn the train. It is now accepted by GWT that the train could have been turned by the use of a "triangle" at Swansea. This would have involved driving the train into a triangular section of siding and then the driver changing ends to drive back onto the Up Main line with power car 43163 facing London. There was some dispute as to the time that would have been necessary to carry out this manoeuvre but GWT accepted, and I accept, that it could have been carried out within the changeover time available at Swansea. GWT further accepted, however, that the train would not have been reversed in this manner even if Control had known of the AWS isolation. The failure to turn the train was therefore due to the absence of an appropriate procedure rather than the failure of any of Driver Tunnock's messages to reach Control.

6.25 As noted above, tests performed on the AWS reset switch recovered from power car 43173 after the crash revealed the reason for its intermittent failure to operate. A contaminant was found on the electrical contact surfaces which produced occasional high resistance in tests performed by WS Atkins. The contaminant was initially thought to be tea, which could have leaked downwards into the switch contacts. Further testing during the course of the Inquiry revealed the presence of chemical traces which ruled out tea. The conclusion reached was that the most likely source of the contamination was from the use of polish. None of the relevant cleaning procedures involved the use of polish and its presence, therefore, remains a mystery.

ATP not switched on

6.26 The reason why 1A47 was running without the Automatic Train Protection (ATP) system operational can be stated shortly. Despite many technical problems which had beset ATP since its introduction as a Pilot Scheme, ATP was operational and could have been switched on in power car 43173. Both Drivers Tunnock and Harrison had undergone basic ATP training but neither had received current refresher training and neither therefore considered himself competent to use ATP. GWT's operating rules in September 1997 did not oblige drivers to keep up their qualification, nor to use ATP. Thus, although services 1B08 and 1A47 were both ATP designated services, neither Driver Tunnock nor Driver Harrison were obliged by the rules to switch the equipment on. Of more relevance is the fact that GWT's rostering procedures did not require or even facilitate the matching of ATP designated services with competent drivers. Unsupervised service running was limited to 30% and, at the relevant time, was actually much lower. It is certain that there were ATP-competent drivers who were rostered to non-ATP designated services on the day in question.

6.27 An additional reason why ATP was not operational for the journey undertaken by Driver Harrison was that, even if he had been qualified to use ATP, the Rules current at the time, would have prevented him from switching on the system at an intermediate point on a journey. The original reason for this Rule was said to be the requirement for a self-test on start-up, lasting 4 minutes. The procedure had been revised in 1996 by limiting the range of tests performed, so that the system could be brought into operation within approximately two minutes. On 19 September 1997, this procedure was not authorised. It appears that drivers had been told of the shorter self-test, but it was still regarded as too long for switching in at an intermediate station.

6.28 Issue was taken as to whether Driver Harrison was, in fact, competent to use ATP. He had undergone the initial training and accepted (he had claimed extra payment on this account) that he had taken a refresher course in September 1995. He claimed, however, that he required additional refresher training and had verbally made such a request to Lester Watts, the Driver Standards Manager. Mr Watts denied any such request and stated that it should have been made in writing and, if received, would have been entered in Mr Watts' records for future action. I prefer Mr Watts' version of events, but it remains the fact that Driver Harrison had never driven a train unsupervised with ATP switched on and could hardly be expected to have done so on this occasion, more particularly, given the unusual situation of an isolated AWS. Driver Harrison was not in breach of any Rule.

6.29 Accordingly, the reason why 1A47 was operating without ATP was that neither of the drivers regarded themselves as either competent or bound to use the system. The Rules did not require them to use it and no one suggested that they should do so. It did not occur to anyone that ATP was a complete answer to the absence of an operational AWS.

CHAPTER 7

WHY THE ACCIDENT HAPPENED

7.1   The relevant events leading up to and immediately following the accident on 19 September 1997 have been set down and analysed in chapters 1 to 6. This has covered the systems and procedures in place at the time of the accident, which may have had an effect on its occurrence and its consequences. More than two years have now elapsed since the accident and it will be necessary in the following chapters to review both the reasons for the delay and the intervening events which have occurred in order to draw conclusions which are relevant at the date of this report. At this stage it is appropriate to address the Terms of Reference (see preface) which require me to determine why the accident happened and in particular to identify the cause or causes.

Track and signals

7.2   No relevant deficiency in the track has been identified. The Up Main line had been adequately maintained. A detected broken rail, which was replaced on the day before the accident, showed that the maintenance system was operating properly. In regard to the signals, the testing of circuits and equipment, together with records from the SSI tapes, established conclusively that the equipment was fully operational at the time of the accident and that the signals had been set correctly for train 1A47 to stop before reaching Southall East Junction. It can therefore be concluded that Driver Harrison passed through two warning signals without taking any action to slow the train. As regards visibility, there is no issue about signal SN254, which Driver Harrison saw and immediately identified as set at red. Signals SN270 and 280, which were the two preceding warning signals, were each located above the normal height now recommended, but this had no material effect on their visibility. Signal SN270 was, additionally, misaligned to "focus" at a point substantially closer to the signal than should have been the case. However, this did not prevent the signal being adequately visible from the minimum sighting distance, 7 seconds before the signal, when running at line speed of 125mph. Despite its misalignment, the signal was adequately visible to others and I cannot regard signal SN270 nor any other approach signal leading up to Southall East Junction as having contributed to the accident. Neither the track nor the signalling equipment are to be regarded as a cause of the accident.

7.3 Two matters relating to signals did give cause for concern. First, post-accident testing of signals was unduly repetitious and prolonged. Signal sighting and alignment should have been the subject of one definitive factual investigation, upon which experts representing different parties could subsequently have given opinions and drawn conclusions. It should not have been necessary for signal sighting tests to be repeated more than 6 months after the accident. Secondly, the failure to correct the misalignment of signal SN270 until November 1999 revealed a potentially serious breakdown in the process of passing on safety-critical information between interested parties. It also revealed, separately, a serious lack of contractual clarity between Railtrack and Amey Rail as to their respective maintenance responsibilities. These issues are considered further in relation to lessons to be learned from the accident in Chapter 16.

Regulation

7.4 It is undeniable that the decision to route freight train 6V17 across the path of the HST created, in the current jargon, a "collision opportunity" which tragically became a reality through train 1A47 not heeding warning signals SN280 and 270. The relevant question to be asked, however, is whether this involved any error of policy or operation, such that the decision made by the signaller can be regarded as a cause of the accident. First, it is necessary to consider the relevant policy of regulation, which is reviewed in Chapter 4 above. Railtrack were responsible for the introduction, in 1996, of a new regulation policy based on minimising overall delay. This was reflected in an addition to the track access conditions which included reference to the protection of "commercial interests", a provision about which Mr Tom

Winsor, the current Rail Regulator, expressed concern. The new policy was introduced without the benefit of a risk analysis. The same is true of the ARS technology which incorporates a similar form of regulation, but involves no intervention by the signaller. As regards causation of the accident, the effect of the new regulation policy, to which Signaller Forde adhered, was that there was no reason to give priority to the HST, which could accordingly be held up in favour of the freight train. In terms of commercial interests, although there was no specific evidence as to the sums involved, it seems likely that delaying an HST in favour of an empty freight train would be commercially disadvantageous. The question addressed by Signaller Forde, however, was how to achieve the freight crossing with minimum overall delay. I do not believe that, in the circumstances, the decision made by Signaller Forde had any safety implications, given that the crossing had to be achieved at some point in the face of regular HST and other passenger services on both main lines. Nor did it involve any consideration of the overall commercial effect. In my view, the regulating policy as applied by Signaller Forde cannot be said to have caused or contributed to the accident.

7.5   In addition to the policy, there was some criticism of Signaller Forde's operational decision to set a route for the crossing of 6V17 at the moment that he did. It was suggested that he should have waited until the last possible moment before setting the route, so as to minimise the "vital interval" during which one train was in the path of the other. In my view, such criticism should be firmly rejected. Any regulation policy must be based on the assumption that trains will comply with signals. Consideration of the consequences of not doing so lies in the field of Layout Risk Analysis, not signalling. It must also be borne in mind that the operation undertaken by Signaller Forde involved overriding the ARS, which would have automatically barred the setting of the route within a short time, had there been further delay. It has been demonstrated that Signaller Forde's decision, in terms of overall delay was at least close to the optimum decision that could have been taken in terms of minimising overall delay. It should be clearly stated that no criticism whatever attaches to the decisions made by Signaller Forde. He had no knowledge of the isolated AWS system on train 1A47 and no reason to believe that Driver Harrison would behave as he did. His actions were not a contributory cause of the accident.

7.6   On the basis of events at Southall, I do not believe that the regulation policy introduced in 1996 by Railtrack had any safety implications. The failure at the time to consider carrying out a risk analysis was remiss, but ultimately of no consequence. In my view, the minimising of overall delay to trains is neutral as regards safety. Nevertheless I believe that reference to commercial interests is quite inappropriate in regard to any regulating decision to be made by a signaller. Furthermore, the interests of safety and security should be paramount and not matters to be balanced with other considerations. To this extent, I agree with and endorse the views of Mr Tom Winsor referred to in para 4.13.

Isolated AWS

7.7   There are a number of different aspects to the issue of AWS isolation. First, it is necessary to identify the reasons why the train in question, then known as set PM24, was allowed to leave OOC on the morning of 19 September 1997 with the AWS in power car 43173 in a state which was likely to lead to a further failure. The earlier failure at Oxford on 18 September 1997 had been entered in the Defect Book of power car 43173 by Driver Taylor. This entry was found late on during the overnight maintenance work at OOC, so that the failure by Driver Taylor to report to the signaller or to fill in a Defect Report or Incident Report form, and the consequent omission of the AWS isolation from the RAVERS computer system, did not result in the fault being overlooked. As regards the testing carried out by Messrs Thomas and McKenzie, this was in accordance with the current practice. Three separate and differing specifications existed covering AWS testing, leading to uncertainty as to precisely what was required. They were ambiguous and obscure, partly as a result of deficient paperwork inherited from BR and partly as a result of GWT's failure to resolve the ambiguities and obscurities, which persisted under their rules. The failure by the maintenance team to make use of the AWS test box and failure to ensure even that the box was in proper working order are superficially reprehensible. Yet it is now clear that the existing test box design was such that it could not have diagnosed the fault in question. This was consistent with the low safety priority accorded to the AWS system, again partly an inherited matter, and partly a failure by GWT properly to assess an issue of safety. There can be no doubt that it would have been within the technical competence of GWT to devise a system for identifying any AWS fault, given the will to do so. The workforce at OOC was working under pressure, as revealed by sloppy paperwork as well as a history of uncorrected minor defects. But I am satisfied that this of itself was not a cause of set PM24 being put into service without the previously reported AWS fault having been rectified. The fault lay in the system being operated by GWT and not with the workforce, none of whom deserve to be criticised for the state in which set PM24 went into service.

7.8   From the time that Driver Tunnock arrived at platform 3, Paddington, and found the AWS in power car 43173 again not working, the question of what went wrong focuses on a number of individuals who had the opportunity to prevent the train entering service at all, or of requiring it to be terminated at Swansea or of turning the train. At this stage, I am not concerned with the proper interpretation of the Rules (which are considered in detail in Chapter 12), which, however, clearly required the fault to be reported to the signalman. On 19 September 1997 all those concerned were content to short circuit the Rules by contacting Swindon Control direct. In the light of all the evidence, which is considered in detail in Chapter 6, I am satisfied that Driver Tunnock did speak to Swindon Control at about 06:30 on 19 September 1997 and that his message, requesting assistance at Swansea, was lost or overlooked, probably as a result of the change of shift that was occurring at about this time at Swindon Control. The recipient of the message cannot now be identified. I am satisfied that Driver Tunnock again contacted Swindon Control from

Swansea Station with a message that the AWS was isolated. This message was taken by Sandra Hallett, who believed that she had passed the message on to Philip Malyon or, more likely, to John Harris. Mrs Hallett had not understood the message and it appears that no note was in fact made of this call. On balance, I am not satisfied that the message was ever passed on. As regards the call-out of the Landore fitters, I am not persuaded that Messrs. Lloyd, Arnold or Bass were aware of an AWS problem, most probably because Mr Palmer, in making the call to the Landore depot did not regard it as his job to specify the work required. The first message which was logged at Swindon Control was received by John Harris at 11:55 from the Landore fitters who, being unaware of the AWS problem, did not report it. In retrospect it is clear that Driver Tunnock's appeals for help in the form of fitters would have been to no avail, since the AWS could only have been attended to by taking the train out of service or by turning it.

7.9   In my view, responsibility for failing to respond to Driver Tunnock's two telephone calls must rest primarily with those having responsibility for the procedures in operation at Swindon Control, particularly the systems for receiving and acting upon messages. No individual can be identified as responsible for failing to act on Driver Tunnock's early morning telephone call. As regards the call from Swansea, Sandra Hallett must bear some responsibility, but the primary fault lay in her lack of training. It is inconceivable that any proper system could allow a safety-critical message to be received by someone whose training did not enable them to appreciate the importance of information which potentially threatened the lives of many people. Had either of Driver Tunnock's messages been received, I am satisfied that it would have been possible (and this was accepted by GWT) to have made arrangements to turn the train at Swansea. Alternatively, the train could have been taken out of service there. However, GWT did not contend that they would, in fact, have taken either of these actions had the messages been received. There was certainly no record of these steps ever being taken by GWT in such circumstances and the level of AWS failures eventually established showed that such occurrences were by no means rare. Consequently, although the failures of communication were serious and reprehensible, the appropriate conclusion to be drawn is that train 1A47 was allowed to run with AWS isolated because this was accepted by GWT, and would have been accepted had they received and considered Driver Tunnock's messages in due time. While these conclusions deal with the actions taken at the time, it must not be overlooked that the Rule Book required notification to the signalman, which (both in the case of the failure at Oxford and that at Paddington) would have brought the matter to the attention of Railtrack. This would have created at least the opportunity for more effective action. The general decision to short-circuit the Rule Book cannot be condoned.

ATP not operational

7.10 The ATP system in power car 43173 was fully operational, as was the trackside equipment over the route from Bristol Parkway to Paddington.. The 10:32 HST service from Swansea to Paddington was a designated ATP service, being part of the then current 30% USSR which had been in operation since December 1996. There were three reasons why the ATP was not in use on the relevant service. First, Driver Harrison considered that he was insufficiently trained. I am not satisfied that Driver Harrison had notified GWT of this and I do not accept his evidence that he had requested refresher training. However, he had never driven a train unsupervised with ATP switched on and GWT cannot have entertained any expectation that he would drive with the assistance of ATP on 19 September 1997. Secondly, even if Driver Harrison had been competent to drive with ATP, GWT's Rules did not then permit the equipment to be switched on in the course of a journey. Driver Tunnock had not switched it on because he too was not trained. There was, in 1997, no reason to maintain this Rule, which was formerly justified by the need for a 4 minute self-test on start up. By 1996, the test had been reduced to some 2 minutes but switching in at an intermediate station was still not authorised. Thirdly GWT's rostering system did not even attempt to match ATP designated services with qualified drivers. The rostering of Drivers

Tunnock and Harrison on the Swansea to Paddington service was therefore not a matter of surprise. These were the immediate reasons why ATP was non-operational on service 1A47. The underlying reasons are discussed at greater length in Chapter 13

Driver Harrison

7.11   His contribution to the accident has been discussed at some length in Chapter 1. In drawing conclusions as to causation and blame, Counsel appearing for Driver Harrison and ASLEF reminded me of the standard of proof to be applied in civil proceedings in the face of very serious allegations and of the danger of drawing damaging conclusions following an inquisitorial process. Reference was made to the approach adopted by Lord Justice Denning in *Baxter v. Baxter* [1951] P35 at page 37 where he said (in relation to a divorce petition on the ground of alleged cruelty):

> "A civil court...does not adopt so high a degree as a criminal court, even when it is considering a charge of a criminal nature; but still it does require a degree of probability which is commensurate with the occasion".

I bear this in mind in relation to the facts which were either admitted or readily ascertainable, as reviewed in Chapter 1. The matter which stands out from the available evidence is Driver Harrison's inability to offer any proper explanation for his failure to respond to signals SN280 or 270. His account of putting things into his bag could not have accounted for more than a few seconds. It is possible this could have been the reason for missing one of the signals, but not both. While Counsel for Driver Harrison put forward various reasons why a signal might have been missed, ranging from poor visibility (particularly of signal SN270) to sunlight, Driver Harrison did not himself give any support to either explanation, both of which I reject. The inevitable conclusion, bearing in mind the required degree of probability to be established, is that Driver Harrison was inattentive at the critical moments of passing the two warning signals.

7.12   Evidence on "human behaviour" was called on behalf of Driver Harrison and responded to by HSE and by W S Atkins. This established the possibility of short periods of inattention referred to as "microsleeps" which may explain but not excuse Driver Harrison's conduct. Of more direct relevance was the evidence suggestive of some form of misconduct on his part. First, an allegation originally pursued by BTP, suggested the possibility of misuse of the driver's bag as a weight to hold down the driver's pedal, thus relieving the driver of the burden of holding down the pedal throughout a journey. Such an allegation merited serious consideration only because of its appalling reflection on the highly responsible task of driving at high speed. There was in fact little to support such an allegation beyond some instances of seemingly eccentric behaviour from Driver Harrison. The use of such a device would in any event still require the pedal to be lifted frequently in response to the DVD.

7.13   One form of eccentricity which seemed to add credence to the allegation concerning misuse of the driver's bag, was the recollection of a number of witnesses that Driver Harrison was seen to drive into Bristol Parkway with both his feet up on the front console. This allegation was challenged on behalf of Driver Harrison on both factual and technical grounds. It is also relevant to recall evidence that Driver Harrison's apparently casual manner caused alarm to passengers. Taking these allegations of misconduct together, I conclude that there is no credible evidence to support the suggestion that Driver Harrison was misusing his bag in a manner that might have contributed to the accident. The allegation is of such a damaging nature that in the absence of clear evidence it should be firmly rejected. Conversely, I find the evidence of Driver Harrison's casual manner, particularly of driving into a station with both feet resting up on the console, to be credible and compelling and I can find no reason to reject this evidence. This particular incident was not alledged to have endangered safety. What is of relevance is that the evidence reveals Driver Harrison as a man capable of a somewhat cavalier disregard of convention. Taken with other events in his past, Driver Harrison can be seen as a man capable of irregular behaviour which might lead to the disregarding of safety Rules.

7.14 There was nothing in Driver Harrison's formal training record to suggest any technical deficiency in his mastery of the job of driving. He passed all relevant tests and scored highly in the obligatory questionnaires. Outwardly Driver Harrison was a competent, skilled and highly experienced driver, yet on one crucial occasion his inattention led to disaster. In these circumstances, it is relevant to pose the question whether the system of training and assessment is capable of identifying effectively drivers who are "at risk". The answer may lie in the emerging study of human behaviour. On the basis of the evidence presented, I would not accept that any driver might have committed the same error in Mr Harrison's shoes.

What caused the accident

7.15 The accident at Southall on 19 September 1997 would not have occurred had ATP been operational in power car 43173. A cause of the accident was, therefore, GWT's failure to roster ATP competent drivers for train 1A47. Had the 07:00 Paddington to Swansea and the 10:32 Swansea to Paddington services been rostered to ATP competent drivers, the Rule which prevented ATP being switched on at Cardiff would not have applied and both services would have been fully ATP protected, as they should have been.

7.16 In the absence of ATP, the AWS system became critical. While drivers accepted the traditional view that AWS was merely an "aid" the reality was somewhat different, as the Southall accident has demonstrated. While it must be emphasised that the primary duty of a driver is to keep a vigilant lookout at all times, there must be a tendency for drivers, to an extent, to become dependent on the security of an automatic warning on the approach to every signal. A full understanding of the effect of such systems depends upon studies of human behaviour in the particular environment of the driving cab, a subject which has so far received only limited attention. It can be concluded, however, that the absence of AWS was a contributory factor to the failure of Driver Harrison to respond to signals SN280 or 270 at the crucial time.

7.17   Responsibility for non-functioning of the AWS on service 1A47 rests firmly with GWT, first in having inadequate maintenance procedures to eliminate known faults, and secondly through inadequate procedures for communicating and taking action following AWS isolation. The existence of ambiguous and confusing Rules as regards action to be taken in the event of AWS isolation is principally the responsibility of Railtrack, who should have initiated a review. The immediate responsibility for the accident, however, rests with Driver Harrison for his unexplained inattention, particularly in the circumstances of operating a passenger train at high speed, knowing that neither of the available warning systems was operational.

7.18   The Drivers' Restructuring Initiative introduced by GWT in 1996 resulted in the removal of the second man from the cab. The question necessarily arises whether this change should also be regarded as having contributed causally to the crash. As noted in Chapter 5, the two risk assessments carried out by GWT, before and after privatisation, were not wholly conclusive, the later DNV report recommending continued monitoring of the situation. No consideration was given to running HSTs without operative safety systems and the EQE report appeared to place some reliance (which was quite misplaced in the circumstances), on the availability of ATP. Given that a second man was subsequently advocated as one possible safety measure on isolation of the AWS (see Chapter 9), the removal of the second man might be seen as a contributory cause to the particular accident at Southall. However, given the conclusion that the HST should have not been running on a normal route with AWS isolated (a conclusion now universally accepted), the removal of a second man cannot be seen as causative in itself.

7.19   It is not my task to determine legal liability. To determine what caused the accident it is necessary, however, to place the alternative causes in some order of ranking. Having carefully considered the contemporary evidence I have come to the following conclusions:

- The primary cause of the accident was Driver Harrison's unexplained failure to respond to two warning signals.

Other causes of the accident which rank equally in their potency were:

- The failure of GWT's maintenance system to identify and repair the previously reported AWS fault in power car 43173.

- The failure of GWT to react to isolation of the AWS on power car 43173 by turning the train or withdrawing it from service.

- The failure of Railtrack to put in place clear Rules to prevent any normal running of an HST service with AWS isolated.

- The failure of GWT to manage the ATP Pilot Scheme such that ATP equipment in power car 43173 was switched on.

7.20   It should be recorded that both GWT and Railtrack, during the course of the Inquiry, accepted responsibility for their part in the accident. Specifically, Alison Forster accepted on behalf of GWT that they had not recognised the risk of running without AWS. GWT specifically accepted that they had the opportunity to turn the train at Swansea, or to withdraw it from service, and on this basis pleaded guilty to the charge under section 3 of the Health and Safety at Work Act, 1974 of failing to conduct their undertaking in such a way as to ensure "so far as reasonably practicable that persons...who may be affected thereby are not thereby exposed to risks to their health or safety". Both Alison Forster and Richard George accepted responsibility for failure to progress the ATP Pilot Scheme sufficiently to ensure that the system was fully operational. On behalf of Railtrack it was accepted that both the Rules and Group Standard GO/OT0013 were unclear and ambiguous with regard to entering and withdrawal from service of trains with defective AWS. Railtrack considered that the train should not have left the OOC depot and that train 1A47 should not have been allowed to run as a normal service with AWS isolated. They accepted, however, that there was lack of clarity about who was in control locally. As for Driver Harrison, he showed somewhat grudging remorse in the witness box. I put this down to having borne, for more than 18 months, the burden of criminal charges with the possibility of imprisonment, if convicted. I prefer to recall Driver Harrison's more frank and open expressions of grief and shock at the time, as a more fitting response to the terrible accident which he had caused (Annex 8).

Response to the accident

7.21 By general consent, the response of the emergency services deserves high commendation. By good fortune, fires which at one stage threatened to spread did not do so. With the exception of coach G in which the majority of the fatalities occurred, the Mark III rolling stock withstood the force of the collision and undoubtedly preserved lives that would otherwise have been lost. All the emergency services provided adequate manpower and equipment at the scene and the emergency medical services are particularly to be commended for the technical skill in the triage of accident victims.

7.22 Organisational problems began to develop, however, within hours of the accident as a result of the large number of interested parties. It should be emphasised that none of the injured suffered as a result but organisational problems did adversely affect passengers who had been rescued from train 1A47. Tensions between BTP and Railtrack staff as well as representatives of other organisations, led to errors in the process of investigation. The organisation of post-accident investigations lacked co-ordination and direction, largely as a result of the overriding demands of the criminal investigation. These issues are considered in more detail later. Sadly, the distress caused to bereaved relatives was made worse by shortcomings in the procedures employed.

7.23   It is remarkable that such a terrible accident did not result in more fatalities, as would doubtless have been the case had more passengers been travelling in the first two coaches.

CHAPTER 8

THE INQUIRY AND DELAY TO PROGRESS

8.1   On the day of the accident at Southall the Health & Safety Commission (HSC) decided to set up an Inquiry under section 14(2)(b) of the Health and Safety at Work Act, 1974. The Inquiry was directed to be held in public and in accordance with the Health and Safety Inquiries (Procedure) Regulations, 1975. The Terms of Reference of the Inquiry were:

> **The purpose of the Inquiry is to determine why the accident happened, and in particular to ascertain the cause or causes, to identify any lessons which have relevance for those with responsibilities for securing railway safety and to make recommendations.**

8.2   This was the first occasion on which the 1975 Regulations had been used, with the exception of an Inquiry in 1975 into an accident at the Houghton Main Colliery. Railway accidents involving reportable damage or injury have previously been subject to Inquiries under the Regulation of Railways Act, 1871, in which evidence was, by custom, taken in public and the reports published. More formal Inquiries have been rare. In recent times only the accidents at Kings Cross in 1987 and Clapham Junction in 1988 have been the subject of full public Inquiries, both of these having been directed by the Secretary of State. The 1871 Act was repealed in May 1997 so that Southall was the first rail Inquiry under the 1975 Regulations. It is of some relevance to note that the 1975 Regulations provide expressly that persons entitled to appear have the right to call evidence and to cross-examine witnesses (Reg.8(5)) and that the persons entitled to appear at the Inquiry include any that were injured or suffered damage as a result of the accident, or their personal representatives (Reg. 5(1)(e)). The Regulations empower the appointed person to require the attendance of witnesses to give evidence or to produce documents (Reg. 7(1)) and allow him to take into account written representations or statements received before the Inquiry (Reg. 8(8)). The procedure is generally to be in the discretion of the appointed person and may include the giving of evidence on oath (Reg. 8(6)). A limited number of notices requiring the attendance of witnesses were served, but generally documents were produced in accordance with directions given and all witnesses attended as requested. All oral evidence was taken under oath or affirmation.

The Inquiry begins

8.3 The Inquiry commenced with a business meeting on 19 December 1997, following which initial directions were given for the provision of lists of documents and for the formal opening of the Inquiry. In anticipation of some delay, the HSE were directed to provide monthly reports on progress. The question of the relationship between the Inquiry and criminal proceedings was extensively discussed at the business meeting. It will be recalled that Driver Harrison had been arrested on suspicion of manslaughter on the day of the accident. Police inquiries were continuing into his position and into the roles of GWT and Railtrack. The view almost universally expressed by the parties was that the Inquiry hearings should await first, any decision to bring manslaughter proceedings and secondly, (if brought) their conclusion. That was in accordance with the view of the Lord Chancellor's Department referred to by the HSE at the meeting, which was that in cases involving "serious criminality" the prosecution should go first. The Inquiry was opened on 24 February 1998 with the keeping of one minute's silence in memory of those who died. The opening hearing proceeded on the basis that there would be some delay. A manslaughter charge was anticipated shortly in respect of Mr Harrison and it was hoped that all criminal matters could be resolved within a few months. A long delay to the Inquiry hearings was not then in contemplation.

8.4 As noted in Chapter 2, the British Transport Police (BTP) had treated the accident site as a scene of crime, as a matter of convention. Larry Harrison had been arrested on 19 September 1997 and released on police bail, which was extended on a number of occasions. A preliminary file was sent to the Crown

Prosecution Service (CPS) in December 1997. From January 1998, the possibility of corporate charges against Great Western Trains and others was understood to be under consideration. BTP continued to collect evidence for possible criminal proceedings in collaboration with HSE, who continued with their investigation into the circumstances of the accident.

Criminal charges and delay to the Inquiry

8.5 On 17 April 1998, Larry Harrison was charged with seven counts of manslaughter and released on bail, which was again successively renewed. Such charges undoubtedly constituted potential "serious criminality" so as to justify further delay to the Inquiry. However, the Inquiry sought to make progress by direct contact with the Director of Public Prosecutions, expressing concern about the delay and seeking the early release of documents. Regrettably, however, during the next 7 months the Inquiry was effectively stalled and could only follow the course of events. On the first anniversary of the accident I wrote to all parties to the Inquiry explaining the position and noting the lack of progress. It was not until 1 December 1998 that the CPS announced its decision on further charges. GWT were charged with corporate manslaughter, but with no named individual being alleged to bear responsibility for the company's acts. They were also charged with offences under section 3(1) of the Health and Safety at Work Act, 1974 and Larry Harrison was charged under section 7 of the Act, these being brought by HSE. Little progress had been made with the Inquiry during 1998, beyond setting up a document-handling system in anticipation of the ultimate release of large volumes of material. The HSE, as requested, provided monthly reports on progress from January 1998 to April 1999.

8.6 The House of Commons Environment, Transport and Regional Affairs Committee had given consideration to delays to Inquiries resulting from criminal proceedings. In their report published in November 1998 it was concluded and recommended as follows:

66. There is considerable concern at the delays to accident inquiries or the publication of their findings caused by the pursuit of criminal investigations into railway accidents. We recommend that the Government, as a matter of urgency, should investigate what procedures should be put in place to expedite criminal proceedings, to ensure that accident inquires may be held as swiftly as possible.

8.7 In order to establish at least a timetable for the Inquiry, I decided, once the extent of criminal charges was known, to set a provisional date for re-opening the Inquiry. On 17 December 1998, therefore, it was announced that the Inquiry hearings would start on 20 September 1999. This took into account the likelihood that the cases would not be heard until the summer of 1999. It also anticipated that some degree of expedition would be introduced into the criminal proceedings to reflect the obvious conflict of public interest resulting from the delay to the start of the Inquiry.

8.8 During the early months of 1999, preparation by the Inquiry team began in earnest, in anticipation of being able to meet the date which had been set for the hearings to start. After a number of adjournments, the criminal trial commenced on 21 June at the Old Bailey, on preliminary legal issues as to whether manslaughter charges were maintainable against GWT. On 30 June 1999, Mr Justice Scott-Baker handed down a written judgment, the effect of which was to reject the prosecution case. The decision was not the subject of direct appeal proceedings, although an Attorney General's reference is proceeding in the Court of Appeal.

8.9 On 2 July 1999 GWT elected to plead guilty to the Health and Safety at Work Act charges. The Crown decided not to proceed against Mr Harrison on any charges and the Judge directed that not guilty verdicts be entered. The case was therefore adjourned for sentencing against Great Western Trains Limited. The final hearing took place on 27 July 1999 and resulted in fine of £1.5 million against GWT. A transcript of the remarks of Mr Justice Scott-Baker is included at Annex 14. These have been referred to during the present hearing by a number of parties.

The Inquiry proceeds

8.10 The way was now clear for the Inquiry to proceed. It had been held up for 17 months. From February 1999 onwards documents were progressively released to the Inquiry by the parties and by the prosecuting authorities. What had been a trickle, rapidly became a torrent and the Inquiry team was provided, within a short time, with documents amounting to some 0.5 million pages. These included extensive documents prepared by BTP in support of the criminal proceedings, together with large numbers of further documents, statements and expert reports disclosed by Railtrack and GWT. Parties continued to provide further documents, statements and expert reports up to the start and throughout the course of the Inquiry.

8.11 During the summer of 1999, the Inquiry's administrative team expanded from the minimum of two to a maximum strength of fifteen who were largely engaged full time for some 6 weeks in printing, sorting and collating documents from 35 CD-ROMs, in which form many documents had been provided to the Inquiry, as well as numerous paper-based files. A list of proposed issues had been sent to the parties on 19 February 1999, reproduced in Annex 20. For the Inquiry hearing, the issues were re-arranged into five groups of topics and the "core" files, comprising some 23,000 pages, arranged accordingly.

8.12 In the light of the criminal proceedings, it was not until the last week of July 1999 that the Inquiry start date could be confirmed. Although all involved in the Inquiry would have wished to start earlier, this was not practically possible. The fact the Inquiry was able to commence hearings on 20 September 1999 is a tribute to the Inquiry Secretariat, led by David Brewer and Laurance O'Dea of the Treasury Solicitor. A list of personnel involved in the Inquiry is at Annex 3. The documents were made available to the parties on 7 August 1999, with extra documents and supplementary bundles being added throughout the Inquiry hearings.

8.13 Having commenced its hearings on 20 September 1999 at the New Connaught Rooms, London WC2, the subsequent course of the Inquiry was not to be smooth. At the end of the second week (30 September 1999) the Inquiry proceedings were adjourned for one week, at the request of passenger groups who required more reading time. Early on 5 October 1999, a major collision occurred at Ladbroke Grove, London W11. The immediate impact of this accident was immense and led, within days, to the announcement of a further public Inquiry chaired by Lord Cullen and a separate technical report on railway safety systems to be prepared by Sir David Davies. The effect of these events is noted in Chapter 10 below. Hearings of the Southall Inquiry resumed on 25 October and were concluded on 25 November 1999, with final submissions of the parties being received in writing and orally on 20 December 1999.

Issues arising from delay.

8.14 The delay to the start of the Inquiry had a significant effect on the way in which the Inquiry was organised. Had it been possible to start hearings within a few months after the accident (as in the case of the Kings Cross and Clapham Junction Inquiries), the proceedings would necessarily have been more inquisitorial in nature, with the issues evolving as evidence and documents became available. In the case of Southall, however, as a result of the long delay and the Secretariat having some months at least to organise the documents, the Inquiry took on more the appearance of major commercial litigation. In addition, the delay meant that the issues had to include events since the crash, during which far-reaching changes have occurred, particularly in regard to safety systems.

8.15   On the last day of the Inquiry hearings John Cartledge, on behalf of CRUCC, raised directly the question who had decided that the Inquiry could not proceed until the criminal proceedings were resolved. He cited a number of earlier public Inquires which had been conducted before criminal proceedings had been brought, including those at Clapham Junction and Kings Cross. Serious charges were never in contemplation in those cases. In the case of Southall, the decision on when to proceed was ultimately a matter for the Chairman of the Inquiry. In practice, however, the Inquiry could not make progress until it was able to obtain access to documents, nor could the proceedings continue without the co-operation of the parties. As noted above, the question of when the Inquiry could proceed was discussed openly with all parties both at the business meeting on 19 December 1997 and at the Inquiry opening on 24 February 1998. All parties then recognised that further progress had to await decisions on charges to be brought. Regrettably, it took until 1 December 1998 for decisions to be made by the Crown Prosecution Service. As a result of these decisions, there could be no question of the Inquiry proceeding before the conclusion of criminal proceedings. I am satisfied that no further avoidable delay occurred after 1 December 1998. The Inquiry was made aware of concerns at all levels of government over delay to the Inquiry. It was not suggested, in any quarter, that the Inquiry could or should have proceeded earlier than it did. It should be recorded that on 27 July 1999 the Attorney General agreed to an undertaking being given by me in the following terms:

> "I have been authorised by HM Attorney General to undertake in respect of any person who provides evidence to this inquiry that no evidence he or she may give before the inquiry (whether orally or by written statement) nor any written statement made preparatory to giving evidence nor any documents produced by that person to the inquiry will be used in evidence against him or her in any criminal proceedings, except in proceedings where he or she is charged with having given false evidence in the course of this inquiry or with having conspired with or procured others to do so".

Such an undertaking was essential before the Inquiry could proceed. It is inconceivable that the undertaking could have been given so as to allow the Inquiry to proceed before the conclusion of the criminal proceedings.

8.16 Other issues were raised during the Inquiry in relation to the criminal prosecution, which included the following questions, posed by Mr John Hendy QC, on behalf of the Southall Train Crash Steering Committee representing many of the dead and injured:

- What steps could be taken in the future to avoid unsuccessful criminal proceedings delaying Public Inquiries after a major disaster?

- Is it feasible to hold an Inquiry before such a prosecution?

- Why did the DPP bring a corporate manslaughter prosecution against GWT without also charging an individual director when it must have been realised in the current state of the law that it was bound to fail?

- Why did the DPP bring a corporate manslaughter prosecution against GWT only when BTP had prepared a case against GWT and a director?

- If the reason was that the prosecution was anticipated to fail against the named director by reason of the fact that he had not personally authorised the train to run without AWS, in other words failed on the proximity test, would it not have been better to have tested this other than on a charge against the Corporation alone?

- In the light of the CPS public commitment to meet relatives of persons killed in a crime which results in a prosecution, why did the prosecution refuse to meet Mrs Petch and Mrs Traynor to discuss their concerns after they had been advised by their own lawyers that the corporate manslaughter prosecution was bound to fail?

- Why was the prosecution of Mr Harrison dropped. Would it have been dropped if he had been prosecuted alone?

The first two questions received some support from Mr Roger Henderson, QC, Counsel for Railtrack. Questions concerning the interrelationship between public Inquiries and criminal proceedings had been raised before the Environment, Transport and Regional Affairs Committee as noted above.

8.17 Counsel to the Inquiry advised that the above questions would require consideration to be given to the interests of many organisations, including the police forces (including in this case, British Transport Police) the DPP, HSE, the Law Officers, the Lord Chancellor's Department, the Home Office, DETR and Coroners, together with Trade Unions, consumer groups and representatives of organisations whose activities might give rise to disasters, and that the questions fell outside my Terms of Reference. Nevertheless, the general question of delay to the Inquiry has given rise to strong and justified concern, and distress to people involved both directly and indirectly in the accident. The majority of the organisations listed above were, in fact, represented at the Inquiry and others who were not have expressed views on the issues of delay which have come to the attention of the Inquiry. While the general question of delay to Inquiries is a matter which must lie in the hands of others, I believe that it is appropriate to address the narrower question of the appropriate means of conducting an effective Rail Industry Inquiry in the face of impending criminal proceedings and inevitable delay to any public Inquiry.

The effects of delay

8.18 The effect of the delay in terms of anguish and frustration does not need repetition. It should, however, be recorded that, as a result of the embargo on dissemination of evidence, victims and relatives of those who died were left in a state of substantial ignorance of the detailed facts until the opening of the Inquiry proceedings in September 1999. Up to that point, they knew no more about the fate of the deceased than had been reported (often inaccurately) in the media. In addition, as appears in the following Chapter and elsewhere in this report, changes thought to be necessary as a result of the Southall crash were formulated on the basis of the Rail Industry Inquiry over a period of more than 2 years after the date of the accident. That Inquiry was based on a partial selection of the available evidence and was conducted before a Tribunal whose appropriateness has been called into serious question. These issues have been fully canvassed at the Inquiry, and it is appropriate that conclusions should be drawn and that recommendations should be made as to the means of avoiding such consequences in future.

8.19 Consideration must be given to the tension between the constitutional duty of the police to investigate crime and the public interest in having lessons drawn from an accident and applied for the benefit of public safety. In this regard the following points emerge from the experience at Southall:

- The criminal investigation imposed an effective block on technical investigation by the rail industry and dissemination of information on the circumstances of the accident.

- Safety issues emerging from the Southall crash were the subject of numerous separate and overlapping investigations involving HMRI and the rail industry itself.

- The relationship between these investigations, the work of BTP and the stalled public Inquiry remained uncertain, was undefined and caused unnecessary diversion of the resources of the Inquiry.

As an illustration of the these points, Group Standard GO/RT3252, which covers the investigation of SPADs, requires the driver to be interviewed by a "competent person to establish the facts of the incident" (para 7.2.1(a)). The intervention of BTP prevented any such interview and the pending criminal proceedings prevented the Rail Industry Inquiry interviewing Mr Harrison either. The public Inquiry heard oral evidence from Mr Harrison more than 2 years after the event, at which time he was unable to give any proper account of his actions.

8.20   In the result, the present Inquiry has had the task of reviewing the facts largely on the basis of written statements prepared over a substantial period of time, many of which must have been affected by hindsight. In addition, the Inquiry has had the opportunity to review the many different investigations carried out into the accident, including the internal Rail Industry Inquiry. Some have questioned the usefulness of conducting a formal public Inquiry so long after the event and following many other forms of inquiry into the same accident. That issue ought to be addressed, including the possibility that an Inquiry which is no longer serving a useful purpose should be abandoned. In this regard, it should be recorded that the delay and overlapping Inquiry processes at Southall resulted in proceedings which were inefficient and wasteful of public resources and finance.

8.21   One proposal was that a new accident management body should be created, which could take over all aspects of investigation and direct the taking of appropriate action, including criminal proceedings. The Chairman or Director would conduct all such proceedings, and would therefore have to have the status of a judge of the High Court. It was pointed out that such proposals involved far-reaching considerations which would require wide consultation. They were also plainly beyond the remit of the present Inquiry. They illustrate, however, the level of concern which exists over the situation at present. The general solution advocated by the parties at the Southall Inquiry was for a different form of investigation capable of avoiding overlap and inefficiency, possibly including the creation of a new rail accident investigating body. The issues to be considered are therefore the following:

(1)   What form should any such investigating body take and what steps would be appropriate to identify its composition and powers.

(2)   What steps are appropriate to avoid delay to the investigation where criminal proceedings are under consideration.

These issues are discussed further in Chapter 15.

Televising the Inquiry

8.22 Prior to the Southall accident, HSE had made arrangements with Blakeway Associates Ltd for a major incident involving an HSE Inquiry to be filmed, for educational and training purposes. From the day of the Southall crash, Blakeway began work and subsequently filmed many different aspects of the investigation and Inquiry process. For the business meeting on 19 December 1997, Blakeway requested permission to film the proceedings. After taking note of the views of all parties present, I gave permission for the filming of that meeting and requested written submissions from all interested parties as to whether filming of the Inquiry itself should be permitted. Detailed submissions were received during January 1998. Legal advice was received from Counsel to the Inquiry that there was no legal impediment to the Inquiry being televised, nor would any private law rights of persons involved be infringed. On 10 February 1998, shortly before the opening of the Inquiry, a Draft Ruling was given allowing the opening of the Inquiry to be televised, and concluding that television coverage of the Inquiry could be permitted provided that adequate safeguards were put in place to avoid possible prejudice or abuse

8.23 The Draft Ruling was stated to be subject to the drawing up of an adequate protocol for television coverage, in the light of comments submitted to the Inquiry. In addition, further comment was invited on public interest issues and on the form that any television coverage should take. After further consultations, a draft protocol for broadcasting of both sound and vision was circulated. Extensive comments were received and the Inquiry was able to consider similar protocols developed elsewhere, including the Florida Protocol and the Scottish Court Protocol.

8.24 After further extensive exchanges, I was satisfied that the views of all relevant parties had been obtained. It was noted that passengers and relatives of those killed in the accident lived in many different parts of the country, and had a genuine interest in maintaining the closest possible contact with the Inquiry proceedings. It was noted that vigorous argument over some decades in the USA had eventually been resolved in favour of increased public access to the court system. It was considered inescapable that television would play a key role in public awareness of the Inquiry, and that the public interest would be better served by the opportunity to witness the actual proceedings, rather than second-hand accounts, necessarily given by those representing a particular interest. Taking all these matters into account, a ruling was given in June 1999 permitting television coverage in accordance with the finalised protocol. This envisaged that filming would be undertaken by an independent production company, which would provide a pooled feed to all broadcasters. In fact, the intended production company decided not to proceed and broadcasters were left to provide their own camera crews and to arrange filming independently.

8.25   It is to be noted that the protocol gave some concern to broadcasters, particularly the requirement for a 60 minute delay before transmission. A letter taking issue with this requirement was sent on behalf of a number of broadcasters. The embargo was nevertheless maintained, but other elements of the protocol were relaxed during the Inquiry. The letter and protocol are included at Annex 15.

8.26   The issue of televising court and other proceedings had been reviewed extensively by a working party set up by the General Counsel of the Bar. The report of the Working Party, Chaired by Jonathan Caplan QC, concluded that televising of the courts should be permitted on an experimental basis, following in the well worn steps of several countries which have carried out their own Inquiries. Televising of Parliament itself commenced on an experimental basis in 1989 and continues. No further progress has been made on the televising of judicial proceedings in England and Wales but there has been filming in a Scottish court in 1994 following the issuing of a practice direction and protocol.

8.27　The proceedings of the Public Inquiry were not, as originally anticipated, televised on a regular or systematic basis. That was a matter of decision for broadcasters, who were given free access throughout the Inquiry proceedings. Those involved in the Inquiry will have formed their own views as to the merits and effectiveness of permitting the proceedings to be televised. It is appropriate, however, to record that:

- There was no occasion when any witness appeared to be prejudiced or pressurised by the presence of television cameras or by the fact of televising the proceedings.

- There was no occasion when the behaviour of any advocate or other person involved in the Inquiry appeared to be adversely affected or influenced by televising of the Inquiry.

- There was no occasion on which any party requested, or I considered it necessary, that recorded material should not be broadcast.

- Television coverage was, however, spasmodic and apparently concerned more with personal or human issues than with technical or management issues.

- Despite the opportunity to film the actual proceedings, the parties to the Inquiry continued to give interviews, commenting on the Inquiry proceedings, which were often given prominence over televising of the actual Inquiry proceedings.

8.28　The experience of televising of the Inquiry gave no support whatever to fears expressed by many parties that witnesses would be prejudiced or that advocates would play to the cameras. The extent of serious television coverage was, however, disappointing. Broadcasters still appeared to find staged interviews more convenient than televising the actual proceedings. While the televising of the Inquiry should not be seen as setting any precedent or as circumscribing further debate on the issue of media coverage, it may be seen as having dispelled some illusions about the effect of television coverage.

8.29   It should also be noted that the daily placing of the transcript on the Internet was widely welcomed and, in contrast to the press and television coverage, provided a serious means of publicising widely the actual proceedings of the Inquiry. An average of well over 2000 daily requests were logged by the Inquiry web site during the hearings, totalling in excess of 200,000 to date, including requests from many countries around the world. Many people who could attend the Inquiry only occasionally expressed their warm appreciation of the ability to read the transcript daily.

Procedure for meeting criticisms

8.30   In common with the practices of other public inquiries, steps were taken to ensure that both organisations and individuals who might be the subject of criticism in this Report were given a reasonable opportunity to meet such criticism. The steps appropriate to ensure fairness in this regard must, of course, depend upon the circumstances and procedures adopted. In the case of the Southall Inquiry, the issues which I was concerned to investigate were identified in a letter sent to the parties on 19 February 1999 (Annex 20). It was to those issues that the parties were asked to direct their disclosure of documents and provision of witness statements The scope of the Inquiry was further refined in letters following the Ladbroke Grove Accident (Annex 21).

8.31   The opening statements of Counsel to the Inquiry and those of the represented parties gave notice of many areas of potential criticism, as did also the witness statements distributed in advance of the oral evidence. Other criticisms were put to witnesses in the course of their evidence and responded to. As new points arose, the represented parties took the opportunity to submit further evidence in the form of documents or witness statements. During the course of the proceedings all the parties were invited to submit to the Inquiry a considered list of criticisms they wished to advance against other parties or individuals. Most, but not all parties, did so.

8.32 After the conclusions of the oral evidence, the Secretariat prepared and served collated lists of potential criticisms to both organisations and individuals. Notice was given to individuals through their employers or trade unions. The parties responded to potential criticism in the course of two rounds of written submissions and in the final oral submissions heard on 20 December 1999. The relevant individuals, to the extent that they wished to do so, responded separately. In so far as this report contains criticisms of organisations or individuals, in each case I am satisfied that a reasonable opportunity has been provided for that criticism to be met.

CHAPTER 9

REACTIONS TO SOUTHALL

9.1 There was a swift response to the accident on 19 September 1997. The investigations at the site of the crash and subsequent technical investigations have been described in Chapters 2 and 3. A public Inquiry was announced by the Chairman of HSC on the day of the accident and on 24 September 1997 the Deputy Prime Minister said:

> "A report will be published by the Health and Safety Commission, which will advise me on the findings and recommendations. Meanwhile, the Health and Safety Executive has comprehensive powers to take any immediate remedial or enforcement action if the need becomes evident during its investigation."

Action on AWS isolation

9.2 HSE did not deem it necessary to take any enforcement action, but reacted quickly to the discovery that 1A47 had been travelling with its AWS isolated. On 30 September 1997, HM Deputy Chief Inspector of Railways, Vic Coleman sent a circular letter to all TOCs and to Railtrack dealing with rules covering AWS isolation. The letter stated that:

- Trains should not commence a journey without the AWS working in the driving cab.

- Every effort should be made to either repair or replace the defective locomotive or unit or otherwise provide effective AWS (for example by turning the train).

The letter further stated that it was not accepted that there could be any other reasonable interpretation of the Rules contained in Appendix 8 of the Rule Book and Group Standard GT/OT 0013. It was stated that HMRI regarded AWS as "an extremely important safety system" and that all train companies were expected to ensure that it was available for use to the maximum extent possible, and that any decision to keep a traction unit in service with AWS defective must be fully justifiable. A full copy of the letter is included in Annex 16.

9.2   HMRI received various responses from TOCs to the letter of 30 September, suggesting that there was interest in looking at further risk reduction measures. Mr Coleman also wrote to Railtrack on 30 September 1997 suggesting further clarification of issues relating to the failure and isolation of AWS, and proposing urgent consideration of mitigating steps where trains were operated without functioning AWS. David Rayner replied on behalf of Railtrack, stating that steps were being taken to ascertain the frequency of actual AWS failures, as distinct from those reported, before further steps were considered. As noted in Chapter 12 below, the true level of AWS failures on GWT proved to be elusive and required extensive research before reliable figures were identified.

9.4   ASLEF reacted to the Southall crash by advising its members that, where the AWS was defective/isolated, they should be accompanied by a person "validated for safety". ASLEF's advice was circulated throughout the rail industry and on 12 November, by way of response to Mr Coleman's letter of 30 September, Lew Adams, General Secretary of ASLEF, provided a list of responses which varied from agreement (Central Trains, Eurostar, RfD) to objection that such action would make the situation worse (Anglia). Most operators reiterated their intention to comply fully with the Rules and Group Standard. These reactions have relevance to the continuing question of amendment to the Rules. Mr Coleman responded to the ASLEF initiative on 17 November 1997, pointing out that there were risk consequences for and against the proposed measures and adhering to the approach set out in the letter of 30 September.

9.5   Mr Coleman, now Chief Inspector of Railways, gave oral evidence in support of HMRI's actions following the accident. It was pointed out that the issue of AWS had been raised in the report following the Cowden accident in October

1994, where the Inspector recommended that the instruction to report isolation of AWS should be stiffened to require such reports immediately, either by radio or telephone (Recommendation 2). It was suggested to Mr Coleman that the ambiguity in the Rules was apparent to all parties, yet neither HMRI nor Railtrack had thought it appropriate to change or clarify the Rules. It was also suggested that the Rules were ambiguous and that HMRI had reacted only as a result of the Southall crash. As noted below, the review recommended by the RII did lead to some revision of the Rules, but not to AWS being classed as vital to the continued running of the train. Nor did it lead to any clear and generally accepted interpretation of the Rules. Mr Coleman, nevertheless, reiterated that AWS was an extremely important safety system as stated in his letter following the accident

Rail Industry Inquiry

9.6   As required by Railway Group Standards, an internal Rail Industry Inquiry (RII) was set up into the accident within days. The appointed panel members of the Inquiry were John Ellis (Independent Chairman), Alison Forster (Operations and Safety Manager, Great Western Trains), Les Wilkinson (Production Manager, Railtrack, Great Western Zone) and Tom Birch (Operations Safety and Standards Manager, EWS). The Inquiry was conducted in accordance with Group Standard GO/RT3434/3, which came into force only on 4 October 1997. The remit for the Investigation was defined, as follows:

> The investigation and subsequent report must identify and state the immediate cause(s), any underlying causes of the accident and any recommendations necessary to prevent a recurrence.

> Particular attention must be given to:-

> (i)   To establish (sic) the circumstances and immediate causes of the fatal accident at Southall on Friday, 19th September 1997.

(ii)   Pending the HSE formal inquiry:-

- to identify any actions that ought to be taken in the short term, by any of the parties, to prevent a recurrence;

- to identify any secondary issues regarding the accident that ought to form part of the HSE inquiry.

(iii)   To present a written report as quickly as possible.

9.7   The panel met at Ambrose House, Swindon and heard evidence on Friday, 26 September through to Wednesday, 1 October 1997 (4 days). The Investigation proceedings, of which a full transcript is available, took an inquisitorial form with 25 witnesses being called (not under oath) and questioned by the panel. Most of the witnesses subsequently gave evidence to the Public Inquiry and in some cases their statements at the RII formed part of their written evidence. A 40-page report, including conclusions and recommendations (Report No.97/RTGW/JI/08) was issued on 20 March 1998 to a limited circulation list, including the rail companies involved, Trade Unions, HMRI and W S Atkins. The report was provided to the Inquiry Secretariat on 5 May 1998 on a confidential basis, in view of pending criminal proceedings. The conclusions and recommendations are included at Annex 17.

9.8   The RII was able to conclude that track condition was not a factor in the accident; also that the signals were operating correctly and that signal sighting was not a factor in the accident. No conclusive evidence was available about the performance of the braking system but it was established that the train was operating within its maintenance schedule and had operated satisfactorily up to the point of the accident. Evidence concerning the accident itself was taken from Signaller Forde (Slough IECC) and from Drivers Alan Bricker (EWS Freight) and James Tunnock (GWT). Larry Harrison (driver of 1A47) produced a written statement and Tim Mayo (Railtrack), who travelled in the cab between Swindon and Reading, gave evidence about Mr Harrison's performance. Lester Watts (Driver Standards Manager, GWT) gave evidence about Mr Harrison's training and fitness for duty. A recommendation was made for review of human factors or alternative control measures.

9.9   The RII heard limited evidence concerning maintenance work at Old Oak Common, and no conclusion was drawn as to the adequacy of the examination which had been carried out before the accident. For the events at Swindon Control and at Swansea Station, the Panel had written statements together with the evidence of Driver Tunnock. They were able to conclude that, while both drivers were aware of the AWS isolation, it had not been reported to the signaller, and that Driver Tunnock's attempts to report direct to Swindon Control had not been effective. A recommendation was made concerning communication of AWS and other faults.

9.10   The RII did not examine policy on action to be taken following AWS isolation, but had evidence on provisions of the Rule Book. They recommended a review of Rules on AWS isolation, to include Group Standard GO/OT0013. The review was to include SPADs involving AWS isolation and the level of AWS failures. The Panel heard evidence about changes to signalling and regulation policy. Noting that there had been no formal risk assessment, it was recommended that S&SD should consider the safety implications.

9.11   The RII received limited evidence concerning the Great Western ATP Pilot Scheme and noted that overall system performance was substantially below the target set. They considered that safe operation was not dependent on the Pilot ATP Scheme, but recommended a review of the effectiveness of the project. As regards events after the crash the panel noted a lack of co-ordination and that restrictions had been imposed on investigations. Recommendations were made as to post-incident arrangements.

Response to RII

9.12   A substantial amount of evidence was called at the Public Inquiry as to the
        steps taken by all parties for the implementation of the recommendations of
        the RII.   The principal witnesses were Alison Forster on behalf of GWT and
        Garth Ratcliffe on behalf of Railtrack, with additional evidence being given by
        Rod Muttram, Aidan Nelson, Clive Burrows and others.   Railtrack also
        commissioned Audits of Train Operators' levels of compliance with the RII
        recommendations.   The relevant actions taken by Railtrack and GWT are
        noted below under the summarised recommendations of the Panel.

Recommendation 1.1

Railtrack S&SD should review human factors or alternative control measures
when Driver support systems are isolated, including proposed Train
Protection Warning System.

9.13   Railtrack have developed a number of options including training for
        "defensive driving" (i.e. driving so as to anticipate signals at caution).
        Railtrack have developed alternative control measures where safety systems
        become inoperative. They have also obtained a report from Mr Hugh Gibson
        of Birmingham University on SPAD records and patterns of behaviour. This
        has so far led to revision of the SPAD investigation procedure. Railtrack have
        set up a National SPAD Focus Group which, at the time of the Inquiry was
        engaged in considering the HMRI SPAD report issued on 2 September 1999.
        Railtrack are also carrying out work on cab environmental conditions. GWT,
        before the Southall crash had commissioned work on human behaviour as part
        of the Drivers' Restructuring Initiative. They have subsequently carried out a
        risk assessment on options available to drivers in the event of failure of a
        safety system.

Recommendation 2.1

GWTC and other operators should review arrangements for the communication of AWS faults and other safety-related issues to ensure that verbal messages are dealt with and recorded.

9.14 Recording of calls to and from GWT's Operations Control (now Service Delivery Centre) was introduced in January 1998. Tapes are retained for three months and are monitored on a monthly basis with corrective action being taken as appropriate. Railtrack have taken steps to improve verbal communication procedures through mandatory speech protocols, including use of the phonetic alphabet. GWT's procedures were consolidated into an Emergency Response Plan in February 1998. A new post of Fleet Performance Manager was created in August 1998 with responsibilities covering all incidents and failures involving the fleet, with a view to drawing up action plans for each depot. Similar steps should be taken by other TOCs where such facilities do not exist.

Recommendation 2.2

GWTC, Train Operators and Railtrack should review the adequacy of training and competence of controllers and supervisors in transmitting, receiving recording and acting upon safety-related messages.

9.15 GWT have introduced a new training programme and competency assessment procedure. It is to be noted that the controllers had formerly been designated safety-critical but this had lapsed by 1997. The importance of their work is such that this designation should be reinstated. Both the training and safety-designation of controllers are matters of general importance and application.

Review of the management and reporting structure for Control led to transfer of responsibility to the Operations and Safety Director in 1998 and amalgamation with the Resource Centre to form the new Operations Centre. Evidence to the Inquiry also revealed that, from shortly after the Southall Crash, GWT Swindon Control began to keep an additional and confidential log to record reported faults, seemingly because of press attention directed at the "official" log. No proper explanation was forthcoming for this decision.

Recommendation 2.3

Railtrack S&SD with members of the Railway Group should consider whether a communication system similar to GM/RT2250 should be instituted for operational safety matters.

9.16 Railtrack are proposing to introduce mandatory requirements for dealing with advice on urgent operational safety matters through a new Group Standard analogous to GM/RT2250.

Recommendation 3.1

Railtrack and S&SD should review the contents of Appendix 8 to the Rule Book and Railway Group Standard GO/OT0013 in particular to avoid ambiguity and to ensure that the reporting chains for failures and required actions are clarified to reflect fully the responsibilities of Railtrack, as Infrastructure Controller, and Train Operating Companies. The review should incorporate risk assessments of any proposals for change.

9.17 Group Standard GO/OT0013 was replaced on an interim basis by a Rapid Response document GO/RT3437, Issue 1, in June 1998. A further version, Issue 2 was published in February 1999 coming into effect on 3 April 1999. Appendix 8 to the Rule Book was also revised with the aim of removing ambiguities and is now included in the Rule Book, section C. A Working Group has been established to undertake a wider review of all Rules and Regulations relating to trains entering and being taken out of service. Further revisions are therefore inevitable. GO/RT3437 mandates the provision of a contingency plan for taking trains out of service as a result of defective on-train equipment. It remains the case, however, that AWS isolation is still not regarded as a Category A matter, requiring the train immediately or as soon as practicable to be taken out of service. Current proposals are likely to abolish the present categories, but not to mandate the withdrawal from service. Considerable concern was expressed on behalf of Passenger Groups at the slow pace of this review and that trains were still permitted to run in service with AWS isolated (see also the remarks of Mr Justice Scott-Baker at Annex 14). Conversely, it was argued that diversity and local solutions to such problems were acceptable and more appropriate, provided that safety was maintained.

Recommendation 3.2

Train operators should urgently review their application of the requirements of GO/OT0013, in particular, in respect of AWS.

9.18   GWT, in advance of the RII, issued document OPS0123 on 24 September 1997 to clarify decisions on withdrawal of trains from service. OPS0123 has subsequently been amended. The Service Delivery Centre were required to obtain approval of proposed action from a Second-line Operations On-call Manager. GWT have now introduced a policy by which AWS isolation is effectively treated as Category A, i.e. trains are to be taken out of service as soon as practicable. Provision is made also for running at reduced speed and with additional staff in the cab.

Recommendation 3.3

Railtrack S&SD to undertake a national review of SPADs in respect of those involving AWS isolations or AWS non-fitted areas to determine any rail industry lessons.

9.19   A report was produced for Railtrack in April 1999 which indicated that approximately 1% of SPADs during the review period involved traction units with AWS fitted but not working. The need for significant improvements in the quality of reporting was also identified. This is consistent with the difficulty encountered in assembling data on AWS isolation on GWT pre-Southall.

Recommendation 3.4

Railtrack S&SD to audit compliance of TOCs with GO/OT0013 and Appendix 8 to the Rule Book.

9.20   These Rules have been amended and are subject to further amendment as noted in para 9.17. Railtrack commissioned an audit of the revised Rules for which the final report was issued in November 1999. A summary of the findings is set out at Annex 18. This reported that 30 of 33 relevant operating companies (including GWT) had developed contingency plans as required by GO/RT3437. The remaining 3 had provided insufficient detail. S&SD continued to monitor the delivery of contingency plans. HMRI have carried out a survey of train drivers which revealed wide variations between TOCs in the procedures for actions to be taken after AWS failure. In some companies, drivers were not consistent in their responses and in particular cases gave opposite answers in equal proportions. These matters were brought to the attention of the relevant TOCs (HMRI Annual Report 1997/98, para 58).

Recommendation 3.5

GWTC and other operators should review their instructions and check procedures to ensure compliance with Appendix 8 to the Rule Book requirements for the provision of the isolating handle seal.

9.21   GWT issued a Maintenance Instruction in October 1998 expressly incorporating the checking of the AWS isolating handle seal during each S (daily) Exam. This was incorporated as a permanent revision in May 1999. This requirement was also covered in the audit commissioned by Railtrack (see Annex 18) which reported that 22 of 25 relevant train operating companies had adequately addressed the issue.

Recommendation 3.6

GWTC and other train operators should review the nature and level of AWS failures to determine whether present testing arrangements are appropriate to reduce risk to a level as low as reasonably practicable.

116

9.22　GWT commissioned a review by Halcrow Transmark, in December 1997, of all existing AWS maintenance and testing procedures and instructions. This led to the production of a new composite procedure which was implemented from October 1998. GWT further invited equipment suppliers NRS and Howells to design an improved AWS test box. After carrying out trials, GWT have purchased Howells' test boxes for use at all five depots. GWT also made representation to the Public Inquiry as to the need for improved maintenance arrangements for AWS parts and components, as to which see Chapter 12 below. S&SD has initiated a review of safety assurance in the vehicle supply chain, including train-borne AWS equipment. This work is ongoing.

Recommendation 4.1

Railtrack S&SD should consider the safety implications of changes of substance to regulation policy, train timetabling and increases in numbers of trains, and give guidance to Railtrack Line and Train Operators.

9.23　Railtrack commissioned a risk assessment of regulation policy which was undertaken by Messrs Pickett and Maidment and has been reviewed at para 4.12 above. S&SD have commissioned a further report on regulation and timetabling. A further qualitative assessment is planned in 2000.

Recommendation 5.1

All parties involved in the BR-ATP pilot scheme for GW Main Line should urgently review the effectiveness of the project to ensure its full conclusion

9.24　This recommendation had already been overtaken by the report commissioned in 1997 by Railtrack from Electrowatt (see Chapter 13) which was not considered by the Panel. Steps subsequently taken by GWT are reviewed at para 13.26.

Recommendation 6.1

As a matter of urgency, Railtrack S&SD, HMRI & BTP should seek to establish arrangements for the gathering of evidence, the commissioning of further testing and investigation to ensure that all appropriate evidence is preserved, gathered and assessed, including that from witnesses, and appropriate results made available to the various inquiry processes.

9.25   Difficulties encountered in gathering evidence are reviewed in Chapter 2. At the time of the RII, the only relevant protocol which permitted release of safety-related information by BTP was that between BTP and HMRI, pursuant to which HMRI could not themselves release information without the authority of an Assistant Chief Constable (see para 2.27). No relevant safety-related information from the Southall investigation was released by BTP. In particular, Railtrack were not made aware of the findings of WSA about misalignment of signal SN270. Discussions took place between Railtrack and BTP as a result of this recommendation throughout 1998 and 1999 but it was reported that progress was dependent on revision of the BTP-HMRI protocol which, in turn, required approval of the CPS. No conclusion had been reached at the time of the Ladbroke Grove crash. Whether as a result or by coincidence, BTP and Railtrack reached an accommodation shortly afterwards which was expressed in a Protocol for Information Sharing, signed on 22 and 23 November 1999. This included the following:

> The standing presumption shall be, that evidence and technical reports (including written 'interim' reports) provided by the above-named organisations to British Transport Police, shall be disclosed promptly to Railtrack for the purpose stated in this document unless any of the conditions set out above prevent this.

The conditions referred to require that disclosure is to have "no significant prejudicial effect on the ongoing police investigation". The full text of the Protocol is included in Annex 19.

Recommendation 6.2

Railtrack S&SD should consider whether in circumstances requiring the appointment of a Rail Incident Commander, GO/RT3434/2 should be amended to place on the R.I.C. specific responsibility for agreeing and commissioning expert testing arrangements, and for co-ordinating arrangements for the recovery and preservation of all appropriate evidence.

9.26   This recommendation was not accepted by Railtrack and no action has been taken.

Recommendation 6.3

Railtrack Great Western should review its arrangements for the application of GO/RT3434/2 in respect of the appointment of an appropriately senior RIO in the event of a major accident, and for the provision of suitable Bronze level support and communication.

9.27   Railtrack has reviewed and amended its arrangements for appointment of an appropriate RIO and for suitable Bronze support. The effectiveness of these measures will be assessed in relation to the Ladbroke Grove crash.

Recommendation 6.4

Railtrack Director Operations should review the arrangements for post-incident liaison to ensure that emergency authorities involve the RIO in all Silver meetings.

9.28   Railtrack have taken steps to draw to the attention of all emergency services the role of RIO as the Railtrack representative at site through the issue of the Railtrack Liaison Manual for Emergency Services. An independent review of these arrangements has been carried out by Roger Miles and a report has been issued to the Railway Group. Again, the effectiveness of these proposals will be assessed in the Inquiry into the Ladbroke Grove crash.

Recommendation 7.1

The Panel did not take evidence on the crashworthiness of Mk3 vehicles, but recommends that Railtrack S&SD should review this, together with the contributory crash damage implications of lineside structures, particularly OHLE.

9.29   Evidence on crashworthiness is reviewed in Chapter 11. Railtrack have commissioned a further study by AEA Technology to assess the tear resistance of Mark III vehicles in relation to lineside structures and freight vehicles. This work has been delayed by the Ladbroke Grove accident.

Effectiveness of RII

9.30   Given the serious delay in proceeding with the Public Inquiry it is relevant at this point to consider whether the RII was effective, in the light of the facts as now fully revealed in the Public Inquiry. The importance of this question lies in the fact that the RII recommendations formed the basis of changes to practices in the rail industry, as noted above, which have now been largely carried out. Any criticism of the RII itself must be seen in the context of the considerable difficulties created by the virtual embargo on expert reports from W S Atkins and AEA Technology imposed by BTP. In addition, the Terms of Reference of the RII contemplated its role as being to produce an urgent report pending the Public Inquiry.

9.31   The facts now available show that the RII Panel correctly ruled out of account the track and signals. Although not germane to the accident, they did not have access to the W S Atkins report on the alignment of signal SN270 and were therefore unable (as doubtless they would have done) to make a recommendation in this regard. Similarly, the Panel were not able to rule out any contribution from the braking system since they did not have access to the relevant W S Atkins expert report. Conversely, there is no reason why the Panel could not have taken more detailed evidence concerning maintenance work at OOC, and have made recommendations for review of working practices and/or levels of supervision. With regard to the events at Swindon Control and at Swansea, although the Panel could have taken more detailed evidence, they were able to draw appropriate conclusions concerning the loss of messages transmitted by Driver Tunnock and to make recommendations accordingly.

9.32 As regards AWS, the Panel were properly concerned about ambiguity within the Rule Book and Group Standard 0013 and were also concerned to establish compliance with existing Rules. The failure to achieve a satisfactory review of AWS Rules was that of the industry, not the RII. The view of the panel on regulation policy did not address the question of possible conflict between commercial interests and safety, as subsequently raised at the Public Inquiry. The Panel spent little time on ATP. Given that the history of the pilot project was well known to some at least of the Panel members, this was surprising, but the reasons were not investigated. In contrast, the Panel's review of post-incident issues was, even in hindsight, measured and reasonable.

9.33 At the Public Inquiry GWT, and Alison Forster in particular, volunteered the opinion that the RII should have had an independent panel and that this was the case in regard to the Ladbroke Grove Inquiry, which was being set up during the third week of the Southall Public Inquiry. That view must be endorsed as a matter of obvious necessity, not least so that the public can be assured that any urgent safety measures needed will be identified after proper and independent scrutiny of the relevant events. In regard to the RII for Southall, although no conscious impropriety was suggested or is to be inferred, it is impossible to conclude that the interests of one or more of the Panel members did not influence the coverage of the Inquiry or the conclusions reached. The Group Standard should have required the Inquiry be conducted by a panel which was wholly independent of parties principally involved in the accident.

9.34 In conclusion, while the RII did its job conscientiously and reasonably in the circumstances, the public would be justifiably alarmed to realise that the bulk of technical evidence concerning details of the crash, the state of the infrastructure and the rolling stock involved was withheld from the Inquiry, whose recommendations formed an important element in rail safety for some two years following the accident.

CHAPTER 10

LADBROKE GROVE AND ITS AFTERMATH

10.1 The Southall Inquiry adjourned after nine days hearing, on 30 September 1999, to allow the parties more preparation time. During the adjournment, early on the morning of 5 October 1999, a further serious accident occurred two miles outside Paddington, at Ladbroke Grove Junction. At 08:11 there was a collision between the 06:03 GWT Cheltenham to Paddington train 1A09, travelling on the up main line into Paddington, and the 08:06 Thames Trains Paddington to Bedwyn service, 1K20, which had been travelling on Line 3. The accident occurred as 1K20 crossed a high speed connection which linked Line 3 to the up main.

10.2 A first Interim Report issued by HSE on 8 October 1999 stated that the immediate cause of the accident appeared to be that the Thames train had passed a red signal number SN109, some 700 metres before the collision point. The GWT train had been travelling on green signals. The routes for both trains had been set by the ARS system at the Slough IECC.

10.3 By 8 October 1999 30 people had been confirmed as having been killed in the accident, including both drivers, and 160 injured, some critically, as a result of the rapid outbreak of fire in some of the HST carriages. The number of dead subsequently rose to 31. On the day of the accident it was announced that there would be a Public Inquiry. On 7 October 1999 it was announced that the Inquiry would be Chaired by Lord Cullen and also that a report was to be prepared on train protection systems by Sir David Davies, President of the Royal Academy of Engineering.

Review of Southall Inquiry issues.

10.4   As previously directed, the Southall Inquiry re-convened on 11 October 1999. On that occasion, I stated that the Ladbroke Grove collision would unavoidably impact on the Southall Inquiry, particularly in that there would be overlap between the two Inquiries. Oral submissions were received from parties and further written submissions were requested. It was stated that a decision on the future conduct of the Southall Inquiry would be communicated to the parties on the following day.

10.5   By letter dated 12 October 1999 directions were given as to particular issues with which the Southall Inquiry would continue, by reference to the list of issues circulated on 19 February 1999 (Annex 20). It was confirmed that the Inquiry would deal fully with ATP Issue 5(b) to the extent it related to the Southall accident. Wider issues involving ATP, train protection, TPWS and SPAD prevention measures (Issue 5(c)) would not be dealt with in the Southall Inquiry. It was directed that the Inquiry would resume its hearings on 25 October 1999.

10.6   By further letter to the parties dated 19 October 1999 it was confirmed that the Southall Inquiry would not hear evidence on questions of general railway safety (Issue 6) which was to be fully investigated in a separate Inquiry, also to be conducted by Lord Cullen. After further correspondence and meetings, including consultations with Mr Bill Callaghan, Chair of HSC and Lord Cullen, the final form of the different Inquires concerning rail safety then underway were clarified in a letter dated 5 November 1999 from Mr Callaghan. The effect of this letter was as follows:

(a)   The Southall Inquiry would continue and complete its hearings in accordance with the letters dated 12 and 19 October 1999.

(b)   A further Inquiry (the Joint Inquiry) would be conducted under Section 14(2)(b) of the Health and Safety at Work Act, 1994, Chaired by Lord Cullen and myself.

(c)   Issues of general railway safety (Issue 6) were to be the subject of an Inquiry by Lord Cullen but would be considered by the Southall Inquiry in the direct context of the Southall accident.

10.7   The Joint Inquiry was to consider the following subjects:

(i)   Train Protection and Warning Systems;

(ii)   The future application of Automatic Train Protections systems;

(iii)   SPAD prevention measures;

Taking account in particular of:

-       the Southall rail accident on 19 September 1997;

-       the rail accident at Ladbroke Grove Junction on 5 October 1999;

-       the technical assessment for the Deputy Prime Minister of rail safety systems by Sir David Davies,

with a view to making general recommendations in regard thereto.

It was also stated that the HSC expected the Chairmen of the Southall and Ladbroke Grove Inquiries each to deal separately with matters that it was considered appropriate to investigate within the existing Terms of Reference, subject to the matters to be dealt with in the Joint Inquiry. A copy of the letter of 5 November 1999 is at Annex 21.

Action following Ladbroke Grove

10.8   HSE issued a further report on 29 October 1999 listing action to be taken or in hand following the Ladbroke Grove collision, consisting of enforcement actions taken by HMRI and other initiatives taken or in hand to improve safety. The actions are referred to below. They were also discussed at a Rail

Summit meeting convened by the Deputy Prime Minister on 25 October 1999.

10.9 By an exchange of letters dated 7 and 8 October 1999 between Dr Smallwood, HMRI, and Richard George, it was confirmed on behalf of GWT that the use of ATP had been increased to 80% of services where necessary trackside equipment was available and GWT were committed to a target of 100%. In the weeks following, partly as a result of restrictions to services, GWT achieved, for the first time, 100% running and have since continued to achieve figures well in excess of 90%.

10.10 On 8 October 1999 Dr Smallwood sent a circular letter to all TOCs seeking assurance that effective means were being implemented to ensure that all drivers were fully briefed, particularly as to the likely causes of SPADs and the ways to avoid them. Drivers were additionally to be clearly advised of signals which posed a particular SPAD risk. Briefing was to include reminders on the need for defensive driving techniques. TOCs were requested to review driver training and assessment arrangements.

10.11 HSE had, on 2 September 1999, circulated their report on SPADs which revealed a rise after several years of steady decline. It was noted on 29 October 1999 that Railtrack and all TOCs had submitted plans which had been reviewed by HMRI. Following such review, improvement notices in respect of safety briefing procedures had been served on two TOCs. HMRI also expressed concern at the standard of briefing offered to safety-critical staff, including drivers and were considering whether further notices should be served on TOCs to ensure consistency of delivery.

10.12 HMRI issued three enforcement notices on 8 October 1999 which:

(i) required Railtrack to install additional controls at 22 signals recording the greatest number of SPADs (5 or more) or to devise other agreed means of securing safety;

(ii)   required Railtrack to produce a plan for means to reduce risk to all remaining signals with a recent history of repeated (more than one) SPADs;

(iii)   prohibited the use of routes leading to signal SN109 until effective means were provided for preventing further SPADs.

Railtrack appealed all three notices. The prohibition notice was upheld by the Employment Tribunal in January 2000. Other appeal proceedings are continuing at the date of this report.

10.13   HMRI pursued a number of initiatives to help improve driver competence, including revisions to Group Standard GO/RT2531, Driver Training. It was agreed at the Rail Summit on 25 October 1999 that training standards generally should be reviewed to restore commonality of delivery. HMRI commissioned the development of a training package in support of defensive driving from the Railway Industry Training Council (RITC), which included "top-up" training for all drivers. To support longer-term training, RITC had also been commissioned to develop a new standard for defensive driving, to ensure consistency across the network. There was also to be monitoring of implementation of new training standards and briefing for drivers, to be carried out independently of HMRI.

10.14   The report of 29 October 1999 noted that HMRI were pursuing competence issues for all safety-critical staff, including drivers, on which a report would be published shortly. It was noted also that HMRI and Railtrack were each promoting the introduction of the Confidential Incident Reporting and Analysis System (CIRAS) and its nationwide expansion (see Chapter 14). The Chief Inspector of Railways had written to all TOCs on 21 October advocating the use of CIRAS and the matter had been taken up at the rail summit on 25 October 1999. HMRI additionally called for a speedy retro-fit programme for On Train Data Recorders (OTDR) (see Chapter 14), which should become a routine tool for monitoring driving standards. This would aid the implementation and monitoring of proper driving and would be a major additional tool to help reduce SPADs. It was stated that HMRI would regard any failure to ensure use of OTDR and other safety systems as potential management failures in future. It had been agreed with the Deputy Prime Minister that HMRI would release a monthly report on SPADs from November 1999.

CHAPTER 11

CRASHWORTHINESS AND MEANS OF ESCAPE

11.1   This topic refers to the performance of rolling stock in accidents, primarily in terms of the protection of persons on board. In regard to the Southall crash, the main issue was the structural integrity of the carriages, or trailer cars, involved in the collision. Also of concern was the means of exit from vehicles involved in a crash. This is of particular relevance where a crash involves fire, which fortunately had little impact in the Southall crash. The relevant coaches were owned by Angel Train Contracts Ltd (ATC) and leased to GWT.

Rail vehicle design issues

11.2   Rail vehicles are necessarily of heavy and durable construction and have a typical life of around 40 years. This poses problems for the timely introduction of new designs and improvements to existing stock. A new regulatory regime for vehicle design, together with new certification procedures, was introduced in 1994. These apply, generally, only in the case of new vehicles. The great majority of railway stock at the present time and for some years to come will not conform to the new standards, except where mandatory requirements have been introduced to cover existing vehicles. Consequently, one of the most significant developments in recent years concerning crashworthiness has been the introduction of regulations, in August 1999, providing for withdrawal of Mark I coaches, which have an inferior safety record to other stock. Normal Mark I coaches are to be withdrawn in 2003, and those with modified couplings to prevent over-ride, in 2005

11.3   The coaches involved in the Southall crash were Mark III, a design which was introduced in the 1970s. The roof, floor and sides consist of 2mm thick pressed steel plates assembled in a "monocoque" construction, so that the carriage operates as a strong all welded structural tube: see Annex 22. Mark III vehicles have been found to behave well in many accidents, notably that at

Colwich in 1986, when a head-on collision between a locomotive and a hauled train at a combined speed of over 100mph led to one fatality.

11.4   In addition to structural strength of the carriage, there are a number of other important issues concerning the performance of vehicles in crashes. The design, including couplings between carriages, is now required to prevent or minimise "overriding" by a following carriage, which has in the past resulted in many casualties. Locking arrangements for external doors have been the subject of much debate and necessarily involve a compromise between providing easy exit and the prevention of fatalities or injury by passengers falling out accidentally or intentionally, or the causing of injury inflicted by the opened door. Carriage window design involves a similar compromise between permitting exit but also preventing passengers being thrown out. The internal design of carriages involves a number of important safety issues, including the design of internal doors. A particular design feature which has proved controversial is the introduction of "crumple-zones", as energy-absorbing measures at the ends of coaches. This was opposed by some who considered that it represented a new hazard in view of the possibility of passengers being located within these zones. No issue concerning crumple zones arose from the Southall crash and it is recommended that the matter be considered further in the Ladbroke Grove Inquiry. Those factors relevant to the Southall crash are reviewed further below.

11.5   Although crashworthiness and means of escape are evolving topics, the historical development of the railways, including recent changes, has not been conducive to the steady development and implementation of new ideas. New designs have been evolved in response to orders for new stock, often with substantial gaps between orders. BR did not maintain systematic records on crashworthiness until 1986, when a database was created containing an analysis of over 1700 accidents. This is revised annually and holds data going back to 1973. An updated review of crashworthiness issues was undertaken by Mr J H Lewis of BR Research in June 1996, where it was estimated that improvements in the crashworthiness of vehicles up to 1996 had the potential to reduce the numbers of casualties in accidents to between half and one quarter of the level at that time. Particular hazards responsible for significant numbers of deaths were identified as overriding of carriages and passengers being thrown through broken windows.

11.6   Current vehicle design is governed by Group Standard GM/RT2100, Issue 2 April 1997. This requires vehicles to be designed and maintained so that "the safety of occupants is ensured so far as it practicable under both normal operating conditions and abnormal conditions... Should structural failure occur as a result of a collision or derailment, the possibility of injury to people both inside and outside the vehicle shall be minimised". The standard then sets out more detailed provisions as to structural requirements. A separate Group Standard governs the design of windows (GM/TT0122). Freight wagons are governed by GM/RT2100 together with other standards. HMRI are involved in the introduction of new stock at three levels involving conformance certification, engineering acceptance and route acceptance. Railtrack are also involved in engineering acceptance of new stock. In addition, the trans-European Inter-operability Regulations contain provisions covering vehicle design which will affect both new orders and existing stock using cross-border routes. At the present time there is no single body empowered to set common standards for safety features. While differences will naturally occur between the type of rolling stock used by different operators, it should be possible to achieve a common set of standards for interior safety features.

11.7   While new safety measures are capable of dramatically reducing the numbers of fatalities resulting from accidents, the speed of trains has progressively increased during the same period. Statistically, there is a linear proportionality between speed and numbers of fatalities. However, it should be emphasised that the statistical base on which such a conclusion is to be drawn is very limited. Up to the 1960s few trains travelled above 75mph and almost all of the casualties analysed in the BR database up to 1989 involved collisions at less than 40mph. It is possible that high speed crashes could lead to substantially increased casualties, despite higher levels of physical security. The accidents at Eschede in North West Germany in June 1998 and at Ladbroke Grove in October 1999, resulted in very significant numbers of fatalities, both being accidents which occurred at high speed. The Southall crash would have resulted in more fatalities had more people been travelling in the two leading coaches. The effect of higher speeds on accidents is a matter which should be kept under careful review.

Issues specific to Southall

11.8   There was general agreement among experts that the performance of the Mark III coaches in the Southall crash had been good and that their structural design had made significant contribution to keeping casualties relatively low. The progress of the accident and the fate of the different vehicles involved is described in summary form in Chapter 1 and in more detail at Annex 6. Thus, coach H, although having separated from the rest of the train and falling on its side, remained structurally intact. Two passengers who were killed appear to have been thrown through shattered windows. Those who remained inside coach H survived, some sustaining injuries which were severe, but from which they subsequently made substantial physical recovery. Coach F sustained largely end-on impact with the side of coach G and subsequently with a hopper wagon. In the course of the collision, Coach F was penetrated along the right-hand side by a freight wagon, but fortunately not into a space occupied by passengers. Occupants were severely shaken but none suffered serious physical injury. Coach F remained structurally intact.

11.9   The largest number of fatalities and serious injuries occurred in coach G, the structure of which was damaged, so allowing the coach to undergo gross distortion. This appears to be the only occasion in which a Mark III coach has suffered such severe structural damage in the course of a collision. Given the increasing speed of train travel, and therefore the increasing likelihood that accidents which occur will be at high speed, it would have been relevant to make a detailed examination of coach G. It should have been possible to ascertain precisely how and why the right hand side of the coach was torn off in the course of the accident, the extent to which this caused or contributed to the subsequent gross distortion of the coach, and the changes in design and construction that might have avoided these consequences. Regrettably, while a substantial number of photographs remain, coach G itself, after being removed from the tracks, was cut up and scrapped at the site within days of the crash without any detailed structural investigation having been carried out. At the end of the hearings documents were produced by ATC showing that, after the remains of Coach G had been removed to a site adjacent to the line, GWT requested approval to cut up the remains for disposal. ATC stated that they required confirmation that all interested parties had completed their investigations. This was given by GWT on 24 September, noting that AEA representatives would be allowed access on 26 September, as long as this did not stop the disposal work. It was in these circumstances that Coach G was inspected, and briefly reported on, by Winston Rasaiah and Mick Barradell of AEA. Examination of photographs and reports on coach G suggests that the right hand side was torn out by collision with a freight wagon and that buckling followed impact damage to the solebar. No evidence of a major welding failure was seen.

11.10 As already noted, persons were thrown through broken windows in coach H, but others subsequently had difficulty in getting out. Window design involves drawing a balance between these two dangers. Code of Practice GM/RC2504 comments on this issue as follows:

"A significant cause of death and serious injury in vehicle overturning accidents has been the breakage of side windows, which has allowed vehicle occupants to fall out. It is therefore important that windows are constructed so that containment of occupants is assured in such circumstances as far as is practically possible. Laminated glass, which is currently being specified with the new rolling stock will help achieve this end"

The current Group Standard for windows, applicable from June 1993, requires windows to be provided with laminated glass or similar, except for windows designated for emergency egress, which are to have toughened glass or similar. The Mark III coaches in the Southall crash were built before 1993 and would have had toughened glass windows. There is no suggestion that the material was in any way defective.

11.11 An issue relevant to Southall was the means of breaking or otherwise removing windows. Special hammers are provided which are capable of breaking the windows at an appropriate point. It does not appear that anyone, following the Southall collision, managed to find the hammers or to break an otherwise unbroken window. Access to the hammers, particularly in the circumstances immediately following a major collision appears to be a serious problem which awaits solution. One possibility which should be considered is some form of warning light which will at least reveal the location of hammers in conditions of restricted visibility and confusion. This possibility should be considered along with the provision of exit lighting indicators, as now routinely fitted in aircraft and to be mandated by European regulation for some trains. An important element in emergency evacuation is training and briefing of train crew and the verification of planned measures by trials involving representative groups of passengers.

11.12 The passengers within coach H found themselves in the wholly unexpected situation of the coach being turned on its side. The same occurred to one of the coaches in the Ladbroke Grove crash. As a matter of basic design, consideration ought to be given to the effect of this on passengers and how they are likely to react when the coach is thrown onto its side. This applies both to means of escape and to moving within the coach. One particular aspect of this question is the ability to pass through internal sliding doors. It was pointed out by Dr John Boddy, one of the passengers who managed to exit from coach H through one of the windows, that the sliding doors were jammed shut. Some work has been carried out to ensure that such doors will always provide exit from a coach on its side by providing for one of the doors to fall away. This is, again, an elementary design issue that ought to be applied to every high speed coach. Quick exit from coaches involved in crashes is of paramount importance in the case of fire.

11.13 Consideration has been given to the introduction of safety measures common through other modes of transport, such as seat belts and air bags. While these should be kept under review, freedom of movement within and between carriages is regarded as an important factor by most travellers and this effectively precludes the practical use of such measures as well as their enforcement. It was also pointed out that, unlike air travel where safety briefings are given by staff at the commencement of every flight, rail travellers receive no such briefing and most are unaware of safety measures. Consideration should be given to appropriate means of communicating safety information to passengers. If this cannot be achieved through the posting up of notices, consideration might be given, in later generations of rolling stock, to the provision of seat-back screens which could display such information in a form more likely to be taken into account by passengers. Such measures are already in use in modern rail systems such as the new Hong Kong airport link. The feasibility of safety announcements on main line services should also be considered.

11.14 It was noted that significant parts of the damage to coaches F, G and H were caused by sharp protruding edges and other "aggressive" features of the freight vehicles involved in the collision. It was suggested that their design might take into account the need to minimise damage in a collision. On behalf of EWS, the operators of train 6V17, it was stated that sharp corners were not deliberately included in vehicle design and that manufacturers did avoid sharp corners, but that restrictions on the shape or design of these vehicles might impact on their utility. Bearing in mind that side-on collisions are the least common types of accident, it is doubtful whether a requirement for freight wagons to be so designed would be justified. However, EWS proposed that a risk assessment should be carried out on whether freight wagon design could avoid aggressive features without detriment to their primary function. Of more direct relevance are the couplings employed: had the freight wagons involved in the crash become detached less readily, the penetration damage which occurred, principally to coach G, might not have happened. It was stated that, where possible, auto-couplers were now used, which could keep wagons connected and in line in the event of collision. A risk assessment should be carried out to consider whether there are disadvantages in the general use of more secure couplings.

11.15 As noted in Chapter 2 and Annex 6 both coaches H and G came into contact with OHL stanchions in the course of the crash, which caused the vehicles finally to come to rest. The impact of a freight wagon with a stanchion was part of the sequence of events which resulted in coach G undergoing severe distortion and which almost certainly contributed to the number of fatalities. The collision was of such violence that the stanchion was bent into a horizontal position near ground level. The impact of coach H was of far less moment and this may have caused little additional damage to the vehicle.

11.16 Railtrack have commissioned a report into the behaviour of the stanchions, five of which in total were involved in the accident. The report, by AEA Technology, is not yet available but this remains a topic which should be kept under review. Specifically, consideration should be given to whether the response of OHL structures in accidents can be improved without detriment to their primary role.

CHAPTER 12

AUTOMATIC WARNING SYSTEM (AWS)

Development and operation

12.1   A control system which would apply brakes at a distant (warning) signal, if not appropriately cancelled, was first introduced on the British railway network by the original Great Western Railway Company (GWR). Known as Automatic Train Control, the system operated through a ramp fixed between the rails which made contact with a spring loaded shoe beneath the locomotive. An early version, first piloted in 1906, delivered an audible warning at the signal and this was soon developed to apply the brakes if the warning was not acknowledged by the driver. The success of the system in reducing accidents soon led to its adoption throughout the GWR network, and later to the development of systems by other railway companies. Automatic Train Control was seen as a device which would allow drivers to proceed at normal speed in conditions of poor visibility and would also provide protection against incapacity of the driver. It was not seen in any way as a substitute for careful driving. At the time of post-war nationalisation, there was no single nationally accepted control system.

12.2   London Midland and Scottish Railway (LMS) had, by the 1940s, developed their own Hudd system for use on the London-Tilbury-Southend Line using magnets in the track, rather than the ramp contact as employed by GWR. This development had the potential to allow the system to work at higher speeds. The LMS version also included a visual warning, as in the present-day system. In the 1950s a BR team developed the LMS system into the AWS currently in use over virtually the whole British railway system. Advances in the design of magnetic materials allowed the use of much smaller track magnets, mounted on end rather than laid horizontally as in the Hudd system. On the locomotive, a bell is now used to indicate clear (as in the GWR system) rather than the horn signal employed by Hudd. The new 1950s equipment was renamed Automatic Warning System (AWS). The basic mechanics of the system, however, remained the same as in the Hudd system which was itself based on the original concept of Automatic Train Control.

12.3   Development since the 1950s has consisted mainly of adaptations to meet changes in locomotive and multiple-unit design. BR were slow in installing the new system across the country. The accidents at Harrow and Wealdstone (1952) in which 112 people were killed, and at Lewisham (1957) in which 90 people were killed, finally gave enough impetus to ensure nationwide fitment of AWS on main lines which was, however, not complete until the late 1970s. There remain about 1000 miles of track not fitted with AWS, most of which does not involve passenger traffic. In his report on the Harrow disaster the Inspector acknowledged the early introduction of Automatic Train Control on the Western Region and the notable safety record which had been achieved. One change made to the equipment since 1970 has involved modifying the receiver to use reed switches and relays in place of the original magnet armature, the inertia of which was too great to give reliable operation at high speed.

12.4   The operation of AWS in the driver's cab was described in Chapter 1. A schematic drawing of the equipment is contained in Annex 23. The technical operation of the system can be described briefly. Mounted below each HST power car, inside a metal housing, is a "receiver" consisting of reed switches and a reset relay. The switches are wired to electrical devices within the cab comprising the audible warning device (which can be a bell or a horn) and the visual "sunflower" indicator. Also located on the driver's console is the cancel, or reset, button which is referred to in Chapter 6. The technology is based on the fact that opposite magnetic poles attract, while like poles repel. The reed switch is designed to respond to a magnetic field, its normal position being in North contact. Within the running rails located at a distance 200 yards in advance of a signal is the AWS "lineside" equipment. This consists of a strong permanent magnet with its South pole uppermost and an electro-magnet which, when energised by passing current through its winding, presents a North pole uppermost.

138

12.5   When the AWS receiver passes over the track equipment, the magnetic field from the permanent magnet (South pole) causes the reed switch to move into the South contact position. If the electro-magnet is energised, its magnetic field then places the reed switch back in its North contact position. The electrical signal briefly passed from the switch rings a bell in the driver's cab. If the signal is set to any warning aspect (double yellow, yellow or red) the electro-magnet is not energised so that the reed switch, when passing over the track magnets, receives only the South pole magnetic field, moves into the South contact position and remains there. This gives the driver an audible horn which continues to sound until cancelled by the driver's reset button. The cancellation of the horn signal is accompanied by a visual black and yellow "sunflower" aspect. The key feature of the AWS lies in its linkage to the braking system. If the warning horn is not cancelled by the driver within two seconds, an automatic brake application occurs, which cannot be cancelled other than by isolating the AWS unit. Even when the audible warning has been cancelled, the visual warning remains until cancelled by the next signal. Another important feature is that failure of the signal to energise the electro-magnets in the track leads to a warning being given even when the signal is clear. This is referred to as a "right-side" failure.

12.6   As noted in relation to the events of 18/19 September 1997 in Chapter 6, the AWS system may be isolated by operating a lever which is situated in the engine compartment, behind the driver's cab. This is necessary to release the brakes after they have been applied by the AWS system, either because a warning signal was not cancelled or because of malfunction, such as failure of the reset switch. The isolating lever should be "sealed" in the ON position, so that any isolation must break the seal, which is then required to be re-applied when the unit has been serviced and any fault corrected.

12.7   On taking a train from the depot, therefore, the Rule Book requires that the driver should check that the AWS lever is in the ON position and sealed. The AWS will be tested when passing over a ramp on leaving the depot. After arriving at its destination and switching off the engine, the AWS cab equipment will again be automatically tested when the driver's key is inserted to re-start the engine. It was at this stage that Driver Tunnock discovered the AWS system in power car 43173 not to be working, in that the warning horn could not be cancelled, leading to application of the brakes. There are a number of different types of failure which can occur on AWS, including faults in trackside equipment. The great majority of AWS faults lead to right-side failure i.e. the system fails safely. The statistics available on AWS failures are referred to below.

12.8   One of the underlying issues concerning AWS is whether the system is to be regarded only as an aid to drivers' vigilance, or as vital safety equipment, without which trains should not be permitted to run. The former undoubtedly represented the view both of drivers and managers during most of the life of AWS and since the original introduction of Automatic Train Control. By the time of the Southall crash, however, there had been a shift of opinion. Operating speeds had increased progressively and significantly since the demise of steam. The use of interlocking systems and the virtual elimination of signalling errors produced significant advances in safety, such that driver error began to emerge as the most significant cause of accidents and AWS as an important means of avoiding driver error. The issue of AWS status can be seen to crystallise in the Rules relating to the operation of trains with AWS isolated, and the imperative with which those Rules require the train not to run (see below). No risk assessment had ever been carried out on the consequences of running with AWS isolated. After the Southall crash, no one was to be heard justifying the decision to allow service 1A47 to run normally between Swansea and Paddington with its AWS isolated. Yet with very few exceptions, such concerns were not being expressed before the accident. This demonstrates both the spread of opinion that existed and the ambiguity within the Rules.

Shortcomings of AWS

12.9   At first sight AWS would seem to have the potential to eliminate signals being passed at danger (SPADs) unless the system fails or is isolated. Yet the reality is the reverse. Statistics for SPADs indicate that some 99% occur with the AWS functioning, necessarily leading to the conclusion that the driver will have cancelled the warning and then proceeded without adequately applying the brakes. Preliminary reports from HMRI indicate that this may have occurred with such tragic results at the Ladbroke Grove collision in October 1999. SPADs with AWS isolated seem to be rare, yet this appears to have occurred in an incident at Derby North Junction on 4 June 1997 when a Virgin HST with AWS isolated over-ran a stop signal by one mile. Ironically, the Rail Industry report on this incident was not published until October 1997, after the Southall accident, nor did the incident come to the attention of HMRI until publication of the report.

12.10   The reasons for drivers cancelling but then apparently ignoring the AWS warning are complex and lie in the field of psychology and human behaviour, which is touched on in Chapter 1 in relation to the Southall crash. It is readily understandable how drivers could become conditioned to cancelling the AWS warning as a reflex reaction, given that all drivers will encounter many such warnings daily, and given the automatic brake application following a failure to cancel the warning. It was said that some drivers on suburban services rarely encountered a green signal and consequently spent virtually the whole of their working shift cancelling warnings. A search for safer means of control has therefore concentrated both on driver training (to encourage appropriate response to warning signals) and on development of alternative "driver-proof" systems. These include ATP which is considered in more detail in Chapter 13.

12.11   Alternative train control systems are still some years away. The Railway Safety Regulations, brought into effect in August 1999, require that train protection systems be installed at signals falling within the applicable criteria by 1 January 2004. In the interim, safety on the railways will be primarily dependent (with the exception of ATP protected lines) on AWS and appropriate driver vigilance. AWS is one of the systems that should have prevented the Southall crash.

12.12 As has been seen above, the AWS system is simple and based on reliable and tested technology. It is also old technology which has not been able to take advantage of new developments. It uses materials (such as Bakelite) hardly encountered today and is being used in conditions, particularly in terms of speed and intensive use of rolling stock, which were hardly envisaged by the original inventors. John Hawkins, currently GWTC Fleet Engineering Manager, drew attention to the problem of servicing and replacement of AWS parts. The three key components of the train-borne system, the receiver, the voltage converter and the relay panel, as well as various cab devices, are supplied and overhauled by Railpart as successors to the BR component section.

12.13 The train operators are unable themselves to service the individual units and have no control over the extent to which parts are renewed. Repaired components are issued on a common-user basis with no means of traceability. Planned preventative maintenance is not achievable. One of the companies principally concerned with the overhaul of AWS equipment is NRS Limited, who are successors to BR Signalling and Telecommunications, formerly based at Crewe. GWT commissioned an independent audit of NRS, carried out by Halcrow Transmark in conjunction with Railpart. They found the work of NRS satisfactory, but noted certain shortcomings in the consistency of documentation maintained and made certain recommendations. Mr Hawkins considered that AWS equipment did not meet the levels of reliability to be expected from current technology.

12.14 Any proposals for changes in AWS maintenance must take into account the proposed introduction of TPWS, which will utilise much of the AWS system. For both present and future applications, it is important that AWS be maintained and its reliability enhanced. Mr Hawkins has suggested the establishment of a "System Authority" with responsibility for central control of AWS, through monitoring of standards to which the equipment is manufactured and serviced, including the establishment of traceability of parts and components. Although Mr Hawkins did not give high priority to AWS failures as a cause of train delays in service, it emerged that the actual number of AWS defects greatly exceeded the numbers which were formally reported. In my view, any technical failure of AWS equipment should be regarded as a cause for concern, and to be avoided.

AWS Rules and Standards

12.15   Isolation of the AWS is dealt with in the Rule Book current in September 1997 in Appendix 8, which provides as follows:

> "6.1   A traction unit must not enter service if the AWS is isolated or the seal is broken on an AWS isolating handle in any driving cab which is required to be used".

> "6.3   If it is necessary to isolate the AWS the driver must inform the signalman at the first convenient opportunity. The train <u>must be taken out of service at the first suitable location without causing delay or cancellation</u>". (emphasis added)

An earlier (1982) version of the underlined words was " should be taken out of service at the earliest opportunity commensurate with the avoidance of cancellation or delay".

12.16   These provisions are, and were perceived to be, ambiguous. Was the train to be kept in service under Rule 6.3 if delay or cancellation would otherwise be caused?   It is difficult to conceive of circumstances in which delay or cancellation could be avoided unless another train was immediately available at the point of AWS isolation.   Where this was not so, did the word "must" nevertheless indicate that the train was to be taken out of service irrespective of causing delay or cancellation? It is equally difficult to see whether the wording of Rule 6.3, which was introduced in 1993, added clarity or confusion to the old Rule. It is certain that the Rules were interpreted in more than one way.

12.17 Rule 6.1 was known to be equally ambiguous in terms of the expression "enter service". Many different opinions were given at the Inquiry by highly experienced railway experts, which simply confirmed the ambiguity. First, there were different views as to whether Set PM24 had entered service on leaving OOC, or whether it had entered service only on leaving Paddington as train 1B08. Secondly, there were different views on whether 1B08 "left" service on arrival at Swansea and again "entered" service on leaving Swansea as 1A47; or alternatively whether the train remained in service once it had left Paddington (or OOC). Perhaps the ambiguity of Clause 6.3 renders the precise meaning of Clause 6.1 less critical. Nevertheless, it remains important to know whether, under the Rules, service 1B08 should ever have left Paddington. All experts were in agreement that there was nothing "unsafe" about driving 1B08 to Swansea. But it is clear that if "entering service" occurred only at OOC or Paddington, so that the train had to return from Swansea (subject to Clause 6.3), then it is equally clear that the driving cab in power car 43173 was one which was "required to be used" and accordingly, the train should not have entered service.

12.18 There were different versions of the Rule Book for drivers and signallers together with a master copy. In the case of AWS faults and malfunctions, all required the driver to advise the signaller, who was required to pass on the information to Operations Control. However, it was contended that there was inconsistency as to whether the decision about taking the train out of service was to be taken by the driver or by Control. No serious case was made for placing the burden of decision on the driver, but it was recognised that the same result could be achieved through the driver's right to refuse to work on safety grounds, which has been considered in Chapter 5. Further doubt arose as to the meaning of "Operations Control", which is considered in para 12.21 below. It should be appreciated that the bulk of the Rules applicable had been drafted in the days of BR when the driver, the signaller and the control staff were within the same organisation and answerable to the same authority. One of the potential difficulties created by privatisation was the split, first between the driver and signaller, who would work respectively for the train operating company and Railtrack; and secondly, between the signaller and Control, which might refer to either Railtrack or the train operating company. The signaller, when informed by a driver, would be expected to pass the information to Railtrack Control, whereas any direct reporting by the driver would necessarily be to the TOC Control. While the two Control authorities were in contact, their different existence was hardly recognised by the Rules.

12.19 The Rule Book made provision for the action to be taken in the event of equipment being defective. The Rule Book provided two possible courses of action as follows:

> A.　　= The train must be taken out of service immediately or as soon as practicable.

> B.　　= The train must be taken out of service at the first suitable location, without causing delay or cancellation.

The Rule book designated the appropriate action for AWS failures as B. It will be noted that this precisely replicates the wording of Rule 6.3 in Appendix 8. It is also clear that AWS isolation was not intended to lead to the train being taken out of service "immediately or as soon as practicable".

12.20 In an attempt to add clarity to Rule 6.3, BR in 1993 issued Group Standard GO/OT0013, having the stated purpose of defining the arrangements to be made to deal with traction units/vehicles which need to be taken out of service in accordance with relevant Rule Book and Rule Book Appendix instructions. The Group Standard gave the following definitions of the words "take out of service at the first suitable location, without causing delay or cancellation":

6.1   The following should apply where non-availability of equipment or facility is undesirable, but its absence does not present a serious safety risk or, similarly, where replacement of the traction unit/vehicle may result in provision of another vehicle which is not fitted with the equipment which has failed.

6.2   Operations Control must decide the location where the vehicle can be replaced.

6.3   More time is available in these circumstances to organise an alternative at a suitable location as the circumstances are not as urgent as those shown in Section 5 of the this Standard.

6.4   The emphasis must be to provide a replacement traction unit/vehicle or some alternative means as soon as possible. The traction unit/vehicle must be removed from service at the destination of the train, unless replacement can be arranged before that point. Where replacement cannot be arranged at the destination (i.e. the end of a branch line or similar) it may be appropriate, when all factors are taken into account, to allow the train to return from the destination to a location where replacement can be arranged.

6.5   It is not the intention to allow a traction/unit vehicle to continue in service with multiple journeys until arriving at the next stabling point.

The foregoing "definition" begs the question whether or not AWS isolation presents a "serious safety risk". This was again the subject of conflicting views. It may be concluded, again, that before the Southall crash most experts regarded the Group Standard as permitting the continuation of a train (once in service) with AWS isolated, whereas after the crash there was virtual unanimity that other actions had to be taken.

12.21 A debate took place on the meaning of "Operations Control" under Rule 6.2 above. This is defined under the Group Standard as follows:

Operations Control – Any organisation, position or individual specifically nominated for this purpose by the local manager.

At the time of drafting this Standard, Operations Control meant the relevant BR Control Office. At the time of Southall, it could be taken to refer to Railtrack or to GWT (see para 12.18 above). At the time of the accident, their respective GW zone control organisations shared the same room within the Railtrack office building at Swindon, but the two are now in separate buildings although with connected systems. There were thus three entities who might potentially be empowered under the Rules to decide whether a train should should remain in service i.e. the driver, Railtrack or GWT. I am confident that all parties expected the decision to come from GWT Control, but the choice as between Railtrack and GWT was far from clear under the Rules.

12.22 On the day of the Southall crash this potential degree of confusion was not further put to the test since Driver Tunnock (as I have found) reported direct to GWT Control at Swindon, rather than reporting via the signalman. On the previous day, the attempted report by Driver Taylor did not reach either the signalman or GWT Control. The confusion was, therefore, academic and has now been addressed. The lack of precision and clarity throughout these Rules is regrettable. Given that the Rules, whatever their precise meaning, did not prevent train 1A47 running without AWS, the lack of precision was not, of itself, a cause of the accident.

AWS statistics

12.23 Evidence was presented to the Internal Inquiry in October 1997 by Geoff Hudson (GWT Fleet Technical Manager) of AWS faults recorded on 63 power cars during the period 1 January to 20 September 1997. Data taken from the RAVERS system revealed 97 reported AWS defects in the period, of which 60% were recorded as "no fault found". The Internal Inquiry was also given a spreadsheet prepared by Sue Mundy (GWT Systems and Compliance Manager) showing the total number of defects in the period as 210 with 54 in-service isolations. She had considered additional data sources and additional power cars. She subsequently revised her figures to a total of 304.

12.24 For the BTP investigation, PC McQuilliam produced evidence of 64 AWS isolations in the same period. His statement claimed that there was no evidence that on any such occasion an HST had been turned, received a power car change, was cancelled or had a second man in the cab. Further, he found that only ten RT3185 forms had been lodged with Railtrack during the period. This is the fault report form required to be filled in by drivers. GWT challenged the number of isolations recorded, but the figures were overtaken by further research.

12.25   For the Inquiry, David Tubb (on behalf of GWT) prepared a review of the available statistics. He concluded that all were questionable and that the most accurate figure for reported AWS faults was 354 in the period from 1 January to 17 September 1997, including 83 recorded in-service isolations. He also concluded that there was no evidence that an HST had been turned, received a power car change, was cancelled, or had a second man in the cab. The statistics did not include power car 43173. It may be concluded that, during the 9 months preceding the accident at Southall, AWS faults on GWT were running at a rate of almost 10 per week and isolations at more than 2 per week.

12.26   The sources of faults leading to AWS isolation as finally analysed by Mr Tubb are set out in Annex 24. It may be concluded that the running of HSTs with AWS isolated was by no means a rare event. Given the proportion of services running with ATP, it can be confidently concluded that the majority of trains running with AWS isolated were not protected by ATP. As noted in Chapter 9, urgent measures were taken after the Southall crash and following recommendations of the Rail Industry Inquiry. These have led, in effect, to AWS being treated on GWT services as a vital safety system.

12.27   Strong submissions were received from passenger groups to the effect that action upon AWS isolation should be re-designated as Category A (see para 12.19). Action which has been taken is reviewed in Chapter 9 against the recommendations of the RII, where it is noted that this now involves local variations. The only operating rule now common to all TOCs appears to be the requirement which limits driving to 40mph in snow and fog with isolated AWS. It is to be noted that, despite the discussion of swift action in

September and October 1997, the process of Rule changing has proved, not unexpectedly, to be painfully slow. These matters are reviewed further in the concluding chapters of this report.

CHAPTER 13

AUTOMATIC TRAIN PROTECTION (ATP)

13.1   In the 1985 annual report of the Chief Inspecting Officer of Railways, it was noted that safety on Britain's railways would, in the future, require some form of automatic train protection. By 1988, before the accident at Clapham Junction, BRB had already approved plans for the development of an ATP system, then known to be in use on the continent. Although the accident at Clapham Junction on 12 December 1988 was caused by a wrong signal aspect, and was not therefore ATP preventable, the Inquiry under Anthony Hidden QC was asked also to take into account two further accidents which occurred, both in March 1989, at Purley and at Belgrove, each of which was ATP preventable. The Hidden Inquiry therefore heard evidence about the development of ATP and included a recommendation (para 46) that ATP should be fully implemented within five years after the specific type of ATP system had been selected, with a high priority given to densely trafficked lines. This recommendation was endorsed in two further reports following the rail accidents at Newton in 1991 and at Cowden in 1994. As will be seen, after this relatively uncontroversial beginning, ATP was to take on very different aspects in the decade to follow.

How ATP Works

13.2   ATP differs from AWS and other warning devices in that it is designed to limit the speed at which the train can be driven and to take over control of the train if warnings are not complied with. Unlike AWS, it is not capable of cancellation or being overridden. In contrast to devices fitted to driverless trains, ATP does not automate the driving process and driving continues to require the skills of experienced drivers. If the train is driven normally, ATP provides warnings of present and future speed restrictions, but does not otherwise intervene. The system is designed to calculate a designated speed for the train having regard to the signal settings and other information received, and to display this to the driver. Exceeding the designated speed by 3mph results in a warning and the ATP system intervenes if the speed is exceeded by 6mph. A brake application by ATP (unlike AWS) does not bring the train to a halt, but slows it back to the designated speed. With the system operating as designed, the train cannot pass a signal at danger. A schematic drawing of the equipment is contained in Annex 25.

13.3   ATP hardware comprises both lineside and train-borne equipment. Lineside beacons are linked to the signals, feeding information to a loop located within the track which transmits information to the passing train. Below the power car is mounted an antenna which picks up signals from the track loop which are passed to the on-board computer. Data from the tachometer, which measures wheel speed, is also fed to the computer, which calculates distance and position. At the beginning of a route, the computer is provided with data about the train, including its length and weight. The computer calculates braking curves which give, at any point, the indicative speed at which stopping at a signal set to danger can be ensured, as well as the speed at which a warning will be given and that at which the system will intervene if not heeded. Within the cab, the driver is provided with a purpose-designed speedometer with a green light to indicate maximum speed and a flashing green light indicating any speed limit ahead. ATP can be made to operate in different modes including, e.g. shunting.

The GWT ATP Pilot

13.4   BR moved swiftly on the installation of ATP after publication of the Hidden report, in November 1989. Their objective was to have two trial sections of track fitted and in operation by 1991. This was achieved on Great Western Zone by the fitting out of 5 power cars and the provision of lineside equipment between Wootton Bassett and Bristol Parkway (Phase 1), by May 1991. A trial section was fitted on the Chiltern line a few months later. The original intention was to place contracts for the Great Western and Chiltern Projects with different suppliers, that for Great Western being let to ACEC and that for Chiltern to GEC AS/SEL. However, ACEC were subsequently bought by GEC so that the opportunity of achieving competition was lost. The Project Director between 1988 and 1998 was Bob Walters. He worked initially for BR Projects, which became known as TCI in 1997, following a management buy-out in 1996. TCI were themselves later bought out by AEA Technology in 1998, but the essential staff remained in place, including Martin McMillan who was Project Manager from 1993. There was, therefore, some continuity of personnel during and after privatisation.

13.5   Intensive testing was performed on the first installation under the direction of Messrs Walter and McMillan. At this stage, BR had full control of track, vehicles and operations. Driver training commenced in August 1991 and the fitting of further power cars proceeded: 25 had been fitted by March 1992 and 69 by September 1993. Phase 2 lineside equipment between Wootton Bassett and Uffington was commissioned in June 1992. Supervised Service Running (SSR) commenced from August 1992. For this purpose the second man was replaced by a Driver Leader as ATP supervisor. Initial problems which emerged during this period included unrecorded wiring modifications to HSTs, which had to be brought back to standard. Some problems were also experienced with failure of the specially designed antennae which later was to lead to major modification work. Phase 3 lineside equipment, Uffington to Reading was commissioned in June 1993 and others followed, the last of the 7 phases (12 miles west from Paddington) being deferred, to be completed as part of the HEX project, in 1996.

13.6   By 1994, on the eve of privatisation, the trackside infrastructure was complete (except for the final 12 miles into Paddington) with a total of 358 signals fitted. The whole of the GWT HST fleet of 87 power cars had been fitted. The bulk of the installation costs were, therefore, already incurred and what remained was to bring the Pilot Scheme (together with that on Chiltern) into full operation. HMRI were, and continued to be, enthusiastic about ATP. However, just before Railtrack took over as infrastructure controller, BR on 31 March 1994 delivered to the Secretary of State a report on ATP which set out their conclusions on its economic viability. It was reported that the cost of ATP was substantially in excess of normal safety investment criteria (cost per equivalent fatality avoided). The concerns of BR and Railtrack were given public expression at a major conference in July 1994 on Value for Money in Transport Safety. By this date it was becoming increasingly apparent that ATP was unlikely to be fitted nationally. The BR report had been referred by the Secretary of State in May 1994 to the HSC. In December 1994 the Chairman responded, expressing qualified support for the report's conclusion. Further correspondence followed between the Secretary of State and the Chairmen of Railtrack and HSC in which reference was made to new safety initiatives within Railtrack's SPADRAM project, including TPWS. Finally, the Secretary of State on 29 November 1995 made a statement listing the safety measures being pursued by Railtrack and BR, with ATP being limited to the two existing pilot schemes and main line re-signalling projects. Extracts from the above documents are contained in Annex 26. From this point ATP was no longer a national solution. It had been effectively replaced by the SPADRAM programme including TPWS, for which trials were then already under consideration. Railtrack remained committed to the Pilot Schemes as they stood in March 1994, but considered they had no commitment to fit ATP more widely, nor to extend the Pilot Schemes. Those involved in the Pilot Schemes remained optimistic about their technical capability, but were unaware of substantial problems which were to develop in the following years.

13.7   The Great Western and Chiltern pilots were thus left, in 1995, in a position of some uncertainty. Both Railtrack and the Secretary of State had stated publicly that the pilots would proceed. The purpose of doing so was not obvious, however, and was not plainly addressed, as it should have been. Various reasons had been suggested for continuing the pilots, the most compelling being that ATP was, by 1995, already at an advanced stage of fitment to the new HEX and was already operational on Eurostar (although not running on any ATP-fitted track on the English side). But little consideration was given to the impact of the proposed TPWS system on the two pilots or on other ATP lines. By 1995, plans were rapidly advancing for sale of the first rail operating franchises, which were to commence in 1996. Privatisation remained contentious and inevitably the abandonment of ATP altogether in 1995 would have had political implications. In those circumstances, and given that the ATP pilots represented enhanced safety on Great Western and Chiltern lines, there was no realistic alternative to their going ahead, as they did. However, as various witnesses who were familiar with the situation at the time accepted, ATP lost its urgency and impetus and, as HMRI saw it, "went off the boil". The fragmentation to be brought about by privatisation was also an obviously negative factor, involving the ownership of ATP equipment being split between the infrastructure controller (Railtrack), the operator (GWT) and the vehicle leasing company (ATC).

ATP after Privatisation

13.8   GWT gained their franchise in February 1996 following a management buy-out. However, despite further public statements as to continuing with the ATP pilots, it was not established what, if any, legal obligation existed on either Railtrack or GWT to do so. Nor was it established, if they were to be continued, by what measures progress of the pilots would be judged satisfactory or not. As regards legal obligations, GWT were given access to a "roomful" of papers, but subsequent examination of the Track Access Conditions failed to reveal any such obligation, nor was there any provision relating to ATP in the franchise agreement. ATP was referred to in the original 1995 Great Western Safety Case, but not in mandatory terms. In the July 1997 Safety Case it is stated that "GWTC is piloting an automatic train protection system over Great Western main lines. The system links on train and signalling equipment to ensure the safe braking of trains and the avoidance of SPADs" (para 6.15.3(xvii)). Richard George, Deputy MD of GWT in 1996, accepted that the company had taken on an obligation to continue with the Pilot Schemes, but without legal obligation. This somewhat confused position was reflected in the debate conducted by the Parliamentary Transport Committee in July 1995 (which pre-dated the announcement by the Secretary of State), in which delay in implementing the ATP Pilot Schemes was referred to as "deeply disturbing".

13.9   This was the background to continuation of the ATP pilot after privatisation of Railtrack in April 1994 and granting of the Great Western franchise in February 1996. Messrs Walters and McMillan continued their work through TCI who, throughout the whole development of ATP produced reports on progress, initially every 2 weeks and from November 1995 every 4 weeks. From 1995, they were engaged by Railtrack, and had to obtain separate authority from GWT and ATC. Unsupervised Service Running (USSR) commenced in September 1995 at an intended rate of 10%, which was subsequently increased in July 1996 (20%), and December 1996 (30%). Reports of actual percentages of services running are contained in TCI reports. Mr McCulloch (of Railtrack) expressed the view that these reports overstated the true percentages running since the figures were based on negative reporting, i.e. reports of when services did not run. Positive reporting, introduced only in August 1997, revealed significantly lower figures than those reported to that date. Of even greater significance were the reported reasons for services running without ATP, which are considered below.

13.10   ATP was overseen by a number of groups set up during and post privatisation, including the ATP Steering Group, which changed its name to the Train Protection Steering Group (TPSG). In addition, a separate User Management Group (UMG) was set up, which included Railtrack, GWT, TCI and latterly ACEC and HEX. After their formation, GWT applied to join TPSG but were refused on the ground that the group dealt with matters extending considerably beyond ATP and, in any event, had operator representation through Thameslink. It was subsequently accepted on behalf of Railtrack that GWT ought to have been given access to this group also in view of their central role in the ATP pilot.

13.11 In addition to, and perhaps partly as a result of the reduced priority given to the ATP pilot post-1995, specific technical problems were increasingly encountered which can be summarised as follows.

Speed sensor

This is attached to an axle end on the trailing bogie of the power car. Initial difficulties had been experienced in 1993/4 with a failure of the cable which required the units to be shipped back to ACEC and progressively modified and replaced. In 1995, further failures were attributed to water ingress through the upwards facing cable gland. ACEC accepted responsibility and provided a team of Engineers at Landore where the sensors were removed and modified to reduce water ingress. Further problems occurred in June 1997 with defective rubber O rings. Yet further problems attributed to vibration and failure of the axle drive manifested themselves in 1998. This finally led to the conclusion that a more robust model was required which was subsequently put on order.

Wheelslip/slide

The tachometer was fitted to a driven axle (all axles on HST power cars are driven) and were subject to slipping of the wheels, introducing errors in the distance apparently covered. Vehicle parameters were provided by BR in 1992 and were programmed by ACEC to operate the system software when necessary. Up to 1995, with very little ATP operation, there had been few instances of excessive wheel spin. In October 1998, when USSR was in theory running at 100%, GWT experienced conditions of poor rail adhesion which the system failed to accommodate, leading to many emergency brake applications. ATP had to be isolated fleet-wide. Tests were carried out with changed parameter values to reduce the effect of wheel spin, but these were inconclusive. The poor conditions were of short duration, and further work was carried out in 1999 leading to a risk assessment of new optimised parameters. Updated parameter plugs have been installed and this has drastically reduced the number of such faults.

Antennae

A decision by BR in 1990 to retain the space reserved for long-range fuel tanks meant that the limited space available precluded fitting of the original ACEC antennae. These had harness cables at the top but those on the new design had them at the sides where the cables were subjected to higher aerodynamic forces and to damage from items thrown up. Initial antennae failures were attributed to the antennae bracket which vibrated loose but by 1995 it was apparent that the main cause of failures was damage to the antennae body and cables from ballast. Trials were carried out with a GRP shield but further discussions led to the conclusion that the original ACEC design with the cable harness at the top was to be preferred using a stronger bracket and GRP shield. Accordingly, laboratory tests were carried out on the new and old antennae design during 1996. The success of these led to discussions as to funding which are considered below.

Two channel shutdowns

The on-board computer uses triplicated logic with two of three channels voting to achieve required integrity levels. The system continues to operate with one channel inoperative, but loss of a second channel leads to failure of the system. In the great majority of cases it was found that failed channels required merely to be reset. Further, it was evident that most of the occasions on which ATP was operating with two channels only were due to the failure to re-set a failed channel as part of routine examination. This defect therefore goes to issues of maintenance rather than equipment reliability.

13.12 The problems experienced with on-board antennae gave rise to protracted exchanges which can, in retrospect, be seen as going to the root of the whole project. After successful bench tests had been carried out during 1996 on a prototype, it was intended first to fit one of the new antennae to a power car to run service tests for a number of months. Power car No. 43017 was fitted out and established the viability of the new antennae during the first half of 1997. These events ran in parallel with a well-documented series of exchanges between the parties involved in the ATP project. At a meeting on 6 September 1996 GWT are recorded as stating that they would not, at that stage, fund any part of the antennae modification programme "as the system belonged to Railtrack". Mr George stated in evidence that this was "posturing" as he knew that GWT had to pay for the antennae, and the meeting ended with agreement to fund the installation of a new antennae to one HST as a trial. Mr George stated that he wanted to use the issue of antennae funding as a lever to find out what was happening with the project as a whole.

13.13 Subsequently a meeting took place on 28 January 1997, minuted by Mr Dearman, and attended by Richard George of GWT, David Rayner of Railtrack and others, at which the possibility of abandonment or "pulling the stumps" was openly discussed. Again, both Railtrack and GWT said in evidence that they had no intention to abandon the Pilot Scheme. But just as the possibility of abandonment had been brought into the negotiation, so Railtrack raised a veiled threat that ATP might be made mandatory, which GWT realised would lead to loss of a large proportion of their services and, possibly, to loss of their franchise. As both parties knew, this was no more than negotiation, and the meeting ended with agreement that GWT would fit the new antennae to their power cars. Christopher Adams of ATC was also at the meeting and agreed in principle to share the funding with GWT. The new antennae were to be attached to ATCs vehicles, but they knew that the cost would not be reflected in any additional rental.

13.14 Mr Walters of TCI, apparently at Railtrack's request, placed an order for 100 new antennae in December 1996 somewhat ahead of the decision on funding. ACEC were uncertain as to whether they had received a valid order, but nevertheless proceeded to manufacture the antennae. The story became even more confused when, in August 1997, Mr Walters had cold feet and tried to cancel the order he had placed, only to be informed, subsequently, that the antennae had, in fact, been manufactured. By this time the single HST test had been successfully completed and GWT (now post-Southall) placed their official order in December 1997 (after ATC had formally confirmed their agreement to share the cost) and the antennae were delivered and fitted during 1998, more than two years after the new design was settled on. This whole episode well illustrates the lack of priority and commitment which undoubtedly contributed to the serious delays suffered by the ATP project since its effective downgrading in 1995.

13.15 In the latter part of 1996, while the antennae problem remained unsolved, Railtrack decided to commission an independent report on the ATP pilots, both on Great Western Zone and Chiltern. Evidence from a number of senior managers revealed lack of clarity as to the purpose of the report, its intended scope and terms of reference. Railtrack did not go to recognised experts in the field, but sought competitive tenders which led to delay. Electrowatt was eventually appointed but were not enabled to commence work until April 1997, partly as a result of a need to re-tender. Various parties subsequently expressed surprise at the nature of the investigation, which was largely documentary and not involving any engineering assessments, being based on interviews together with a study of the relevant documents. The principal author was Andrew Johnstone, who is qualified in chemical engineering with experience in risk assessment and transport safety. Two drafts of the report were circulated to Railtrack in June and July 1997. The final report had been completed at the date of the Southall crash and was issued very shortly afterwards. It provides a contemporary factual snapshot of the position of all the major players in the four months immediately prior to the accident. Issue was taken as to whether the purpose of the report was to justify abandonment of ATP. The statements and conclusions embodied in the report, based on documentary research and interviews conducted by Mr Johnstone, were challenged both as to their accuracy and emphasis. I am satisfied that Mr

Johnstone was a careful and assiduous reporter, but it must be recognised that the report was of limited ambit given the time and budget and given the fact that much of the material reported to Mr Johnstone had a subjective element.

13.16 Reading the report in this light, however, it is fair to conclude that, while Railtrack were generally in favour of continuing the pilot, both GWT and ATC regarded it with a degree of disfavour and would have been content to see the project abandoned. Mr Johnstone did indeed examine and cost a range of options including continuation on the present basis, acceleration and abandonment. He recommended acceleration and bringing of the scheme into full use, while recognising that an economic case for continuing the project could not be made in accordance with normal cost-benefit principles. Somewhat prophetically, Mr Johnstone analysed, on the basis of standard statistics, the chance of an ATP-preventable accident occurring during the following 10 years, which he quantified at 26%. It is fair to say that the tragic accident which occurred within days of the final draft being prepared had the galvanising effect on the ATP project that no words could have had.

Lack of ATP trained drivers

13.17 General issues of driver training and competence are discussed in Chapter 5. Specific programmes were introduced for ATP training at the outset of the project consisting of a two-day residential course conducted at a Swindon hotel. It subsequently became clear that driver training in ATP was closely interconnected with equipment failure and reliability problems, in that drivers were not able to build on their training and many lost confidence in using ATP, which was optional. Refresher courses were needed but these were not pursued vigorously or systematically. There was no requirement or incentive for drivers to use ATP nor for GWT to match competent drivers to working equipment. A few drivers were enthusiastic but the majority were not. Most of the Driver Standards Managers (DSMs) were not insistent on drivers using

ATP and one (David Hockey) was not himself trained in ATP at the time of Southall. Driver Harrison on 27 June 1997 underwent a cab assessment of his driving technique by Antony Cardall, but there was no mention of ATP. At the time of the Southall crash Driver Tunnock, as a result of sick leave, had not received refresher training and had never driven with ATP unsupervised; and Driver Harrison, while ATP trained and refreshed, considered that he needed further training and was therefore not competent to use ATP. These are some of the cumulative reasons why the ATP system on power car No. 43173, in full working order on 19 September 1997 and on an ATP designated service, was not switched on.

13.18 During the course of the Inquiry, other more fundamental problems concerning drivers and ATP training emerged. First, it was accepted that GWT rostering procedures, by which drivers were allocated to particular services or "diagrams" did not take into account ATP training, and did not, therefore, even attempt to match ATP-trained drivers with ATP designated services. No doubt this could be explained by practical difficulties, but it was another example of the cumulative effect of the low priority accorded by GWT to the running of ATP designated services. Secondly, a number of documents came to light showing surprisingly large numbers of non-ATP-trained drivers within the GWT network in 1997. The figures were difficult to reconcile, but after a careful collation of the records it was accepted by senior representatives of GWT that, in fact, no (or virtually no) basic ATP training had been carried out at all since 1996, when GWT obtained their franchise, and little refresher training. Given the turnover of drivers within the company, this inevitably meant a steady decline in those competent to use ATP.

13.19 The evidence of lack of trained drivers cast doubt on the regular 4-weekly reports of TCI, which continued during 1997 to report high levels of technical faults and not driver training as the cause of services not running with ATP. Bob Walters and Martin McMillan of TCI were responsible for drawing up the reports, which were received on behalf of Railtrack by Richard McCulloch who also chaired UMG meetings. Neither TCI nor Railtrack was in a position to check the information provided which asserted that, for May 1997, only 2% of non-running services were due to non-availability of trained drivers, the remainder being substantially attributed to faults. The reports repeatedly stated, during 1997, that "Driver training has continued with the majority having now received full ATP training course (3 days). A small number of drivers still require refresher training, and this is currently being progressed". It was untrue that driver training had "continued" or that refresher training was being "progressed". In fact, a paper presented to UMG dated 22 April 1996 by Clare Kitcher stated that "Basic training cannot re-commence until mid-June due to commitments to AC overhead line training". This paper was accompanied by a programme which provided for USSR (then 20%) to rise rapidly to 100% by January 1997. This proved hopelessly over-optimistic, and the target figure remained at 30% at the date of the Southall crash. The documentation being presented to UMG, however, continued to suggest that there was no problem with driver training, and on 27 January 1997 Clare Kitcher prepared a briefing paper for Richard George's use for the meeting on the following day (see para 13.13) in which it is stated "All GWT drivers have received ATP training". Mrs Kitcher stated that this was her belief. Both Mr McMillan and Mr McCulloch recalled that Mrs Kitcher had given verbal assurances on more than one occasion to UMG meetings to the effect that ATP training was continuing. Mrs Kitcher accepted in her evidence that this was so. A number of explanations for this misinformation were subsequently put forward on behalf of GWT. It was pointed out that the repeated reference to driver training having "continued" in the 4-weekly TCI reports was due to the same paragraph being carried over from one report to the next, and I accept that this is so, on the face of the reports. It was then pointed out that ATP training had become subordinate to AC overhead line training to a much greater extent than suggested in April 1996 and that the failure to achieve anything like the predicted USSR programme meant that ATP training did not require high priority. This pre-supposes that the TCI reports were correct in their basic assertion that the main concern about ATP remained the

162

availability and reliability of the equipment, a conclusion reiterated by Mr McMillan.

13.20 During her evidence Mrs Kitcher suggested that she may have acquired information about ATP training from internal Driver Management Team meetings. She identified Ivan Davenport and Antony Cardall as the possible sources of this information. Further statements were subsequently received from Mr Davenport, Mr Cardall, Mrs Kitcher and Mr McMillan. Both Mr Davenport and Mr Cardall denied being the source. Both said they were aware that basic driver training had, in fact, ceased, though not as a result of any direct instruction. I accept their evidence. Both had direct responsibility for driver training and must have known the position. I do not believe that either would have set out deliberately to deceive Mrs Kitcher. However it follows that the statements put forward by Clare Kitcher over some 18 months concerning ATP driver training had no proper foundation. I accept that Clare Kitcher had no intention to mislead. The presentation of GWT's case has led me to conclude that the revelations regarding driver training came as a genuine surprise. The question remains why no senior person within GWT sought to question the figures at the time. The gap between what I accept was common knowledge between Driver Managers and the information being circulated by Clare Kitcher was startling. The question whether driver training was material to GWT's inability to increase USSR was hardly insignificant nor was it something which could easily have been overlooked. No further conclusions are appropriate on this issue, save to record that the lack of ATP competent drivers must have been an important factor in GWT's ability to run ATP services, and that GWT management must bear responsibility for the omissions or errors which allowed the situation to occur.

Lack of commitment to ATP

13.21 During 1997, documents produced by the parties revealed a number of factors which were contended to show a further lack of commitment to ATP, if not outright hostility. Although the question of funding for the new antennae had seemingly been resolved at the 28 January meeting, no order was then placed and the only commitment undertaken was the testing of the new antenna on one power car. While this proved to be a success, other technical problems continued to dog the pilot project, to which GWT attributed most of the non-running ATP services. On 12 September 1997 Antony Cardall chaired a driver/manager team meeting at Paddington which referred to the awaited Electrowatt report and the anticipated conclusion that ATP was running well and that "most services run with it on and working". In the manuscript meeting notes, the discussion was reported in the following terms: "Drs still not reporting probs. Soon run at 100% Disaster. DSMs check reporting procedure". Mr Cardall when cross-examined, refuted the suggestion that he regarded ATP as a "disaster" and I accept his explanation that it would have been a "disaster" for ATP to become mandatory at a time when it remained unreliable, and that it was therefore important for drivers to report defects. This exchange did, however, throw further light on GWT's attitude and the state of knowledge within the company. Both Mr Cardall and others who were providing information to TCI for their 4-weekly reports, appeared to believe that the major obstacle to ATP running lay in its unreliability. Ironically, lack of driver training was the sole reason why ATP was not able to prevent the crash which was to occur just one week later at Southall.

13.22 It was also sought to cast a portion of blame on the equipment suppliers, ACEC. It was suggested that the turn round time for repair and replacement of damaged components was excessive and demonstrated lack of commitment. HMRI did not share this view and the Inquiry heard evidence from Dominique Hausman, Managing Director of ACEC (Belgium). He emphasised ACEC's commitment to the pilot projects and expressed the hope that ACEC might provide equipment for other parts of the British rail network. Significantly, ACEC's Maintenance Contract for train-borne equipment, taken out in 1994, expired at the end of March 1997. It was not renewed by GWT but extended informally on the basis that all parties were aware that ATP was then under review by Electrowatt. ACEC continued on this basis to carry out maintenance and, in my view, it would be wrong to attribute any lack of commitment to them.

13.23 Railtrack themselves are credited in the Electrowatt report as being in favour of continuation of the ATP pilot project. Yet, in June 1997, at a private meeting with the then Chief Inspecting Officer of Railways, David Rayner, Director of S&SD is recorded as having raised the question of the future of ATP in the light of the planned introduction of TPWS, which would also impact on HEX. The position of HMRI was firmly in favour of a move to full service running on the ATP pilots as soon as possible. Railtrack had, however, taken the opportunity to pass on their doubts about the future of ATP to HEX, who were reported to be "shaken" by what was said to them. Railtrack's support for ATP, could not, therefore, be regarded as unqualified and there is little doubt that GWT senior management were also aware of these complexities.

13.24 In the period immediately before the Southall crash, therefore, the position of ATP lay in the balance. GWT had not, by 19 September 1997, seen a draft of the Electrowatt report so that they did not know the recommendation to accelerate full implementation of the pilot. Mr Johnstone himself said that he had changed his mind during the course of preparing the report. While Mr Cardall feared there might be a recommendation for ATP to become mandatory, Railtrack were prepared to contemplate its abandonment. By whatever process this occurred, GWT internal data was creating a false picture, concealing the major influence which lack of driver training was having on ATP running. Mr Cooksey's summary that ATP had been allowed to "go off the boil" was an understatement. Given the time that had elapsed since the first running of ATP in 1991, and since full fitment of the equipment in 1994, the problems which were subsequently encountered and which were allowed to occur inevitably relegated ATP to a position of low priority. A significant factor which cannot be overlooked is the apparent *volte face* of BR in 1994, subsequently indorsed by the Chairman of HSC and leading to the statements by the Secretary of State in March and finally in December 1995. The expressions of commitment to continuation of the ATP pilot projects must have been seen by GWT, when they took up their franchise in 1996, as somewhat hollow, given the absence of any binding obligation or apparent sanction. In these circumstances, in September 1997, it was always going to be a matter of chance whether ATP was switched on for an ATP designated service. Even on GWT's flawed figures, the chance was no more than 50%. The moment that an unqualified driver was allocated to the start of service 1A47, there was no chance.

13.25 The suggestion was made to the Inquiry that the lack of commitment to ATP in 1997 was attributable to privatisation of the rail industry, on the basis that BR had originally been committed to vigorous pursuit of ATP throughout the network. It is appropriate to conclude that the fragmentation brought about by privatisation exacerbated the problems of ATP implementation. It divided the obligations and benefits between three parties with no co-ordinating authority exercising delegated powers over all those with interests. TCI, as successors to BR Projects, remained in place as project managers, but as the servant of Railtrack and with no executive power. It was also suggested that Railtrack's cost benefit analysis of 1994 was inspired by anticipation of privatisation. Whatever the reason for its timing, however, it cannot be supposed that ATP would have proceeded towards network-wide fitment without an appraisal of cost-effectiveness, which is expressly referred to in the report of Anthony Hidden, QC at para 48 of his Recommendations, immediately following those relating to Automatic Train Protection. Given that such an appraisal was inevitable, it is only surprising that it was not made earlier. The resultant downgrading of ATP and the search for alternative safety measures would surely have occurred, whatever form of management had been chosen for the railway industry.

ATP after Southall

13.26 The progress of ATP after the Southall crash can be stated shortly. USSR was progressively increased from 30% to 100%. Technical problems and driver training were tackled with new energy and a progressive increase in ATP use was brought about, but not without great difficulty. Fitment of the new antennae to HSTs commenced only in January 1998 and was complete by December. In July 1998, GWT appointed Clive Burrows as Engineering Director. He was a man of wide experience and proven ability who was able to oversee the progressive implementation of ATP services. It was clear that Mr Burrows fully appreciated the many technical difficulties involved in fitment of an off-the-shelf electronic system to relatively old power cars. Mr Burrows succeeded in replacing the troublesome tachometers with a more robust version and in building up stocks of spares to facilitate uninterrupted running. Railtrack added to their technical expertise by bringing in Peter Mason as their Senior Project Manager to oversee the ATP project. GWT also authorised Mr Mason to act on their behalf leading to significant improvements in progress.

13.27 Applications were made for HMRI approval of the ATP system, the lineside equipment being approved on 12 January 1998. Train-borne equipment is approved by the Railtrack Safety Review Group and formal HMRI approval is anticipated. Despite the increase in resources and priority, major problems continued to be encountered. In October 1998, the problem of wheelslip occurred throughout the system resulting in ATP being isolated on all of GWT's HSTs for a period of more than a week. The difficulties encountered by GWT and Railtrack post-Southall, and the time taken to bring ATP into full service, are clear indicators of the poor progress made during the three years following initial fitment. In April 1999 ATP usage reached a peak of 94% but then dropped back to 80% as a result of continuing tachometer problems. At the time of the Inquiry and partly as a result of the Ladbroke Grove accident and consequent restricted services providing more spare sets, GWT were able to operate at 100% ATP. This will reduce when full service is resumed, but it is anticipated that HMRI approval will be forthcoming when tachometer reliability is finally solved.

13.28　The inescapable conclusion is that all the foregoing problems and their resolution could have occurred within a very much shorter time span had there been greater commitment and allocation of resources in the period before and following privatisation. The delay which occurred can be explained but not excused. GWT bear a major responsibility for the delays, but the actions of BR, Railtrack and HMRI all played their part as explained above and the absence of any co-ordinating system or authority was pivotal. It can now be seen with clarity that the effect of privatisation was to leave no one in the driving seat. In retrospect, it was inevitable that the ATP pilot project should be brought into full service. It is a matter of the greatest regret that the Southall collision had to be the catalyst that finally brought this about.

CHAPTER 14

RAILWAY SAFETY ISSUES

14.1 This chapter reviews general safety issues on the railways as they existed in 1997 and up to the date of the start of the Southall Inquiry. In the light of the review to be carried out by the public Inquiry chaired by Lord Cullen into the accident at Ladbroke Grove on 5 October 1999, this report does not deal with wider rail safety but will consider matters which have relevance to Southall. These issues form part of the context in which the events at Southall should be seen, and from which recommendations are to be drawn.

14.2 Rail safety has, both before and since the Southall crash, generated a high level of public concern and awareness. Some have seen this as disproportionate, for example, to the level of press coverage given to road safety issues. The point was addressed in the report of the Environment, Transport and Regional Affairs Committee of November 1998, where it was stated:

> Although rail is the safest form of land transport, a single accident can cause many deaths and injuries and the publicity it attracts can damage public confidence in the safety of rail travel. When public policy is to attract travellers off roads, the safety of rail travel must be firmly based on robust and impartial regulatory systems. This is particularly important when the fragmentation of the railway has led to a host of new companies, contractors, sub-contractors and individuals working on the railway, some of whom have little or no railway experience.

Safety and privatisation

14.3 British Railways (BR), during the 1980s, was reported to be subject to both financial and organisational problems which could not be divorced from safety issues. Anthony Hidden, QC criticised specifically the re-organisation of the Signal and Telecommunications Department on Southern Region in 1988, prior to the accident at Clapham Junction. While this had not made matters worse, he identified poor working practices, unsatisfactory training and incomplete testing as having existed both before and after the re-organisation (para 10.34 to 10.39). BR were then in full control of the rail network, the great majority of work, including design, maintenance and provision of rolling stock, being undertaken by direct BR employees.

14.4   At the time of the Clapham Junction accident BR's safety policy was based on quality management. The aim, in 1988, had been to introduce quality initiatives at all levels within 5 years. Policy documents existed and some staff had been appointed, but the system had not been certified under BS5750 and much work required to be done. From 1992, privatisation of the rail industry was under active review and some of their workshops had already been sold off. HSE were commissioned to develop proposals for a new safety regulatory regime, intended to maintain safety through the process of privatisation. This project included producing new sets of Regulations under the Health and Safety at Work Act, 1974. Their investigations included drawing on experience from other industries in which the Safety Case regime had been introduced and operated. Recommendations were published jointly by HSC and the Department of Transport under the title "Ensuring Safety on British Railways", January 1993. During this period, HMRI moved their base from the Department of Transport, where they had operated on an agency agreement with HSC, to become part of HSE.

14.5   The controversial Railways Act 1993 was passed on 5 November 1993 and empowered the Government to put into effect rail privatisation. New Regulations were then introduced to provide a firm legal basis for the new safety regulatory scheme. The principal sets of Regulations are now the following:

• Railways (Safety Case) Regulations 1994

• Railways (Safety Critical Work) Regulations 1994

• Carriage of Dangerous Goods by Rail Regulations 1994

• Railways (Miscellaneous Provisions) Regulations 1997

- Railway Safety Regulations 1999

In addition, the provisions of the Health and Safety at Work Act 1974, as well as other statutory provisions, apply to the railways. It will be recalled that charges were brought following the Southall accident against the driver and the operating company under Sections 3(1) and 7 of the 1974 Act.

14.6 The model finally chosen for privatisation involved transfer of virtually the whole rail infrastructure, including stations, to Railtrack plc, initially in public ownership. Train, and the majority of station, operations were subsequently allocated to separate operating companies (TOCs), passenger and freight rolling stock being transferred to separate leasing companies (ROSCOs). After re-structuring, the Government decided to float Railtrack in advance of the granting of franchises. Great Western Trains secured their franchise in February 1996 following a management buy-out. Subsequent to the Southall crash, the company was taken over by First Group and at the time of this Report are known as First Great Western.

14.7 Under the new safety regime, each railway operator is required to produce a Safety Case setting out its safety policy, risk assessment, management, maintenance and operational arrangements. HSE were given the duty of validating the Safety Case of the infrastructure controller. Railtrack, in turn, validate the Safety Cases of operators under the "cascade" principle and carry out audits of their performance. The issue of a licence to operate is conditional on having a properly validated Railway Safety Case.

14.8 Detailed safety issues applicable to each railway operator are set out in Group Standards, which cover every significant activity or item of equipment. These were initially based on BR specifications and documentation but are being progressively updated into a common format. Group Standards are also subject to detailed audits, which are carried out for selected activities. The resources devoted to audits are limited and necessarily place restraint on the process. Railtrack have only some 15 to 20 auditors whose work must cover all companies holding a Safety Case and the many hundreds of Group Standards current at any time.

14.9 The Annual Report of HM Chief Inspector of Railways for 1997/98 provided comparative figures for rail safety in terms of numbers of casualties, fatalities and accidents. The figures suggested no increase following privatisation, particularly when figures for 1998/9 were included, during which period no passenger fatalities occurred. However, the Ladbroke Grove rail crash may create a different picture and illustrates the need to interpret statistics over a sufficiently wide base.

Audited performance of GWT

14.10 Audits were carried out on the former Inter-city Great Western from 1993, at which stage they had responsibility for both track and operations. From 1 April 1994 Railtrack took over as Infrastructure Controller and a separate Railway Safety Case for GWT was drawn up, which was subsequently subject to audit in 1995. Mike Siebert, then Controller, Safety Assurance with Railtrack, considered that the audit, still prior to privatisation, revealed their performance to have slipped somewhat. In December 1995, GWT put into place an action plan for improvement, covering eleven areas, one of which was a written procedure for dealing with SPADs. In February 1996 the privatised GWT acquired its franchise. Mr Siebert did not consider the transfer of ownership to be material in terms of the Railways (Safety Case) Regulations, but pursued the audit process which had been started in 1995.

14.11 A second stage audit of GWT was carried out after privatisation, in March 1996. The Auditor, David Parkes, was asked to give attention to outstanding matters from the earlier audit and also actions following a train fire at Maidenhead on 8 September 1995. The second audit was published in April 1996 and found significant areas of non-compliance. On 3 May 1996 Ben Keen, who had taken over as Head of Safety Review, Railtrack, wrote to Brian Scott, Manager Director of GWT pointing out that the results indicated a degree of non-compliance with the accepted Railway Safety Case and requesting a proposed action plan for dealing with outstanding issues in both the first and second stage Audits. Correspondence and meetings continued during the Summer and Autumn of 1996 with Railtrack continuing to express concern. By this time, Railtrack had also become concerned about nine incidents between June and November 1996 which were attributed to defects in GWTs rolling stock. Accordingly, a special investigation was set up, also conducted by David Parkes, to establish reasons for these incidents.

14.12 The special investigation was, in part, a response to the incident at Maidenhead in September 1995, in which the rear fuel tank on the leading power car had fallen off, due to failure of the holding nuts, and caused a serious fire. This accident and the nine additional incidents were thought to be indicative of poor maintenance practices. The special investigation was carried out in late November 1996 and the report published in January 1997. This noted that GWT Fleet Maintenance had been subject to reorganisation earlier in 1996 (see Chapter 6) and since that event some key activities had lapsed and key safety posts had been withdrawn without adequate human resources being provided (para 2.2.1). The report also commented on monitoring and reporting of safety-related defects and noted that GWT had not yet fully introduced robust information gathering systems for this purpose (para 2.4.1).

14.13 On 13 February 1997 Mr Siebert wrote a letter to OPRAF supporting GWT's application for an additional franchise for Regional Railways North West. No mention was made of GWT's recent poor audit performance. Questions were raised at the Inquiry regarding the letter, but it was shortly to be overtaken by other events. Discussions and correspondence concerning the recent audits continued between Railtrack and GWT, in which the latter did recognise the importance of the findings and made proposals for corrective action. In the course of these meetings discussion turned to the next stage RSC Audit due in April 1997.

14.14 The Third Stage Audit was undertaken, again by David Parkes and was published in June 1997. This showed very material improvements both at management level and on the shop floor. HMRI wrote to Railtrack on 27 May 1997, seeking confirmation that the latest audit revealed no major weaknesses or non-compliance, which Railtrack were able to confirm on 1 July 1997. GWT produced their Compliance Audit Action Plan on 3 July 1997 which was being put into effect at the time of the Southall crash. GWT witnesses at the Inquiry, notably Richard George and Alison Forster maintained that GWT had turned a corner in 1997 and that the Third Stage Audit showed their commitment to safety and to compliance with their Safety Case. GWT's Safety Case itself underwent a 3-yearly review in 1997 in which it was completely re-written and submitted for approval. The new document was said to contain firm commitments that were measurable and auditable, to identify key risks, actions and responsibilities, based on a Major Risk Assessment as well as the applicable Regulations. The revised Railway Safety Case was accepted by Railtrack in May 1997.

14.15 It was accepted by Railtrack that the Stage Three Audit revealed very material advances in GWT's compliance with their Safety Case and that other measures, including actions following the rolling stock audit of January 1997, showed a high level of compliance with safety requirements. However, a new internal audit system was introduced by GWT in January 1997 covering fleet maintenance. An audit carried out at OOC in June 1997 reported concern over documents and data control, control of quality records and training. In August 1997 the new audit system was allowed to lapse.

14.16 Audit procedures are substantially paper-based and can do no more than demonstrate that systems exist capable of achieving compliance with safety requirements. An issue which will receive further consideration in a later Inquiry is the extent to which such a system is capable of guaranteeing or achieving safe operation in practice. Judged against the failings recorded in Chapters 6 and 12, it must be concluded that the Safety Case system and the audit process are not of themselves sufficient to guarantee safety. As regards

ATP, although mentioned in the GWT Safety Case, no measurable requirements were laid down and no audit of the system was attempted. This was a notable omission, but for which attention would have been drawn to the problems of the Pilot Scheme at a much earlier date.

General approach to safety

14.17 Submissions were made to the Inquiry on behalf of passengers, to the effect that safety on the railways should be regarded as an absolute requirement, relying on passages from the Hidden Report (para 17.1, 17.4). Safety was not to be regarded as a matter of degree or involving assessment of what was reasonable or affordable. The latter concepts are often expressed in terms of Cost Benefit Analysis (CBA) or the principle that risk should be reduced to a level As Low As Reasonably Practicable (ALARP). As noted in Chapter 13, Recommendation 48 of the Hidden Report refers to a study of appraisal procedure for safety elements of investment proposals "so that the cost-effectiveness of safe operation of the railway occupied its proper place in a business-led operation". In relation to measures that reduce risk, Rod Muttram in his oral evidence described CBA as :

"a way of ranking those measures so that one pursues the measures that will give the maximum value of risk reduction. One does the things that improve society's safety overall".

14.18 More than one expert at the Inquiry said, and I accept, that there was no such thing as absolute safety. That does not mean, however, that rail travel must be accepted as risky. In most situations there will be found to exist overlapping safety systems so that the failure or malfunction of one does not of itself lead to an accident or even to materially increased risk. Rail accidents are said usually to be attributable to a combination of several unplanned occurrences. The collision at Southall was a clear example of this. Even where all relevant safety devices are fully operational the possibility of component failure

175

remains, as in the case of the collision in Eschede, North West Germany in June 1998.

14.19 Railtrack, through S&SD are limited in the introduction of new Group Standards to matters where the safety benefit is shown to exceed the costs. Whatever economic system is applied to the railways, the funding available will have limits and managers will need to analyse priorities even in terms of safety measures. Statistics set out in successive Annual Reports of HMRI reveal significant numbers of serious injuries and fatalities occurring to persons other than those travelling in trains. This includes railway workers, passengers on stations, suicides and trespassers, many of whom are children. The latter groups are not directly in the care of the railway and are necesssarily more difficult to control. Absolute safety is unobtainable in these cases also, but they form part of the priorities that must be considered by rail managers.

14.20 A further element of cost-effectiveness is the so called "equivalent fatality" calculation referred to below in relation to data recorders. This calculation allows for numbers of injuries of different severity to be aggregated into the equivalent of a death. Such an analysis formed the basis of exchanges between BR, HSE and the Department of Transport when considering the future application of ATP in 1995. The Inquiry had the benefit of reading a number of papers on this and related statistical topics prepared by Professor Andrew Evans of the Centre for Transport Studies, University of London. Such considerations do not, in the light of the further Inquiries to be conducted following the Ladbroke Grove crash, form part of the present Inquiry. No comment is therefore appropriate other than to note that the question to be addressed is not whether cost or affordability should be brought into account in relation to safety measures, but rather how it should be brought into account. That question is for another Inquiry.

Data recorders

14.21 This refers to the On-Train Data Recorder (OTDR), otherwise the "black box", which records a variety of train functions, to be available in the event of an incident. Additionally, if required, it can act as a means of monitoring driver performance. The subject has been under consideration within BR and the privatised industry for a number of years. There was uncharacteristic unanimity at the Inquiry that such devices should be introduced at an early date. The issues were whether the industry should wait for development of a full specification model the cost of which, including fitment, is substantial; or alternatively, whether some simpler and cheaper device should be recommended. Railtrack stated that they had been inhibited in requiring the introduction of OTDR on the ground that safety benefits did not exceed costs.

14.22 OTDR was covered by Group Standard GO/OTS203, issued in October 1993 and also by GO/OPS280 which dealt with data extraction and analysis following accidents and incidents. The device was required to be fitted to "new, life extended or extensively modified rail vehicles" of certain types including traction units. The Standard applied to existing rail vehicles as specified, insofar as reasonably practicable. In 1996, Railtrack set up the Data Recorder Strategy Group to develop and implement a strategy to encourage effective use of data recorders. This has led to production of a new standard GO/RT3272 which lays down new minimum requirements for recorders. Fitment policy requires all new trains to be fitted and for TOCs to formulate their policy on whether or not retrospective fitting should be carried out, to be based on an assessment of costs and likely safety benefits. A cost-benefit analysis carried out in May 1999 put the cost of installation and operation at £13,000 per unit, while savings in investigations and repairs were assessed at £2,000 and the value of safety benefits at £1,200. Richard Evans, who works within S&SD, estimated the total industry costs of retro-fitting OTDRs would be some £75 million, and would need to be shown to prevent at least two equivalent fatalities for each year of its planned life to show positive safety benefit. Subsequently, an even more pessimistic CBA was carried out showing the benefits to be even less significant.

14.23 In my view, the cost-benefit figures produced and the conclusions that they suggest amply demonstrate the shortcomings of CBA as a decision-making tool. The first question is to ask why the industry is in a position of needing to spend £75 million to install data recorders, which do not comprise new technology. The reason is that much of the unfitted rolling stock currently in use is of an age which would justify replacement, so that retro-fitting would not have arisen. The fact that parts of the network continue to use out of date rolling stock cannot be allowed to support an argument against retro-fitting on the ground of cost. Alternatively, it may be possible to incorporate some form of OTDR within new safety systems to be fitted to existing vehicles. I believe that the general fitting of data recorders is long overdue and that this view is shared by the great majority of the industry. Every opportunity should be taken to incorporate such devices within any modification programme to existing rolling stock.

14.24 If operators and vehicle owners consider the costs of early fitting to be prohibitive, they should be encouraged in the interim to fit a simpler and cheaper device, a possibility supported by Rod Muttram of Railtrack. From the experience of the Southall crash, any measured data on the performance of the train would have been preferable to none and would greatly have reduced the areas of speculation which have taken up much time and expense. Of much more positive benefit, however, is the potential of data recorders for reducing the possibility of driver abuse or error and for collecting hard evidence on human behaviour, which at present remains theoretical and unsatisfactory (see Chapter 1). They also have the capability of providing data which may assist in establishing optimum shift patterns and driving techniques, thereby assisting in both driver welfare and management as well as safety issues. They should be pursued on these grounds alone. The potential benefit of reducing driver error must surely outweigh the costs of this modest addition to available technology.

CIRAS

14.25   A procedure known as the Confidential Information Reporting and Analysis System was pioneered by the University of Strathclyde and sponsored by Scotrail. The system involves the confidential receipt from individuals of safety-related information which might not otherwise be reported, and creates the opportunity to take action outside existing formal procedures. The system was used on a trial basis in 1996 and subsequently adopted in England, initially by GNER and by Virgin. It is now the subject of national development with the appointment of a Project Manager and the introduction of plans for new regional centres and for locally managed systems. CIRAS enjoys the support of both Railtrack and HMRI. The system is relatively low-cost and essentially aims at the more effective collection and use of safety-related information. Reporting is by Freepost on prepared forms and may be followed up by phone or personal interviews. The essence of the system is its confidentiality and independence from the railway companies.

14.26   Sanitised information is submitted to the appropriate companies for action and response. A response is also sent to the person who initiated the report, and this may include a request to make use of normal reporting channels. Dr Lucas of HMRI commented that drivers might use CIRAS to report signal problems, where they might not otherwise wish to fill in a formal complaint. An example of immediate relevance is signal SN270, known to have been misaligned at the time of the Southall crash and for the following 2 years but which was never the subject of any driver's report or complaint. CIRAS was discussed at the Rail Summit convened by the Deputy Prime Minister on 25 October 1999 and has been given new impetus by his endorsement. Compliance will be mandatory from 1 April 2000.

Fragmentation

14.27 Finally it is appropriate to return to a theme mentioned in several different contexts. Has fragmentation of the rail industry, in the light of Southall, compromised safety? A number of criticisms have been made by parties of the effectiveness of the "cascade" system and its underpinning by audits. Some of these criticisms are well founded, and it is right that the system be judged by results, in terms of practical levels of safety achieved. But any failings of the cascade system (which is to be examined in another Inquiry) are not the result of fragmentation.

14.28 The difficulties resulting from fragmentation can be divided into two categories: first, those resulting from overlapping functions and lack of clear boundaries; secondly, those resulting from artificially divided responsibilities. In the first category is the competing safety functions of S&SD on behalf of the rail industry, with the separate function of HMRI and the somewhat indirect safety interests of BTP. This has led to calls for a new free-standing Rail Safety Directorate, a proposal which will be considered by Lord Cullen's Inquiry. In relation to Southall, it can be said that this difficulty was resolved by S&SD and HMRI effectively surrendering a large proportion of their powers and duties to BTP in a manner that was not conducive to safety and which calls for review as to the proper balance to be drawn. The tensions which arose were not, however, attributable to fragmentation, nor would they have disappeared by merger or by abolition of any of the three bodies in question.

14.29 The second category covers a series of difficulties identified during the course of the Inquiry, including:

- Cumbersome Group Standard procedures involving multiple rounds of consultation, delay and inability to achieve rapid action.

- Divided interests in the same equipment, which is used by an operator but fitted to vehicles owned by others.

- Divided interests in equipment which is partly train-borne and partly track-mounted, with different owners.

- Lack of any System Authority or means of binding all necessary parties where technical decisions are called for.

- Difficulty in promoting research and development where different entities are involved or affected.

14.30 As the process of rail privatisation took its course, there was much discussion within the industry as to the future of research and development. At a meeting organised by the Institution of Electrical Engineers on 5 June 1996 chaired by Sir David Davies on the future of UK Railway Research, the conclusion drawn from the discussion was reported as follows:

> Complete-system considerations and interface problems are likely to be dealt with by the creation of appropriate international standards, but how the necessary underpinning research and its funding are to be put in place is not yet clear. The creation of collaborative groups - Industry Associations – to identify, commission and pay for research, represents a possible way forward. There was a complete unanimity in agreeing that future R&D would be undertaken on a pan-European or global basis rather than just with the aim of meeting single-customer or national requirements.

> In the UK there may well be a temporary R&D hiatus, while the fragmented industry comes to terms with operating the restructured railway system. It will be important to ensure that the very extensive R&D expertise and facilities are not allowed to diffuse away during this readjustment period.

14.31   In a further report by a Review Committee established by the Department of Transport and Chaired by Sir David Davies, published in September 1996, it was noted that there were a number of industry-wide research issues which could fall between stools under the new structure of the railway industry. It was felt that in time the industry would devise a mechanism to address such issues, but there was major advantage in ensuring that work to tackle them continued without delay. The committee accordingly recommended that:

- A Railway Research Association be established to tackle non-competitive, collaborative issues which might not otherwise be addressed.

- The Government should consider pump priming the Association for the first few years during which industry would be encouraged to contribute and take over running and funding the Association.

- In addition, there should be established a Railway Strategy Group, able to consider a strategic vision of the future of the railways with links to the Rail Regulator, the Passenger Rail Franchising Director and senior executives in the industry.

These bodies would be ideally suited to consider the technical and strategic issues arising from cross-company projects, particularly ATP. So far as is known, no action has yet been taken on these recommendations.

CHAPTER 15

DISCUSSION AND CONCLUSIONS

15.1 Chapter 7 has considered why the accident on 19 September 1997 happened and has identified the immediate causes of the accident on the basis of events up to that date. Chapters 8, 9 and 10 have reviewed events which occurred during the long delay to which the Inquiry was subject, including the Rail Industry Inquiry and responses to its recommendations, as well as the tragic accident at Ladbroke Grove on 5 October 1999, during the course of the present Inquiry hearing. Chapters 11 to 14 undertake a review, on a broader basis, of the principal railway safety issues arising from the Southall accident excluding (as a result of the Ladbroke Grove accident) any detailed consideration of the railway safety regime and of future train protection policy, which are to be considered in other Inquiries.

Limitation on Inquiry process

15.2 This chapter now draws together the broader considerations including those from Chapters 8 to 14. It is appropriate here to record some concern over the Inquiry process itself and the requirement to make recommendations. The parties to this Inquiry, in accordance with both the applicable Regulations and long established practice, have been limited to the train companies immediately involved in the crash together with those representing other interested parties, particularly passengers and railway staff. Railtrack, who have played a prominent part in the Inquiry, have responsibility for the whole national rail network. Rail operators, however, have been limited to GWT and EWS, whose trains were involved in the crash; and of rolling stock owners, only ATC have been represented. Likewise, of the many contracting companies involved in railway renewal and maintenance, only Amey Railways were represented. This situation necessarily limits the extent to which nationally applicable recommendations should be considered.

Conversely, it was pointed out that Inquiry recommendations as yet had no direct mandatory force

15.3 These two limitations point to the need for a radical re-think of the whole procedure for rail accident investigation. In this context, it should also be borne in mind that a significant part of the task of questioning the actions of rail companies, as well as the roles of statutory bodies such as BTP and HSE, has been taken on by passenger groups representing only those travelling on the particular train involved in the accident. It might be considered illogical that such an unrepresentative group should take on the burden of questioning general aspects of safety on the railways, as well as the particular circumstances of the crash in which they or their relatives were involved. Yet without their contribution, the investigation conducted through the Inquiry process might have been less searching. The representative role of the Central Rail Users Consultative Committee (CRUCC) is not to be overlooked. Nevertheless, their contribution was limited to the personal exertions of one lay representative (John Cartledge) who had the benefit of neither counsel nor instructing solicitors nor experts. Logically, a body representing all rail users should play a much more prominent and positive role, which would not then need to be duplicated by individual passengers, save to the extent of their direct personal interest in the accident. Through historical and administrative accident, the latter are potentially in receipt of public funding for Inquiries while the former are not.

15.4 In addition to the above considerations, which are specific to the present Inquiry, it must be borne in mind that the Inquiry process has, in the past two or three decades, changed almost out of recognition. This may be attributed to heightened awareness of public safety issues as well as the general increase in recourse to lawyers. Ironically, the same period has seen substantial reduction in the number of rail passenger fatalities. This may have resulted in a smaller number of Inquiries which have, in consequence, become focal points for national concern over rail safety. Whatever the true reason, a public Inquiry, whether relating to rail safety or other issues of public concern, seems inevitably to demand consideration of issues on a wide scale, going far beyond the boundaries of the immediate accident. Consideration of the future role of rail accident Inquiries should therefore include, in addition to the foregoing matters, the possibility of severing the immediate issues of causation from broader issues of public concern, which may more properly be the subject of a different form of inquiry involving all necessary interested parties. This issue is returned to later in the context of accident investigation.

15.5   With these limitations in mind, this report now turns to the conclusions to be drawn at the end of the Inquiry, some 28 months after the date of the accident. No supervening events have affected the conclusions to be drawn as to the cause of the accident, which are as set out in Chapter 7.

AWS maintenance

15.6   Failure of the AWS was an important causative element in the accident. The review of maintenance arrangements covering AWS set out in Chapter 6 revealed a procedure which was seriously deficient in detecting and diagnosing an intermittent fault. The accepted practice meant that only those faults which were apparent during the examination would be attended to. The statistics for AWS isolation (Annex 4) show more than half resulted in "no fault found", which may indicate that intermittent faults were common. It was not suggested by the maintenance staff that there was anything unusual in a reported fault leading to a satisfactory magnet test. Set PM24 in fact contained such a fault in each power car, and it must not be forgotten that the true number of AWS failures has turned out to be greatly in excess of the numbers formally reported and recorded. The inadequacy of the test box available in 1997 has already been commented on (para 6.11). It is surprising that the development and bringing into use of a more effective test box was not undertaken with more urgency. The review of AWS maintenance procedures subsequently undertaken on behalf of GWT was long overdue. What has not yet been demonstrated is an ability reliably to detect and cure intermittent faults. The improvement of AWS maintenance procedures must be accompanied by a review of staff competence and levels of workload, and of documentation including procedures for checking the history of reported defects.

15.7 While all train operators have tightened their procedures governing the management of AWS isolations, particularly GWT, AWS failures still appear to be frequent. In the absence of historical data, it is not possible to assess whether the equipment is less reliable in general than it was in the past. The significant increase in speed and vibration coupled with the age of the equipment would suggest this as a possibility. I am concerned with the potential shortcomings in the maintenance of AWS components to which attention was drawn by John Hawkins, GWT Fleet Engineering Manager, including the inability of train operators to carry out or to check AWS maintenance work and the lack of traceability. Part of the problem is the indeterminate "ownership" of this equipment and the apparent monopoly enjoyed by the present servicing companies. There must be proper incentives to continue the manufacture of new parts for existing AWS components and the development of improved components. In this regard I am pleased to note the assurances received from NRS, in response to Mr Hawkins's statement, that both current approved equipment and improved versions are presently being manufactured. I note and share their concern over the length of time taken to secure approval of new equipment.

15.8 The possible future introduction of TPWS may be seen as largely superseding AWS. At the present time, however, no assumption can be made about the introduction of TPWS and, despite the Regulations which now apply, no date should be predicted for its implementation, in the light of experience with other new safety systems on the railways. At the present time and for some years in the future, a large proportion of the rail network will depend upon AWS as its primary safety system for the prevention of SPADs. The cost of ensuring reliability of AWS equipment is trivial compared to the cost of new safety systems. Every effort should be made to ensure that the systems do not fail other than in extremely rare circumstances. Provision should be made for regular replacement of equipment and for the maintenance of full service records and traceability of all such equipment.

Consequences of AWS isolation

15.9 The failure to take appropriate action upon failure of the AWS was also an important causative element of the accident. Urgent action was taken as soon as it became apparent that train 1A47 had been allowed to continue its normal route with AWS isolated in the driving cab. The Rules contained in Appendix 8 to the Rule Book are reviewed in Chapter 12, together with Group Standard GO/OT0013. It is unnecessary to rehearse further the ambiguities and inconsistencies within the Rule Book and the Group Standard existing at the time of the accident. On 30 September 1997, Vic Coleman (now HM Chief Inspector of Railways) sent out a circular to the effect that there was only one reasonable interpretation of the Rule Book and Group Standard, such that trains should not commence a journey without the AWS working in the driving cab. He did not go so far as to suggest that trains should always be taken out of service whenever an AWS failure occurred (Category A in the Rule Book), but stated that any decision to keep a traction unit in service with AWS defective "must be fully justifiable": see Annex 15. At the Inquiry Mr Coleman was challenged on his view that the Rule bore only one reasonable interpretation. Railtrack submitted that the clear effect of the Rules was that the train should not have left Old Oak Common. Others considered that it should not have left Paddington and yet others that it was acceptable to run to Swansea but not to continue. Railtrack also submitted that no experienced railwayman could or should have interpreted the Rules or the Standard so as to believe that the HST should be allowed to complete its diagram, at least in the formation in which it remained. This submission was not disputed, yet this is precisely what happened on 19 September 1997. It is very doubtful, in my view, that any other course would have been taken even if GWT Swindon Control had taken full account of Driver Tunnock's messages. Accordingly, while Mr Coleman's valiant attempt to impose order on 30 September 1997 was to be applauded in the circumstances, the suggestion that the Rules bore only one reasonable interpretation cannot be accepted. Part of the problem in achieving clarity lay in the fact the "the Rules" were to be found in several places, intended to be complimentary but not always so. Drivers did not have access to Group Standards intended to be read with the Rule Book, nor did Swindon Control have a copy of GO/OT0013 available, had they wished to refer to it. Rules should be contained in a single document unless proper reasons exist for use of multiple sources.

15.10 In March 1998, already six months on from the accident, the RII report was issued including recommendation 3.1 which required Railtrack to review the contents of Appendix 8 and the Group Standard to avoid ambiguity and to reflect fully the responsibilities of Railtrack and train operators. Other recommendations were for a review of the application of these requirements (3.2) and an Audit of compliance (3.4). Apart from a specific recommendation for sealing of the AWS isolating handle (3.5), there was no recommendation for change in the status of AWS isolation as a Category B fault. By the date of the RII report GWT had already revised document OPS 0123 to clarify decisions on withdrawal of trains from service and Railtrack were in course of replacing Group Standard 0013 on an interim basis with GO/RT3437. This mandated the provision of a contingency plan for making a decision on taking the train out of service, but did not require withdrawal from service as such. Consequently, some 30 TOCs have developed their own different contingency plans which are reported to reveal wide variations of action to be taken after AWS isolation. GWT's contingency plan accords closely with Category A of the Rule Book, requiring trains to be taken out of service as soon as practicable. Given that GWT were facing corporate manslaughter charges until July 1999 for allowing 1A47 to continue in service with AWS isolated, their reaction is understandable. It is ironic, however, that GWT have now achieved a very high level of ATP protection which, where operative, renders the AWS obsolete. The possibility of running ATP protected trains without AWS should be reviewed. Many other TOCs, necessarily without the benefit of ATP, are permitted to continue in limited service with AWS isolated, subject to Railtrack's approval of their contingency plan.

15.11 In my view, passenger groups were justified in their strong criticism of the way in which the RII recommendations and revisions to the Group Standard have been handled. What Mr Coleman regarded as being clearly required under the Rules applying to every TOC has been turned into a confusing hotchpotch, the effect of which, in my view, is to put the convenience of operators before the interests of safety. The current Rules also create little incentive on operators to avoid isolation of the AWS in service. Given the importance that all parties now attach to the AWS and given that it will for some years to come represent the only available safety system capable of deterring drivers from passing warning or danger signals, the current Rules are inadequate. The Rules should be amended to mandate withdrawal from service as soon as practicable on the isolation of the AWS unless other adequate protection is available. The Rules, including any permitted exceptions, should apply nationally, subject only to company variations where fully justified. Even where a safety device is not regarded as vital to the continued running of the train, Rules should apply nationally with company differences being permitted only where good reason is shown.

ATP Pilot Scheme

15.12 GWT have been criticised in Chapter 7 for their failure so to manage the ATP Pilot Scheme that train 1A47 on 19 September 1997 was driven by an ATP qualified driver and with the equipment switched in. They have been criticised in Chapter 13 for their lack of commitment to the project, but in circumstances which were exacerbated by privatisation and by lack of any external pressure or incentive. The Southall accident immediately created that incentive and, although they have had little choice in the matter, GWT deserve credit for having brought the ATP, within a period of 2 years, from the brink of abandonment to a position of success. In the course of this, they have enabled the industry to identify important lessons concerning the specific problems of retro-fitting new equipment to old rolling stock and generally as to the industry's tendency to be over optimistic and not to allow sufficient contingencies in any development programme. It may be that this is a tendency inherited from the public sector and that such projects will, in future, be better and more realistically planned and managed by the privatised industry.

15.13 Nevertheless, the ATP project, to a much greater extent than the problems encountered with AWS maintenance, has exposed major difficulties in the management of cross-company projects. In relation to the ATP project these problems included the following:

- Lack of any contractual framework governing rights and obligations as between the infrastructure controller, the operator and the equipment owner, including rights of use and ownership of the equipment.

- Lack of any joint or combined Authority capable of instructing project managers, carrying out research and development and placing orders for design, supply and fitting of equipment.

- Lack of any contractual structure by which running, maintenance and renewal costs, as well as further design and development costs are to be shared and/or recouped.

Various parties have proposed and recognised the importance of establishing a "System Authority" to deal with the development and installation of such inter-company projects. The successful completion of the ATP project was brought about only when an informal System Authority was set up (para 13.26). The setting up of a formal Authority, while clearly desirable, requires the resolution of the above legal issues, to which no solution presently exists.

15.14 An important issue for the future is the status of ATP as presently installed on lines operated by GWT. The question of national fitment of ATP or other train protection systems is the subject of another Inquiry and is not addressed here. In relation to the Southall Inquiry, however, the question necessarily arises, what should happen to ATP as presently fitted. No party at the Inquiry suggested that it should be removed or curtailed in any way. In my view, the success of the system is now such that there should be no question of its removal or curtailment until replaced by an equally effective train protection system. The question whether the present GWT installation should be extended should be reviewed.

General issues of rail safety

15.15 In the light of the impending further Inquires to be chaired by Lord Cullen and the Joint Inquiry into rail safety systems and train protection, it is inappropriate to consider general questions of rail safety in any detail. Conclusions arising from the Southall crash are appropriate, however, and may need to be taken into account in the forthcoming Inquiries. The issues concerning on-train data recorders (the "black box") and the Confidential Information Reporting Analysis System (CIRAS) have been considered in Chapter 14. There is a wide measure of support for both. CIRAS has been given new impetus following the Rail Summit called by the Deputy Prime Minister in October 1999 and no further endorsement is needed. The introduction of data recorders has, however, been inhibited by cost-benefit analyses which, in my view, demonstrates the shortcomings of CBA when applied blindly to such a project. The apparent reluctance of some sectors of the industry to proceed with this project demonstrates the inertia which the industry has traditionally faced. Data recorders will be the subject of a recommendation at the conclusion of this report.

Crashworthiness

15.16 Given the creditable performance of Mark III rolling stock in the Southall crash, no general recommendations are appropriate other than as to means of exit. Many of the detailed problems encountered are under consideration and some will become mandatory on certain routes as a result of the European Interoperability Directive. A general concern which should be noted, is the considerable age of many vehicles currently in use and the inevitable fact that many mandated improvements apply only to new vehicles or to existing vehicles kept in service after some future date. The result is that large numbers of passengers will continue to be conveyed in rolling stock which falls substantially short of current standards. Various kinds of pressure are applied to operators and rolling stock companies to update their stock but often with no result. This problem should be recognised and kept clearly in view as a matter of continuing public concern.

15.17 A second aspect of crashworthiness is the tendency for developments and improvements to occur at widely spaced intervals, for example, after an accident or when economic conditions permit, rather than on a progressive and developing basis. Such a tendency may be seen as belonging more to public sector management and it is to be expected that one material benefit of privatisation will be the ability to invest on a more systematic basis and to be more responsive to consumer pressures. This issue is also affected by the current debate on length of franchises, which has not been considered by the Inquiry.

GWT's safety record

15.18 A major issue underlying the whole of the Inquiry into the Southall crash was whether GWT, in the process of privatisation had allowed safety standards to deteriorate. A number of parties put this accusation in terms of "profit before safety". I do not accept this as a necessary relationship and it is of little relevance that changes introduced by the new managers of GWT should have efficiency, and therefore profit, as their primary motive. The question is whether any such changes also had the effect of compromising safety; and also whether GWT's general approach to management allowed a reduction in safety standards. The Southall accident occurred some 19 months after formal privatisation of GWT, but restructuring when still in public ownership extends back to the early days of privatisation. Indeed, in the case of GWT, there was little change in the management structure as a direct result of privatisation.

15.19 Under the Safety Case regime, safety is conventionally measured and assessed through Audit, although the practical effects of the process are from time to time laid bare by accidents and the process of investigation. Such was the case in relation to the 9 incidents considered by Railtrack to be indicative of poor maintenance of rolling stock which occurred during June and November 1996, within months of privatisation, but including also the pre-privatisation incident at Maidenhead in September 1995 which involved loss of life. These issues have been reviewed in Chapter 14. The special investigation carried out in November 1996 noted continuing deficiencies in GWT's maintenance arrangements. The restructuring of Fleet Maintenance Depots overseen by Mr Cusworth started in 1996 and continued during 1997 at OOC. At the time of the Southall crash some 9 months had elapsed since the special investigation. The detailed examination by this Inquiry of maintenance practices at OOC during the period immediately before the crash leaves no doubt that there were continuing deficiencies in the maintenance regime and that lessons had not been learned either from the 9 incidents or from the Special Investigation. Nor did the short-lived Internal Audit System of Fleet Maintenance introduced during 1997 improve matters.

15.20 As regards general safety, the major three-stage audit process of GWT carried out between 1995 and 1997, which straddled privatisation, is reviewed in Chapter 14. The third stage audit published in June 1997 showed very material improvements. Again, it must be concluded that such improvements were not matched by performance when seen in the light of the failures discussed in Chapters 6 and 7. A question which should be raised for consideration elsewhere is whether the audit process, which is selective by its nature, can lead to general improvements, or whether it results only in correction of auditable matters.

15.21 Another significant decision-making tool where safety issues are involved is the so-called "risk assessment". A significant number of such assessments have been referred to in the course of the Inquiry. The situation has been reached where any change not accompanied by risk assessment is greeted with surprise, if not disbelief. In my view, however, this technique has its limitations and should not be seen as a substitute for clear thinking. The risk assessments considered by the Inquiry have revealed a process of somewhat variable quality, which is clearly dependent on the experience and expertise of those involved, including the persons responsible for commissioning the assessment. Comments are included in this report on a number of individual assessments and they are not repeated here. No uniform standard exists for the carrying out of a risk assessment and the widely varying circumstances in which they are required effectively precludes regulation. Helpful remarks are contained within Guidance Notes published by HSE on the Safety Case Regulations. These also contain the following description:

> A risk assessment usually involves identifying the hazards present in the undertaking (both operational and occupational) and then evaluating the extent of the risks involved, taking into account whatever precautions are already being taken and also the likelihood and consequences of precautions failing (either singly or in chance combination) (para 137).

It is axiomatic that any such assessment touching on public safety should be appropriately rigorous and commensurate with the risks perceived to require assessment. Careful attention should be paid to the HSE Guidelines, which should accordingly be kept regularly under review.

Accident investigation

15.22 Finally, it is appropriate to return to the general subject of accident investigation which has been discussed in Chapters 2 and 8 (see particularly para 8.21). The problems of technical investigation present a relatively clear solution. At Southall, too many experts were brought in and their roles quickly became confused. Some of those who should have had free access were impeded and restricted, and there was no overall plan for the technical investigation. Potentially important evidence was overlooked and some was destroyed. Fortunately, this had few overall safety implications, but the position could have been otherwise. In relation to the Southall investigation, the duplication and protraction of technical investigations was extremely wasteful of costs, including public funding for the Inquiry itself.

15.23 It is unacceptable that a technical accident investigation should be directed or controlled by BTP. Their lack of expertise and dependency on outside advice led to most of the deficiencies noted above. A technical investigation is conducted for reasons much wider than potential prosecution. While there may be exceptional cases in which the police should play a prominent role, for example, in cases of suspected terrorism or vandalism, in the case of an accident resulting from the process of running the railways, any technical investigation should be directed by an appropriate expert body. At the present time there can be no doubt that the body which should perform this role is HM Railway Inspectorate. I recommend, however, that, while such a change should be implemented with immediate effect, there should also be an urgent review to consider the adequacy of resources and arrangements for liaison with all other interested parties, including the police forces. The review should include consideration of whether, in the future, some alternative body should be created to direct rail accident investigations and possibly other transport issues as well. The review should cover the adequacy of powers available to HMRI to fulfill this role. For the immediate future I recommend that HMRI should be given powers to require the services of particular experts, as was the case (apparently without specific powers) with the BTP at Southall. This could be accomplished by amendment to existing contracts between the experts and rail companies (principally Railtrack), with matters of funding being negotiated with HMRI. These proposals are not intended to diminish the role of BTP but to define it and to ensure that public safety issues remain paramount, rather than run the risk of their being made subordinate to the investigation of crime.

15.24 One of the important tasks of HMRI and of any alternative rail accident investigating body that might emerge from the recommended review, will be to ensure that a single, thorough and definitive technical investigation is carried out, to include the recording of all appropriate factual data upon which experts, who may be instructed by individual parties, can subsequently prepare reports and opinions. Physical evidence removed from the scene of a crash must be preserved and made available on the same basis. Other important tasks for HMRI or any successor body will be to ensure adequate liaison with the emergency services and other bodies involved with accidents, including the Rail Incident Officer to be appointed by Railtrack; and to decide what data or information emerging from the investigation should be passed to the rail companies for rapid action. There will also need to be a review of existing protocols dealing with accident investigation, between Railtrack, BTP and HMRI.

15.25 Much debate at the Inquiry concerned the adequacy of and appropriate procedures to be adopted for the Rail Industry Inquiry, as conducted both for the Southall crash and subsequently for the Ladbroke Grove crash. This is considered in Chapter 9 where it is noted that, by general consent, all parties concerned now recognise that the RII panel should be independent. In relation to the Southall crash it is important to note that rail safety in the two years following the accident was heavily influenced by the recommendations of the RII, although other far-reaching changes were introduced even before the RII had reported. It is therefore of the highest significance to take note of the deficiencies in the material which was made available to the RII panel and the limitations on the matters which they investigated. For example, no detailed consideration was given to ATP, with the result that the rail industry was left to put its own house in order. To its credit, the industry recognised what had to be done and took the necessary steps.

15.26 In my view, the post-accident Rail Inquiry procedure needs to be strengthened and revised where necessary, so as to be capable of fulfilling its true role as the primary means of implementing the necessary changes which impact on rail safety, at the earliest possible time. There should be the closest liaison between the technical investigation, which I have recommended generally to be under the control of HMRI, and the Rail Industry Inquiry proceedings, in order to ensure that all relevant material is considered and that all necessary recommendations for improvement can be made at the earliest possible time. Consideration should be given to amendment to the Group Standard with the objective of providing for a rapid and effective investigation of the issues arising from a rail accident, which is capable of fulfilling the needs of interested parties, as well as public safety.

15.27 These proposals, if implemented, necessarily dictate a reconsideration of the role of any subsequent Inquiry under section 14 of the Health and Safety at Work Act 1974, whether conducted in private as in the case of the Watford accident in 1996, or in public as in the case of Southall and Ladbroke Grove. Particularly, the purpose of any further investigation following a properly conducted Rail Industry Inquiry should be carefully considered. As discussed above, where the circumstances of a particular accident give rise to wider public concerns, there may be occasion for conducting a subsequent Inquiry so as to involve all sections of the industry which might be affected. In such an Inquiry, further consideration would need to be given to the grouping of interests in order to achieve reasonable efficiency. Fortunately, representative bodies already exist such as the Association of Train Operating Companies (ATOC) as well as CRUCC. Such bodies should be consulted when considering changes to the present Inquiry regime.

15.28 It is axiomatic that the post-accident Rail Inquiry should not be held up or impeded by the possibility of criminal proceedings, nor should the flow of information to the Rail Industry Inquiry be curtailed in any way. Where potential criminal proceedings so require, the Rail Industry Inquiry may be conducted in private and circulation of its recommendations restricted, as in the case of the RII at Southall. Consideration should also be given to whether procedures for the RII can be adapted to become more accessible, particularly to persons who were involved in the accident. The question of whether any subsequent Inquiry should proceed before the bringing of criminal proceedings, and if so whether such an Inquiry should be held in public, are matters which have been considered elsewhere and will necessarily become less critical if a satisfactory and comprehensive Rail Industry Inquiry into safety issues has been conducted in a timely manner and appropriate actions taken.

15.29   It is to be noted that, partly in response to concerns expressed following the Southall accident, S&SD published a paper entitled 'The Future of Accident Investigation in the Railway Industry', dated 14 May 1999, in which some of the foregoing issues were reviewed and comments invited on a range of draft proposals. The review is ongoing. Its proposals are substantially less radical than those above and involve matters of detail not considered here. That process should be integrated with the reviews that I have recommended.

CHAPTER 16

LESSONS TO BE LEARNED

16.1   The Terms of Reference (see para 8.1) require me to identify any lessons which have relevance for those with responsibilities for securing railway safety and to make recommendations. The final chapter of this report sets out my recommendations, organised under the same headings as are contained in the present chapter, which sets out the lessons to be learned from the Southall crash.

Driver training

16.2   No general weakness in driver training, including the systems for monitoring and driver refresher training, has been identified. A number of specific shortcomings are the subject of recommendations. The main issue concerning driver training which emerged from the Southall crash was the potential which clearly exists for the system to fail in its most fundamental task of weeding out drivers who are unsuitable for the heavy task which they have to bear, by attitude or temperament. Research into human behaviour as applied to the environment of the driving cab was not sufficient to pinpoint any palpable reason why Driver Harrison failed in the most basic task of driving his train safely. Yet those who observed his behaviour at Bristol Parkway and Swindon on the day of the accident, even allowing for an element of hindsight, formed the impression that all was not well.

16.3   The most important lesson to be learned, in terms of driver training, is that while passenger safety continues to depend on the vigilance of drivers, and while SPADs continue to occur at a rate of around 2 per day, efforts must concentrate on all possible means of ensuring that drivers act with the maximum of vigilance and responsibility, and that any potential for irregular behaviour is eradicated. Necessary steps include the promotion of CIRAS, the development of simulators and the use of On-Train Data Recorders to assist in gathering evidence of actual behaviour in the cab. Simulators received general support in principle, but it must be accepted that the great variety of cab lay-outs will limit their use to general driving practices. Data Recorders would, in ordinary circumstances, be controversial yet I note that the Unions have generally supported the need for obtaining hard evidence about driver behaviour, and I believe that they have every interest in co-operating with these proposals. At the time of writing this Report it is stated that SPADs have reduced by 25%. This is to be welcomed but it should not be allowed to deflect the major effort which is still needed to secure the highest levels of driver vigilance.

16.4 The Southall accident has revealed that the testing of drivers for their knowledge of Rules does not necessarily equip them to apply those Rules in practice, particularly when the Rules themselves are ambiguous. Testing should therefore include the practical application of Rules. Likewise, where Rules contemplate abnormal procedures (such as driving with AWS isolated), it cannot be assumed that drivers will be competent to drive in such a manner without specific training. A further general lesson to be learned is that drivers may be reluctant to report possible inadequacies in the infrastructure equipment, such as misaligned signals, possibly through a misplaced sense of loyalty or because they think that no action will be taken.

16.5 Evidence about drivers' qualifications and training revealed the absence of a nationally controlled or accredited driver training system; also that some TOCs may be avoiding the considerable burden of training drivers by offering attractive transfer packages to drivers trained by others. Furthermore, there is no centrally controlled system to ensure the guaranteed transfer of all relevant records with a driver who moves between operators. Appropriate recommendations appear in Chapter 17.

Operating rules

16.6 Those sections of the Rule Book and Group Standards which were examined in some detail, relating particularly to AWS isolation, revealed an appalling lack of clarity. The fact that the majority of the problems can be traced back to BR is of little consequence. It may be that the Rules were more capable of being given sensible meaning in the less competitive environment of a publicly owned service. In a harsh commercial environment it must be assumed that Rules will be interpreted and enforced in accordance with their natural meaning. A possible explanation for Rules having been allowed to remain in a state of patent and known ambiguity for so long is that they were thought to reflect a range of different views, in the same way that a political document might be allowed to mean different things in different circumstances. Any such notion should be dispelled at once. Rules are to be given their proper meaning which should not depend on the circumstances unless this is intended to be their effect.

16.7 Another surprising lesson to be learned is from the reaction of the industry to the Southall crash. Despite the demonstrated dangers of running with AWS isolated, the industry sought to find a minimal solution which would put little pressure on TOCs to avoid the root problem of unreliable AWS. In doing so, Railtrack have permitted a situation to develop in which the once uniform Rules have been replaced, effectively, by a hotchpotch of different Rules applying to each TOC, still reflecting the wide range of opinion as to the consequences of AWS isolation.

16.8 An important lesson to be learned is that the fragmented rail industry seems to be disinclined to devising and imposing on itself a clearly expressed solution to the clear problem of AWS isolation, such that the solution can be easily comprehended by drivers. Part of the problem concerns the protracted and convoluted procedures for the introduction or amendment of Group Standards. This problem will need to be considered by the Inquiry to be chaired by Lord Cullen. The lessons to be learned from the Southall crash are expressed in terms of recommendations for changes to the current Rules.

Fault reporting

16.9 Despite the existence of relatively clear Rules, the Southall accident revealed widespread failures of compliance with fault reporting procedures. This included lax performance by individuals of tasks which, at the time, they had no particular reason to regard as significant (but which acquired very high significance in the light of the accident). It revealed also failures to put in place systems that were likely to perform adequately when called upon. In addition, the maintenance system is vitally dependent on reporting and making available to maintenance staff properly accessible data on faults reported. The databases in use (including RAVERS) should be configured to display repeat faults including a 28-day history of defects on any vehicle. They should also be programmed to determine and to display statistically significant trends in fault-occurrence.

16.10 The lesson to be learned seems to be that compliance with Rules cannot be assumed in the absence of some positive system of monitoring which is likely to detect failures. Such a conclusion would, however, be a sad reflection on a fine industry which has been created through the enthusiasm and support of countless individuals who were proud to be thought of as part of "the railway". Perhaps the true lesson is that a different culture needs to be developed, or recreated, through which individuals will perform to the best of their ability and not resort to delivering the minimum service that can be got away with. It is regrettable that a new positive safety culture was developed by GWT only after the Southall crash, in clear contrast to the situation that existed before.

16.11 A particular lesson to be learned in relation to AWS faults is that conventionally accepted practices (at least up to the date of the Southall crash) can result in a seriously misleading picture being created. The true incidence of AWS failures and isolation was not to be discovered without painstaking research. A safe railway cannot be maintained without rigorous reporting of faults and defects. This dictates that fault reporting must be made simple and convenient and that rigorous steps be taken to avoid any failure to provide the means of reporting, i.e. report forms, repair books and the like.

Fleet maintenance

16.12   The major lessons to be learned from the experiences of the Southall crash are that potentially serious deficiencies may develop in detailed maintenance procedures which are not detected by conventional management procedures or by audit.   Thus, sloppy practices went undetected at OOC despite the close attention of management to the re-organisation of the workforce, including a risk assessment.   Most surprising was the fact that management was apparently unaware of the unsatisfactory procedures which existed, both in terms of comprehensible maintenance procedures and equipment for the repair of reported AWS faults.   This was compounded by the fact that the inadequate test equipment was itself not available for use.   A lesson to be learned from the inadequate attempt made by GWT to reconcile the different specifications created by BR for detection and repair of AWS faults, is that the task of achieving clarity and removing ambiguity is not to be taken lightly.   Unclear Rules are likely to conceal unclear thinking and inadequate practices.

16.13   As regards maintenance and renewal of AWS parts, the lesson to be learned is that the cause of defects and unreliability in equipment may be found to lie within the control of one or more companies against which the operator possesses no formal or informal rights.   Such rights could be created in regard to existing equipment but the development of new equipment calls for the creation of an effective "System Authority" (as in the case of ATP) which will require fundamental re-thinking of contractual rights and obligations.

Infrastructure maintenance

16.14   Lessons to be learned in regard to the rail infrastructure are limited to the signals, where 2 out of 3 vital signals were found to be substantially misaligned, one (SN270) being grossly misaligned.   This revealed that errors must have occurred at the stage of installation which were not picked up by routine maintenance during the period of well over two years that they were in use before the Southall crash; nor in the period of some 18 months after they were handed back into normal maintenance. The failure to detect misalignment after installation shows that no adequate testing can have been performed at the time of commissioning. As regards routine maintenance, differences between Railtrack and Amey Rail revealed that no maintenance checks at all had been carried out, owing to differences of interpretation of the contract. These facts also reveal a surprising reticence on the part of drivers, some of whom must have suspected that signal SN270, while adequately visible, was not of the intensity that it should have been. The lesson to be learned is that such faults can survive procedures designed to ensure their detection. It should not take a major accident to reveal their existence.

Regulation

16.15 The lesson to be learned in relation to regulation is that not all changes have safety implications. It was, however, remiss of Railtrack to introduce such a seemingly far-reaching change as the 1996 Regulation Policy without carrying out a risk assessment to confirm that it involved no safety implications.

16.16 The reference to the protection of "commercial interests" in the added Condition H11 of the Track Access Conditions, was unhelpful and potentially misleading. There should be no question of signallers considering commercial interests and Railtrack should emphasise that safety and security are to be the first priority in any regulating decision. Condition H11 should be reviewed and the Level 1 policy statement similarly reviewed in the light of any changes made. While the Layout Risk Method has no place in the general signalling regulation of trains, Dr Murphy's criticism of the ARS system should be carefully considered. Likewise, Dr Murphy's risk analysis should be taken into account in any further review of LRM and both methods of analysis should be considered in regard to Levels 2 and 3 policy statements.

Vehicle design and operation

16.17 The lessons to be learned in relation to crashworthiness were limited to questions of emergency access and procedures. The Southall crash revealed serious deficiencies in the means of gaining egress from a coach on its side, with lighting no longer functioning and internal doors jammed. Recommendations include a number of issues raised in relation to the operation of vehicles. Recommendations are also appropriate concerning the design of freight wagons.

16.18 Two particular matters of procedure need to be considered in terms of any recommended improvement. First, all research and development in the rail industry, as presently constituted, suffers from lack of a "System Authority" capable of co-ordinating the interests of different companies (the same applies in the case of AWS and ATP). Secondly, the question arises how best to promote improvements to existing stock, rather than waiting for a new generation of vehicles to bring in any recommended changes. These matters are significant given the life of rolling stock, often around 30 to 40 years. This usually includes a mid-life refit but the periods during which a vehicle can continue to depend on old technologies is still substantial.

Research and Development

16.19 An important lesson to be learned from a number of different aspects of the Inquiry proceedings is the inability of the rail industry, as presently constituted, to deal effectively with inter-company issues. Thus, while the fragmented industry has been set up to run the railways in their existing state, any research and development issues have been seen to re-open the lines of division between the commercial interests of different parties. The absence of any general contractual or statutory arrangements to deal with the problems which inevitably arise has generally led to inaction, to the detriment of safety as well as to the long term interests of the industry. Such problems were not unforeseen – solutions which were proposed in 1996 are discussed at the end of Chapter 14. Such matters are also likely to be considered in the impending review of railway safety issues by the European Commission.

16.20 Partial solutions have been put in place through the creation of the Railway Group and organisations such at ATOC. Railtrack proposed that the Railway Group should be enlarged to include ROSCOs and component suppliers. There is probably no shortage of groups overseeing the railways at strategic level, now including the Rail Regulator and the Strategic Rail Authority. What is conspicuously lacking, however, is workable inter-company arrangements which can be seen most clearly to be required to promote and facilitate research and development, even of a comparatively routine nature.

16.21 Thus, it has been seen that part of the problem of AWS reliability lies in the artificial separation of the interests of the operator, the vehicle owners and those who have control of parts and components, including their maintenance. The question of "ownership", which is of some significance although by no means decisive, remains wholly obscure. There is an urgent need to define enforceable rights in relation to such vital equipment. Exactly the same lesson is to be learned, although applying over a different timescale, in the case of research and development into vehicle design and into the proposed introduction of data recorders. The problems which arise are largely of a legal nature. They require urgent resolution on an industry-wide basis.

16.22 The lesson to be learned from these matters, which goes to the root of the privatisation process, is that appropriate inter-company structures must be created by means to be determined. This may require review of Safety Cases and franchising arrangements. An alternative approach could involve action by the Rail Regulator in relation to the common industry Track Access Conditions. It is clear that research and development in the privatised industry will need more rigorous programming, cost-projections and funding arrangements, including realistic contingencies, than has hitherto been the case in the publicly owned industry. This too is likely to be achievable only via appropriate inter-company arrangements.

Automatic Train Protection

16.23 The ATP pilot, despite the Electrowatt report, came close to being abandoned before the Southall crash. Although GWT now deserve credit for the effort and investment involved, the willpower and commitment to take the steps which can now be seen to have been required to bring the ATP pilot into full operation simply did not exist before the Southall crash and there was no industry structure which, in my view, was capable of pushing it through to a successful completion. There were many examples of the bizarre consequences of the absence of any proper legal framework for the continuation of the pilot, including the confused negotiations in 1996/7 over payment for replacement antennae for the ATP, as well as the fact that huge investment in the Heathrow Express went forward on the assumption that ATP was to be continued, an assumption which was later seen to be based on very shaky foundations (see para 13.22). This also explains why the industry was unable to respond to the strong expressions of concern over the ATP pilot which emanated from the Parliamentary Transport Committee in July 1995 (see para 13.8).

16.24 Apart from general questions of research and development considered above, the lesson to be learned from the technical experiences of the ATP project is that the industry has tended to over-optimism both in terms of the time necessary to develop new systems and the cost. In an industry based on privately raised finance, projections must be realistic and results must bear proper comparison with predictions. On the positive side, ATP is now nearing formal acceptance. Its very high level of use represents a major safety advance on those sections of the Great Western lines fitted with ATP

General Safety Issues

16.25 In his report into the Clapham Junction accident, Anthony Hidden QC, drew attention (Chapter 17) to the difference between appearance and reality in terms of the commitment to safety and systems intended to achieve safety. An important lesson to be learned from the Southall crash is that the difference persists and had not diminished in any way in its potency to mislead and create false assurance. The railway industry is now overburdened with paperwork, such that it is to be doubted that many individuals can have a proper grasp of all the documents for which they bear nominal responsibility. The stock answer to any problem which is identified is to create yet more paperwork in the form of risk assessments, further Group Standards and the like. Against this, it should be recorded that Railtrack are actively involved in the Herculean task of reducing the thousands of documents inherited from BR to a more manageable number. But the problem of effective communication persists and there were many examples of recently generated paperwork which had the capacity to confuse and obfuscate in just the same way as the old system did . The lesson to be learned, yet again, is that ineffective communication is no communication.

16.26 A specific lesson is to be learned from the secondary checking processes used throughout the industry. First, while the process of audit is essential and generally of considerable value, its shortcomings have been demonstrated through the failure of GWT's maintenance procedures, and their general attitude to safety, to live up to the reports produced through audit. Secondly, risk assessment procedures have been shown to produce variable results, which are seldom rigorous and sometime questionable. No primary or secondary paper-based system is a substitute for common sense and commitment to the job.

Accident investigations and inquiries

16.27 The lesson to be learned from the Southall crash is that accident investigation is not rendered more effective by duplicated and partial procedures. The reverse is the case. At Southall, unregulated and competing interests succeeded in duplicating and confusing both the investigation and inquiry processes. Perhaps most important to record, is that during the two year hiatus between the crash and the start of the Public Inquiry, the rail industry was left to regulate its safety procedures on the basis of a patently imperfect Rail Industry Inquiry which has led to far-reaching changes. Had the RII been differently constituted and had they been given full access to available data, different recommendations would have been made. A thorough review of the process is urgently called for. The details are discussed at length in the report and are reflected in the recommendations in Chapter 17. A review of accident investigation procedures is apposite given the impending review of railway safety issues by the European Commission.

Post-accident procedures

16.28 The principal lesson to be learned from the emergency response to the accident was one of success, particularly in the rescue and treatment of injured passengers. Lessons are to be learned, however, in relation to a number of procedures which did not operate as they should have. These have generally been identified and improvement can be expected. It remains to be seen whether these improvements were manifested at the Ladbroke Grove crash scene. De-briefing exercises were carried out both in relation to the emergency services and the railway industry. It is surprising that no procedure existed for a combined de-briefing, which should have occurred. Some lessons are to be learned in relation to the more sensitive handling of relatives and those enquiring about the fate of victims. Generally, however, the emergency services are to be commended for their dedicated work.

CHAPTER 17

RECOMMENDATIONS

17.1 The final requirement of the Terms of Reference (see para 8.1) is to make recommendations. Many possible recommendations have been considered during the course of the Inquiry and all parties submitted draft proposals with their written closing submissions. These are gratefully acknowledged for the invaluable assistance they have given. The draft proposals have been assessed in relation to the findings and conclusions expressed elsewhere in this Report. The final list of Recommendations set out below has been considered by the Inquiry Technical Assessor, Major A G B King, OBE particularly in relation to the appropriate periods for compliance. They are arranged under the same headings as the lessons to be learned, set out in Chapter 16. Recommendations are not set out in order of priority. Periods for compliance are given for each recommendation, with appropriate cross references to paragraphs of the Report.

17.2 One matter canvassed particularly by Passenger Groups but which will not be the subject of a recommendation as such, was the absence of any obligation to comply with recommendations made by Inquiries such as the present. Given that recommendations potentially affect bodies who may not have been parties to the Inquiry, and given the obvious moral and political pressure to comply with the recommendations in the absence of compelling reasons, I am not persuaded that such a proposal would be appropriate. I do recommend, however, that a review of compliance be conducted on behalf of HSC within six months of publication of this Report and that further reviews be put in hand as necessary after the end of the periods specified for compliance.

17.3 The numbered recommendations below identify the parties to whom they are directed. In a number of cases reference is made to the Association of Train Operating Companies (ATOC). They were not represented at the Inquiry and no information was received as to their resources or their authority. I believe however, that if ATOC does not currently have the power to comply, urgent

210

action should be taken by the rail industry as a whole, either to reconstitute ATOC with sufficient resources and authority to comply with my recommendations, or to establish a body representing TOCs which is so resourced and authorised.

17.4   The time periods for compliance with recommendations are noted in abbreviated form below. Their effect is to be read as follows

- Ongoing: Action should begin now or as soon as practicable. No completion is specified as action should continue

- Now – 6 mths: Action should begin now and be completed within 6 months

- Now – 12 mths: Action should begin now and be completed within 12 months

- 6 – 24 mths: Action should begin within 6 months and be complete within 24 months from start

These periods run from the date of publication of this Report.

17.5   <u>Driver Training</u>

1.	All parties in the rail industry should co-operate in the collection of evidence to support reliable research into human behaviour studies relating to driver performance. Railtrack should co-ordinate this work and TOCs incorporate the results into training programmes (paras 1.25, 7.16, 16.2).	**RT, ATOC** **Now – 12 mths**
2.	Evidence should include that to be provided by CIRAS and from On-Train Data Recorders used to monitor driver behaviour. ASLEF in particular should give their full support to such an initiative (paras 14.23, 14.25, 15.15, 16.3).	**RT, ASLEF** **Now – 12 mths**

3.	Simulators should be introduced for driver training and for the observance of driver behaviour (para 16.3).	ATOC Now – 12 mths
4.	Driver training should include driving in abnormal situations permitted by the Rules and specifically driving with AWS isolated to the extent so permitted, including the use of simulators (para 16.4).	ATOC Now – 12 mths
5.	Testing of driver competence and knowledge of Rules should be extended to cover application of the Rules to practical situations, including all abnormal driving situations permitted by the Rules (para 16.4).	ATOC Ongoing
6.	Drivers should be encouraged to report all actual or suspected faults, whether through formal fault reporting procedures or through CIRAS (paras 14.26, 16.4).	ATOC Ongoing
7.	Railtrack together with ATOC should establish a national qualification and accreditation system for drivers including centrally held records to be available to the current employer (paras 5.5, 16.5).	RT, ATOC 6 – 24 mths
8.	Railtrack and ATOC should monitor the transfer of drivers between operators and the numbers of drivers trained by each TOC and consider whether there are any safety implications involved (paras 5.5, 16.5).	RT, ATOC 6 – 24 mths
9.	Current Rules governing drivers' permitted daily and weekly working hours should be reviewed in the light of current research into human behaviour (para 5.9).	RT Now – 12 mths

212

17.6   Operating Rules

10.   Railtrack must ensure that Rules and Group Standards **RT**
applicable to operators, including drivers, are clear and
unambiguous.   In particular, Railtrack should urgently **Now – 6 mths**
complete the review of operating Rules to ensure they are
workable in the privatised, fragmented industry   (para
16.6).

11.   The use of more than one document (whether Rules, Group **RT**
Standards or otherwise) to cover a single operational issue
should be avoided, save where proper reasons exist for use **Now – 12 mths**
of multiple sources (para 15.9).

12.   All train-borne safety equipment should be clearly **RT**
designated as to whether or not it is vital to the continued **Now - 6 mths**
running of the train (para 15.11).

13.   AWS is to be regarded as vital to the continued running of **RT**
the train (para 15.11).
Now - 6 mths

14.   Clear procedures for steps to be taken on failure of any **RT**
train-borne safety equipment should apply nationally,
subject only to such company variation as is fully justified **Now - 6 mths**
(para 15.11).

15.   All parties must emphasise the need to comply with the **RT, ATOC**
Rule Book and must not condone departures (para 7.9).

17.7   Fault reporting

16.   Railtrack and TOCs must impress on drivers and other **RT, ATOC** staff the need to use formal fault reporting procedures where the Rules so provide, and that the duty to report a **Ongoing** fault must be performed personally and the report delivered to the person or body identified in the Rules, and not to any other person or body (paras 7.9, 16.11).

17.   Fault reporting procedures should be reviewed and made **RT, ATOC** as simple and convenient to use as practically possible. They should include provision for an acknowledgement **Ongoing** and an explanation if relevant (para 16.11).

18.   Failure to provide forms, defect repair books or other **RT, ATOC** means of reporting faults should be regarded as a **Ongoing** disciplinary offence (para 16.11).

19.   Appropriate procedures for receiving and making an **RT, ATOC** automatic record of verbal reports should exist in all control centres, similar to the facilities installed by GWT **Now – 12 mths** in 1998 (Para 9.14).

20.   Level and quality of training for information controllers **RT, ATOC** should be reviewed (para 9.15).

      Now – 12 mths

21.   Controllers' posts in Railtrack and TOCs should be **RT, ATOC** designated as "safety-critical" as defined in the Railways (Safety Critical Works) Regulations 1994 (para 9.15). **Now – 12 mths**

22. Fault data bases (including RAVERS) should ensure that repeat faults are logged and that a 28 day history of defects is available to managers and maintenance staff (para 16.9).

ATOC

Now – 12 mths

23. Databases should be programmed to determine and highlight statistically significant trends in faults reported and to display such information to managers and maintenance staff (para 16.9).

ATOC

Now – 12 mths

17.8   Fleet Maintenance

24. GWT should maintain full records of competencies for all maintenance staff as required by job descriptions and safety responsibility statements (paras 6.8, 15.6).

GWT

6 – 24 mths

25. GWT should   regularly monitor the workload of all maintenance staff (para 15.6).

GWT

Ongoing

26. A current and detailed list of items required to be inspected for each examination should be prepared for and used by maintenance teams (paras 6.8, 15.6).

ATOC, ROSCO

Now - 6 mths

27. Documentation for the A-Exam should require ATP reset and self-test (para 6.8).

ATOC, ROSCO

Now - 6 mths

28. Maintenance staff should be provided with a flow-chart to show the derivation of all sources of repair work, to include RAVERS (with check on repeat items) and appropriate structure for Request, Repair Book and Maintenance Control items (para 15.16).

ATOC,

ROSCO

Now – 12 mths

29. Maintenance procedures should require checking of the history of reported defects, including repeat faults, and the taking of appropriate action (paras 6.14, 15.6).

ATOC, ROSCO

Now – 12 mths

30. An improved AWS test box, capable of detecting faults not revealed by the magnet test, should be provided as standard issue at all maintenance depots (paras 6.11, 9.22, 15.6).

ATOC, ROSCO

Now - 6 mths

31. Efforts should be concentrated on ensuring that AWS and other train-borne safety equipment does not fail in service through preventable causes. This should include regular replacements of equipment, maintenance of full service records and provision for full traceability of repairable parts and components (para 15.8).

ATOC, RAILPART, NRS

Now – 6mths

32. Contractual ownership and other rights in AWS equipment must be clarified and defined (paras 15.7, 16.21).

ATOC, ROSCO

6 – 24 mths

33. ATOC and Railtrack should monitor the supply of new AWS parts and components to ensure continued availability on an indefinite basis, including the introduction of improved components (para 15.7).

ATOC, ROSCO, RAILPART

Ongoing

17.9   Infrastructure maintenance

34. Railtrack should ensure that the alignment and sighting of signals is confirmed at the time of commissioning, both from the signal and from the track, and appropriate records made, including photographs (paras 3.16, 16.14).

RT

Now – 12 mths

35.	Railtrack should ensure that checks on alignment and sighting of signals are made at least annually, and at a greater frequency to be determined on the basis of errors found (paras 3.16, 16.14).	**RT** **Now - 6 mths**
36.	Railtrack should review all maintenance contracts to ensure that all parties are aware of what checks are included and which excluded (paras 3.16, 16.14).	**RT** **6 – 24 mths**

17.10   Regulation

37.	Railtrack should ensure that any further proposed change of regulation policy is preceded by a risk assessment (para 4.6, 16.15).	**RT** **6 – 24 mths**
38.	There should be a review of Condition H11 of the Track Access Conditions which should make clear that no regulating decision is to be made on the basis of protecting commercial interests. Safety and security must be paramount considerations (paras 4.13, 7.6, 16.16).	**RT, ORR** **6 – 24 mths**
39.	Railtrack should review their Level 1 Policy Statement in the light of any amendment to Condition H11 (para 6.16).	**RT** **6 – 24 mths**
40.	More Level 2 and 3 Policy Statements should be introduced having due regard to any relevant risk analysis (para 6.16).	**RT** **6 – 24 mths**
41.	Railtrack should review the operation of ARS to consider whether more green signals should be booked ahead of higher speed trains, and generally whether the speed and length of trains is adequately taken into account (para 16.16).	**RT** **6 – 24 mths**

42. Any further review of LRM should take into account Dr **RT**
Murphy's risk analysis (para 16.16).

6 – 24 mths

17.11 Vehicle design

43. HMRI should keep under long-term review the effect of **HMRI**
speed on numbers of casualties in rail accidents (para
11.7). **Ongoing**

44. A review should be carried out by ATOC, with input from **ATOC**
all interested bodies, on the ways in which internal safety
features may be modified and standardised to provide the **6 – 24 mths**
best practicable means of emergency exit under accident
conditions, including vehicles lying on their side, to
include the provision of emergency lighting and
standardised public announcements (paras 11.11, 11.12,
11.13).

45. The review should consider dates and means for the **ATOC**
introduction of identified improvements to existing stock
(para 11.2, 15.16). **6 – 24 mths**

46. A single body should be empowered to specify common **ATOC**
standards for safety features in the interior of passenger
vehicles and to identify and approve types of vehicles **6 – 24 mths**
and/or operators to which particular standards are to apply
(paras 11.6, 16.18).

47. The design of coaches should be such that internal doors **ATOC**
can be easily opened in a crash situation, in darkness and
irrespective of the attitude of the vehicle; and that **6 – 24 mths**
hammers intended for breaking windows can be easily
located in the same conditions (paras 11.11, 11.12).

48.	Safety briefings or other appropriate means of communicating safety information to passengers should be adopted, including pointing out safety notices to passengers. ATOC should monitor the methods adopted by TOCs and issue guidance documents after a suitable trial period, including recommendations for different types of journey (para 11.13).	**ATOC** **Now – 12 mths**
49.	A design study and risk assessment should be carried out to determine whether freight wagons could be designed with less aggressive features without detriment to their primary function (para 11.14).	**EWS, RT** **6 – 24 mths**
50.	Consideration should be given to the most appropriate form of coupling for freight trains, to minimise damage in the event of collision, including a risk assessment (para 11.15).	**EWS, RT** **6 – 24 mths**
51.	No recommendation is made concerning crumple zones in passenger carriages, save that the matter should be given attention by the Ladbroke Grove Inquiry (para 11.4).	**Ladbroke Grove**
52.	Train crews should be given improved training and briefing on emergency actions, including a practical evacuation (para 11.11).	**ATOC** **Now – 12 mths**
53.	Standards for evacuation of passengers should be proved by practical exercises using typical groups of passengers and train crew, and repeated on a regular basis to be approved by HMRI (para 11.11).	**ATOC, RT,HMRI** **Now – 12 mths**

54.	Consideration should be given to modification to the design of OHL structures to improve their response to accidents, if achievable without detriment to their primary role (para 11.16).	**RT** **6 – 24 mths**
55.	All trains should be fitted with data recorders. All data recorders should record speed, time/location, brake application and AWS cancellation, and should be simple and speedy to download (para 14.23).	**ATOC, RT** **6 – 24 mths**
56.	Consideration should be given to developing a cheaper form of data recorder for retrospective fitment where this will allow earlier fitting (para 14.24).	**ATOC, RT** **Now - 6 mths**

17.12 Research and Development

57.	Steps should be taken to put in place means to resolve inter-company issues relating to research and development at all levels. Specifically, the following issues must be addressed (paras 15.13, 16.21).	**ATOC, ROSCO** **Now – 12 mths**
58.	Rights (including ownership) and obligations in all equipment added to vehicles, together with lineside equipment upon which its operation depends, must be defined in legally enforceable terms (paras 15.7, 15.13, 16.21).	**ATOC, ROSCO** **Now – 12 mths**
59.	The above recommendation to include review of Safety Cases and franchising arrangements and consideration of action by the Rail Regulator (para 16.22).	**ATOC, RT, SRA, ORR** **Now – 12 mths**

60. Consideration should also be given, for the purpose of the above recommendations, to enlarging or re-organising existing inter-company groups, including considering whether the Railway Group should include ROSCOs and component suppliers (para 16.20).

RT

Now – 12 mths

61. S&SD together with HMRI and other bodies having responsibility for accepting or approving new equipment or stock should review their procedures with a view to reducing delay and introducing fast-track procedures where possible (para 15.7).

RT, HMRI

6 – 24 mths

62. There should be a review of progress on implementing the Recommendations of the DTp Review Committee Report (chaired by Sir David Davies) published in September 1996 (para 14.31).

ATOC, RT

Now – 12 mths

63. One or more System Authorities should be created to oversee the specific development of any new project on the railways and to oversee continuation of work on existing projects, including AWS and ATP (paras 15.13, 16.13, 16.18).

RT, ATOC

Now – 12 mths

64. Future R&D must be the subject of rigorous programming, cost-projections and funding arrangements, including reliable contingencies. R&D funding must be on a cross-industry basis, irrespective of whether individual TOCs decide to fit new technology (para 16.22).

RT, ATOC

Now – 12 mths

17.13 Automatic Train Protection

65.	Development of ATP should be managed and funded in future through a System Authority having broad industry representation and support (para 15.13).	**RT, ATOC** **Now – 12 mths**
66.	ATP should be maintained in a fully operational state on Great Western lines currently fitted, until replaced by an equally effective train protection system (para 15.14).	**GWTC** **Ongoing**
67.	GWT and Railtrack should consider extensions to the present coverage of ATP (para 15.14).	**GWTC, RT** **Now – 12 mths**
68.	GWT, Railtrack and HMRI should consider whether trains with AWS isolated can run normal services where ATP is fitted and operational (para 15.10).	**GWTC, RT, HMRI** **Now - 6 mths**

17.14 General Safety Issues

69.	All parties in the industry must ensure that paper-based procedures do not become divorced from reality. This should include senior managers maintaining a direct knowledge of the situation in railway workplaces (para 16.25).	**All** **Ongoing**
70.	Paper-based audits should be backed up by unplanned inspections and other direct observation of the work under review (para 16.26).	**All** **Ongoing**

71. Steps should be taken to ensure that all risk assessments **All**
are rigorous and that those initiating risk assessments are
appropriately qualified and informed. Steps include giving **Ongoing**
attention to HSE Guidance Notes covering risk
assessment, which should accordingly be kept under
review (paras 15.21, 16.26).

72. Consultation procedures and times involved in revision of **Ladbroke Grove**
Group Standards or the introduction of new Group **Inquiry**
Standards, should be reviewed by the Inquiry to be held
into safety procedures (para 16.8).

17.15 <u>Accident investigations and inquiries</u>

73. The technical investigation of serious rail accidents should **HSC**
be controlled by HMRI save in exceptional cases of
suspected crime which is unconnected with the running of **6 – 24 mths**
the railway (para 15.23).

74. HMRI should ensure that a single, thorough and definitive **HSC**
technical investigation is carried out, to include the
recording of all appropriate factual data, the collection of **6 – 24 mths**
physical evidence from the scene of the accident and
decisions as to handing the site back to the rail companies
(paras 2.19, 7.3, 15.24).

75. Standing contracts for the provision of consulting services **HSC**
by recognised railway experts should be amended to make
provision for HMRI to require any appropriate individual **6 – 24 mths**
to provide expert services for the immediate accident
investigation, including the services of any appropriate
laboratory or testing house (para 15.23).

76.	HMRI should decide, irrespective of any ongoing criminal investigation, what data or information is to be passed on to rail companies for rapid action (para 15.24).	**HSC** **6 – 24 mths**
77.	The primary forum for deciding upon appropriate recommendations following an accident should be the Rail Industry Inquiry (RII). Procedures for holding such an inquiry at the earliest possible date should be strengthened, and should include the presentation by HMRI of their investigation (para 15.26).	**RT, ATOC, HMRI** **6 – 24 mths**
78.	Procedure for conducting a RII should be reviewed. This should include ensuring that the RII panel is independent of all parties having an interest in the accident (paras 9.33, 15.25, 16.26).	**RT** **6 – 24 mths**
79.	Consideration should be given to whether procedures can be adapted to make any RII accessible to the public, save where the needs of confidentiality otherwise require (para 15.28).	**RT** **6 – 24 mths**
80.	Nothing should be permitted to delay the opening of a RII nor the completion of their Report and Recommendations (para 15.28).	**RT** **6 – 24 mths**
81.	Consideration should be given to whether an additional independent accident investigation body should be created, to take over the accident investigation functions of HMRI under Recommendation 73 (para 15.23).	**HSC** **6 – 24 mths**
82.	Existing protocols between Railtrack, BTP and HMRI should be reviewed in the light of the above Recommendations (para 15.24).	**HSC, BTP, RT** **6 – 24 mths**

83. Any subsequent Inquiry directed under the Health and Safety at Work Act, 1974 should involve all parties in the rail industry who may have an interest in Recommendations to be made, through the involvement of representative groups including ATOC (para 15.27).

HSC

6 – 24 mths

84. Passenger representation at such inquiries should not be limited to those involved in the immediate accident. Consideration should be given to enlarging the role of CRUCC and the provision of appropriate funding for their full participation in Inquiries (para 15.27).

DETR

6 – 24 mths

85. Responses to the S&SD paper "The Future of Accident Investigation in the Railway Industry" should be taken into consideration in applying the foregoing Recommendations (para 15.29).

RT

Now – 12 mths

17.16 Post-accident procedures

86. Steps should be taken to upgrade the role of Rail Incident Officer and to ensure that the person so designated has sufficient authority and standing for the task in hand, bearing in mind the tensions that can develop in the early stages of an accident response (para 2.15).

RT

Now - 6 mths

87. Consideration should be given to means of speeding up the process of earthing and isolation of traction current following an accident on an electrified section of line (para 2.15).

RT

Now - 6 mths

88. Routes for evacuation away from an accident should take into account the need to avoid distressing scenes (para 2.11).

Emergency Services

Ongoing

89. Further consideration should be given to the sensitive handling of persons rescued from accidents including whether they should be sent onward by train (para 2.14).

ATOC

Ongoing

90. More effective means of liaising with hospital and casualty gathering areas should be considered (para 2.14).

ATOC

Ongoing

91. Identification of victims should be speeded up and information released to relatives at the earliest possible time (para 2.24).

Police Forces

Now – 12 mths

92. Casualty bureaux procedures should be reviewed in order to ensure that they remain open for as long as required and that adequate telephone facilities are available (para 2.24).

Police Forces

Now – 6 mths

93. Post-accident de-briefing procedures should be reviewed to ensure that combined de-briefings are held between all involved Railway Industry and Emergency Services groups (paras 2.25, 16.28).

All

Now – 6 mths

PARTIES & REPRESENTATIVES

FOR THE INQUIRY Ian Burnett QC & Richard Wilkinson
Instructed by Treasury Solicitor

ASLEF/HARRISON A.C. Scrivener QC & G.Forlin
Instructed by Thompsons

AMEY RAIL Tom Custance & David Higgins
of Herbert Smith

ANGEL TRAIN CONTRACTS Hon. Philip Havers QC
Instructed by Cameron McKenna

BRITISH TRANPORT POLICE Richard Lissack QC & Tom Leeper
Instructed by British Railways Board

CENTRAL RAIL USERS CONSULTATIVE COMMITTEE
John Cartledge

ENGLISH, WELSH & SCOTTISH TRAINS
Michael Spencer QC.
George Alliott
Instructed by Davies Arnold Cooper

GREAT WESTERN TRAINS Jonathan Caplan QC & Gregory Treverton-Jones
Instructed by Burges Salmon

HEALTH & SAFETY EXECUTIVE
Kevin O'Reilly. Vic Coleman & Alan Cooksey

NATIONAL UNION OF RAIL MARITIME & TRANSPORT
Barry Cotter
Instructed by Pattinson & Brewer

PASSENGERS Steering Committee
John Hendy QC & Michael Forde
Instructed by Christian Fisher

Southall Kenneth Hamer & Ms Isabella Zornoza
Instructed by Collins

RAILTRACK Roger Henderson QC &.Stephen Powles QC
Roger Eastman & Prashant Popat
Instructed by Railtrack solicitors

Alphabetical List of Witnesses

NAME OF WITNESS	PARTY REPRESENTED	DAY OF APPEARANCE (R) indicates read
Adams, Christopher	ATC	28, 32(R)
Adams, Lew	ASLEF	31
Andrews, Keith	Railtrack	14
Ardiff, Peter	GWT	12
Arnold, Andrew	GWT	04
Balmer, Paul	AMEY	17
Banfield, George	GWT	03
Banfield, Tim	Passenger	06
Barker, David	GWT	08(R)
Barradell, Mick	AEA	32(R)
Barton, Debra	Passenger	08
Bass, Kenneth	GWT	05(R)
Bell, Roy	ASLEF	17
Bilsborough, Gerard	Railtrack	05(R)
Boddy, John. Dr	Passenger	06(R)
Bricker, Alan	EWS	02(R)
Burrows, Clive	Railtrack	30
Buxton, Tim	Passenger	09
Cardall, Tony	GWT	13
Chapman, Kerwin	GWT	13(R)
Clements, Neil	GWT	25(R)
Coleman, Vic	HMRI	20
Cooksey, Alan	HMRI	19,22,26,31
Cope, Andrew	GWT	14
Cross, Andrew	WS Atkins	08(R)
Cusworth, Ian	GWT	23
Dawes, Alan	GWT	21
Day, Peter	AMEY	18(R)
Dearman, Peter	GWT	27
Deller, A	Halcrow Transmark	08
Driver, Annette	GWT	25(R)
Duffy, Michael	AMEY	03(R)
Dufus, Angela	Passenger	06(R)
Edwards, John (chief Inspector)	BTP	09
Ellis, Robert	Railtrack	06(R)
Evans, Martin	GWT	25(R)
Evans, Richard	Railtrack	30
Felton, Michael	WS Atkins	08(R)
Fenner, David	Railtrack	18
Ferguson, Peter	Witness	08(R)
Fitzgerald, Desmond	Railtrack	05(R)
Ford, Michael	GWT	13, 25(R)
Forde, Stephen	Railtrack	05
Forster, Alison	GWT	13, 22, 32

Francis, Oliver	GWT	03
Fry, Graham	GWT	02(R)
Fulford, Nigel	GWT	13
Funge, Ann	Passenger	06
Furness, Nicola	Railtrack	18(R)
George, Richard	GWT	15,27,32
Geoffrey, Stuart	GWT	14(R)
Goff, Anthony	GWT	19
Goodwin, Peter	Expert Witness	24
Gregory, Philip	GWT	25(R)
Groeger. Professor	Expert Witness	23
Gronow, Frank	GWT	15
Haddow, Kenneth	Passenger	06(R)
Hallet, Sandra	GWT	04
Harman, Ian	Railtrack	18(R)
Harris, John	GWT	05
Harrison, Larry	ASLEF	07
Hart, Anthony	GWT	04
Hart, Stanley	HMRI	08(R)
Harvey, Andrew	HMRI	03(R)
Harvey, Douglas	GWT	14
Harwood, Michael	GWT	19(R)
Hausman, Dominique	Expert Witness	28
Hawkins, John	GWT	14, 24(R)
Hellier, Michael. Dr	Passenger	07
Hellicar, John	HMRI	08(R)
Hockey, David	GWT	25(R)
Horan, Philip	GWT	03(R)
Horncastle, Martin	Ambulance	09
How, Francis	Railtrack	18
Howarth, Peter	Railtrack	24
Hudson, Geoff	GWT	14(R) 25(R)
Jeffrey, Stuart	GWT	14(R) 29(R)
Jenkins, Philip	Railtrack	05(R)
Johnson, Asher	Passenger	08(R)
Johnstone, Andrew	Expert Witness	25
Kelleher, Alan	Railtrack	08
Khan, Khalid	EWS	08(R)
Khanghauri, Abdul	GWT	06
Kidman, Nicholas	Amey	18(R)
Kitcher, Clare	GWT	29
Kirwin, Andrew	GWT	04
Lewis, John	Expert Witness	18
Livingston, A	Expert Witness	24(R)
Lloyd, Raymond	GWT	04
Lockyear, Alan	Passenger	06(R)
Lucas, Debra. Dr	Expert Witness	23
Maidment, David	Expert Witness	20
Martin, John	AMEY	18(R)
Mason, Peter	GWT	26

Matthews, Byron	GWT	25(R)
Maylon, Christopher	Witness	08(R)
Maylon, Phillip	Railtrack	05
Mayo, Timothy	Railtrack	05
McCulloch, Richard	Railtrack	05
McGlinchy, Bryan	Passenger	07(R)
McGlinchy, Shelley	Passenger	07(R)
Mckenzie, David	GWT	03
McMillan, Martin	Expert Witness	29
Merryweather. Roger	Railtrack	20
Moodie, Michael	Railtrack	08
Moray. Professor	Expert Witness	23(R)
Morris. Chief Inspector	BTP	08
Murphy, Ian. Dr.	Expert Witness	16
Muttram, Roderick	Railtrack	21
Napier, Alan	Passenger	08(R)
Nelson, Aidan	Railtrack	32(R)
Newstead, Barry	LFCDA	09
Nicholas, Paul (Assistant Chief Constable)	BTP	11,12
Norman, David	Passenger	06
Oatway, Nigel	EWS	16
O'Connor Stephen	Railtrack	05(R)
O'Connor Owen	WS Atkins	08(R)
Organ, Michael	Railtrack	18(R)
Palmer, William	GWT	04
Parker, Richard	Railtrack	03
Parks, David	Railtrack	15
Patterson, Marcia	GWT	06(R)
Portsmouth, Ian	Railtrack	05(R)
Preston, Graham	EWS	20
Rasaiah, Winston	Expert Witness	18
Ratcliffe, Cornelis	Railtrack	30
Rayner, David	Railtrack	24
Rayner, Peter	Expert Witness	24
Rees, Hadyn	Passenger	07(R)
Rees, Mrs Linda	Passenger	07
Reilly, Shaun	BTP	08(R)
Rider, Kenneth	Virgin Trains	05(R)
Robinson, K	AEA	32(R)
Rudd, Amanda	HMRI	08(R)
Ryan, Albert	BTP	07(R)
Sargent, David	GNER	24(R)
Satchwell, Graham (Detective Superintendent)	BTP	11
Saunders, Arnold	GWT	25(R)
Shanahan, Kevin	BTP	08(R)
Sharpe, Andrew	Railtrack	16, 32(R)
Shooter, Tony	Witness	08(R)
Short, Roger	HMRI	08(R)

Shuttleworth, Mary	GWT	06
Siebley, Myles	HMRI	30(R)
Siebert, Michael	GWT	15
Smart David	GWT	09,12
Southwell, Mark	Railtrack	18(R)
Spence, William	BTP	08(R)
Spencer, Matthew	Railtrack	31
Spoors, Richard	Railtrack	18(R), 21(R)
Standish, Michael	EWS	13(R)
Staynings, Mr	LFCDA	09
Stuttard, Janice	Passenger	06
Sugden, Anthony	EWS	08(R)
Suguira, Ann	GWT	25(R)
Sutton, Nicholas	Passenger	08
Taylor, Alan	GWT	03
Tawn, Peter	Passenger	09
Thomas, Austin	GWT	03
Thomas, Mark	GWT	04
Thompson, Derek	Passenger	06(R)
Townsend, Barry	Railtrack	06(R)
Traynor, John	Witness	08(R)
Triggs, Mark	Railtrack	05(R)
Tubb, Dave	GWT	14(R)
Tunnock, James	GWT	04
Twibill, Martin	Railtrack	09
Vandermark, Adam	Passenger	09
Varney, Ann	Passenger	07
Vinnicombe, Gordon	GWT	04
Vipas. P.C	Police	07
Walker, Anthony	Railtrack	18
Walley, Mike	Met Office	07
Walters, Robert	Expert Witness	28
Watts, Lester	GWT	09(R)
Weedon, David	Railtrack	09
Wheeler, C	AMEY	18(R)
White, John	Halcrow Transmark	08(R)
Wilkins, Stephen	Expert Witness	17
Wilkinson, Barry	Railtrack	06(R)
Williams, Glyn	GWT	06
Wilson, John	Railtrack	24(R)
Wilson, Nicholas	GWT	06
Wiltshire, Joy	Passenger	07(R)
Winsor, Thomas	Rail Regulator	17
Winters, Heinz	Railtrack	06(R)
Woodbridge, Peter	WS Atkins	08(R)
Wright, Nicholas	GWT	30(R)

List of Inquiry Personnel

Chairman

Professor John Uff QC

Technical Assessor

Major Tony King OBE

Counsel

Ian Burnett QC

Richard Wilkinson

Dominic Adamson

Mandy Maclean

Sharon Flockhart

Secretariat Team

David Brewer (Secretary to the Inquiry)

Chris Bechervaise (Inquiry Manager)

Laurance O'Dea (Inquiry Solicitor)

Peter O'Connor (Press Officer to the Inquiry)

Heidi Ashley

Jennifer Byrne

Eddie Matthews

Mike Carless

Paul Donahoe

Alvina Francis

Catherine Green

Seema Janab

Matthew Knight

Aimee Lister

Paul McGuinness

Joe Mott

Darren Putland

Abdul Saddique

Catherine Thompson

Natalie Ward

Facsimile of note left in driver's cab of Power Car 43173

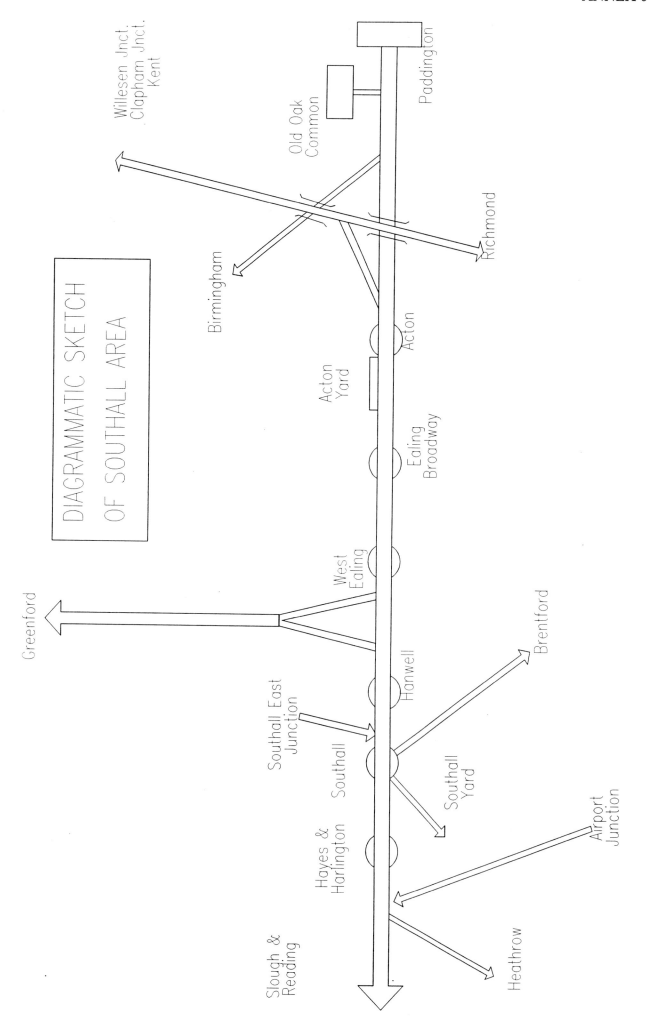

DIAGRAMMATIC SKETCH
OF SOUTHALL AREA

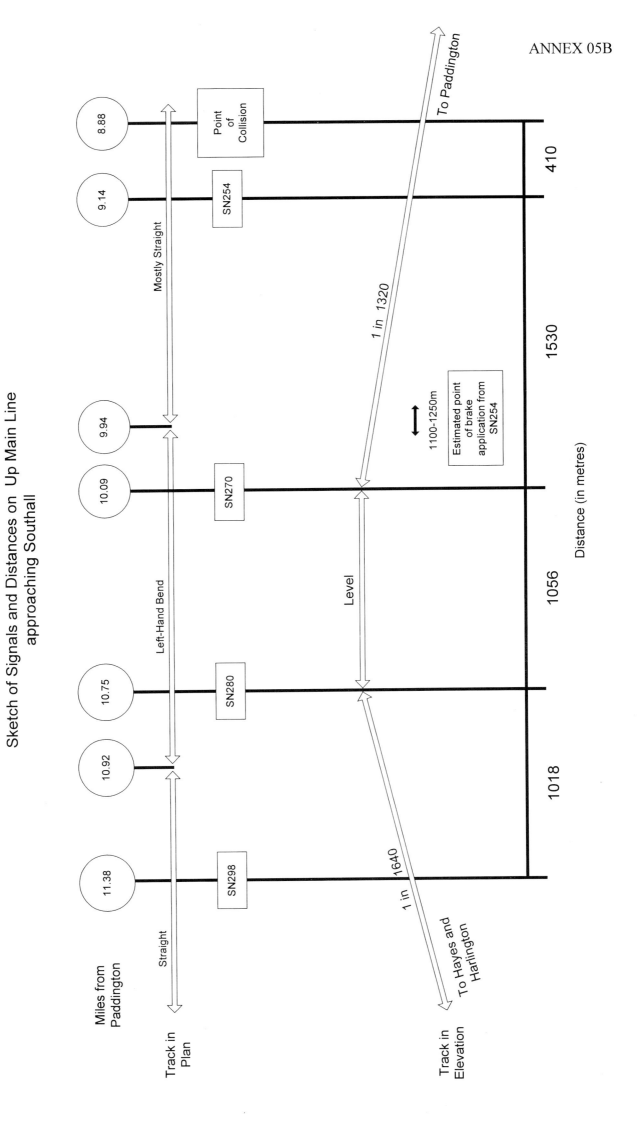

Account of the reconstruction of collision events in the Southall rail crash

Time 0.0 secs	Initial impact at point of crossing (410m East of signal Sn 254) between HST power car 43173 and wagon 17906
Time 0.3 secs	Power car reaches rear of wagon 17906. Lateral interference is 0.5m, resulting in derailment of rear bogie of wagon 17906
Time 0.4 secs	Power car has heavy collision with wagon 17903. Front bogies of both power car and 17903 are derailed.
Time 0.8 secs	Power car has heavy collision with wagon 17919, which derails completely, becomes uncoupled at both ends and subsequently overturns. The rear bogie of the power car is derailed. Wagon 17903 has a collision with coach H, derailing its leading bogie
Time 1.2 secs	Power car has heavy collision with wagon 17926, which derails completely, becomes uncoupled at both ends and subsequently overturns, finally colliding with an OLE stanchion.
Time 1.7 secs	Power car has heavy collision with wagon 19859, which becomes derailed, uncouples and subsequently overturns. This in turn derails wagon 19880 which twists away from the track and suffers no collision damage. Wagon 17903 has a collision with coach G, derailing its leading bogie. Bogie or other debris from wagon 17919 gets under the rear bogie of coach H and derails it to the north. Coaches H and G uncouple.
Time 3.0 secs	Power car and coach H have been derailed to the north and hence miss wagon 19891, which is now almost stationary at the front of the remaining rake of eight wagons, all with brakes applied. Coach H topples onto its left side and slides along the adjacent track.
Time 4.0 secs	Coach G and 19891 collide very heavily in an almost full frontal collision. The freight wagons are driven back and jacknife at the coupling of 19819 and 17907, the latter overturning. Both coach G and wagon 19891 leap into the air at the point of collision. The wagon tears out the front half of the already damaged side of coach G, the side remaining jammed in front of the wagon. The underframe of overturned wagon 17926 penetrates the side of coach F.
Time 5.6 secs	Coach G falls to the ground derailed to the north, minus its front bogie, still being propelled by the vehicles behind. Wagon 19891 remains airborne at its front end, pivoting with its rear end on the ground. It swings clockwise and collides with an OLE stanchion whilst in mid air.
Time 6.9 secs	The impact of wagon 19891 bends the stanchion and before the wagon reaches the ground, the leading edge of coach G, without its front bogie, drives into the space beneath it. This completes the flattening of the stanchion and the wagon drops onto the leading end of the roof of coach G, severely distorting it. The front of coach G is now wedged firmly under the wagon, which itself is partly held in its tilted position by a trailer bogie on the east side.
Time 8.5 secs	The back end of coach G is still attached to (or in contact with) coach F and hence to the rest of the HST. The force transmitted by coach F to the rear of the weakened coach G is sufficient to bend the coach to the point where coach F can pass its rear, the front end of the coach being firmly held by wagon 19891. Coach F is deflected from its path and collides head on with wagon 19819, pushing both it and wagon 17907 back to their final positions. The following coaches and power car came to rest with coaches E, C, and B derailed. Coach H collides with the next OLE stanchion as it comes to rest. The power car comes to rest upright next to the remaining wagons.

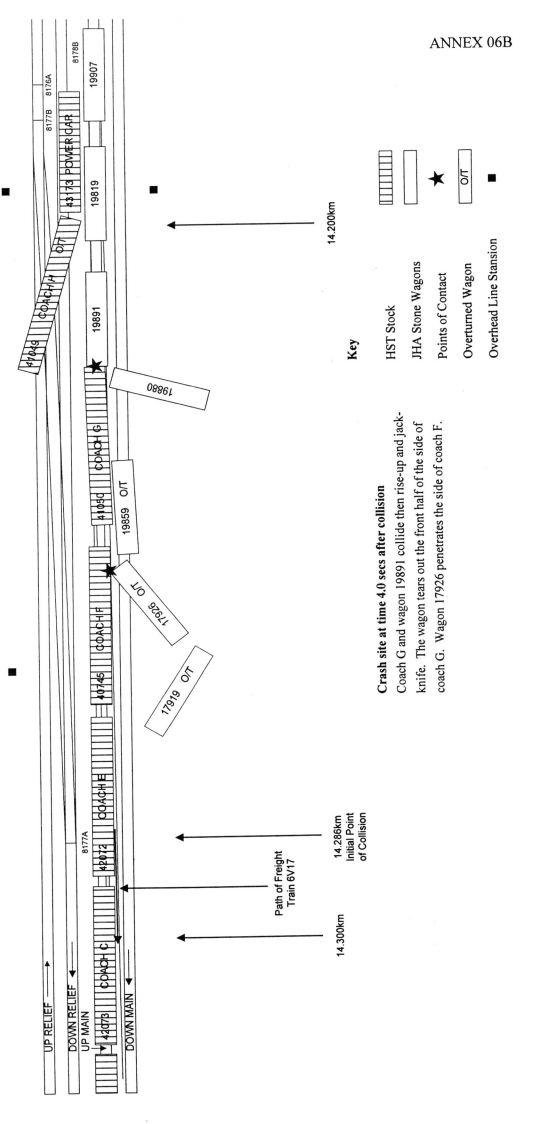

ANNEX 06B

TO PADDINGTON

FROM READING

Key

HST Stock

JHA Stone Wagons

Points of Contact

Overturned Wagon

Overhead Line Stansion

Crash site at time 4.0 secs after collision

Coach G and wagon 19891 collide then rise-up and jack-knife. The wagon tears out the front half of the side of coach G. Wagon 17926 penetrates the side of coach F.

14.200km

14.286km Initial Point of Collision

14.300km

Path of Freight Train 6V17

UP RELIEF
DOWN RELIEF
UP MAIN
DOWN MAIN

8177B   8176A
8178B
8177A

41049   COACH H   O/T
43173 POWER CAR
19907
19819
19891
COACH G   41050
19880
19859   O/T
17926   O/T
COACH F   40745
17919   O/T
COACH E
42072
COACH C   42073

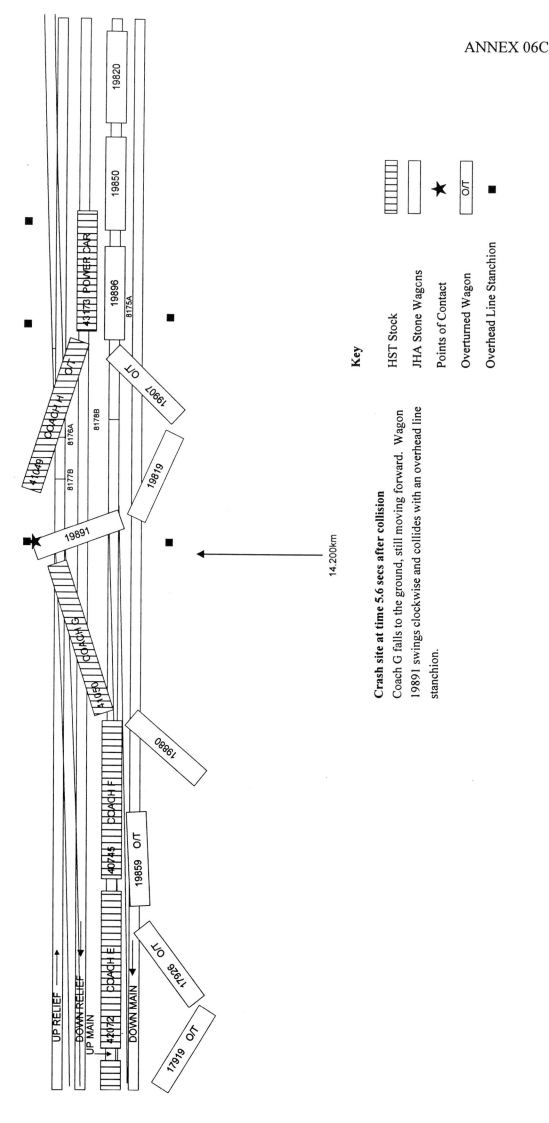

ANNEX 06C

TO PADDINGTON

FROM READING

Key

HST Stock

JHA Stone Wagons

Points of Contact

Overturned Wagon

Overhead Line Stanchion

Crash site at time 5.6 secs after collision

Coach G falls to the ground, still moving forward. Wagon 19891 swings clockwise and collides with an overhead line stanchion.

14.200km

UP RELIEF
DOWN RELIEF
UP MAIN
DOWN MAIN

43173 POWER CAR

19820

19850

19896

8175A

8178B

8176A
8177B

41049 COACH H O/T

19907 O/T

19819

19891

41050 COACH G

19880

40745 COACH F

19859 O/T

42072 COACH E

17926 O/T

17919 O/T

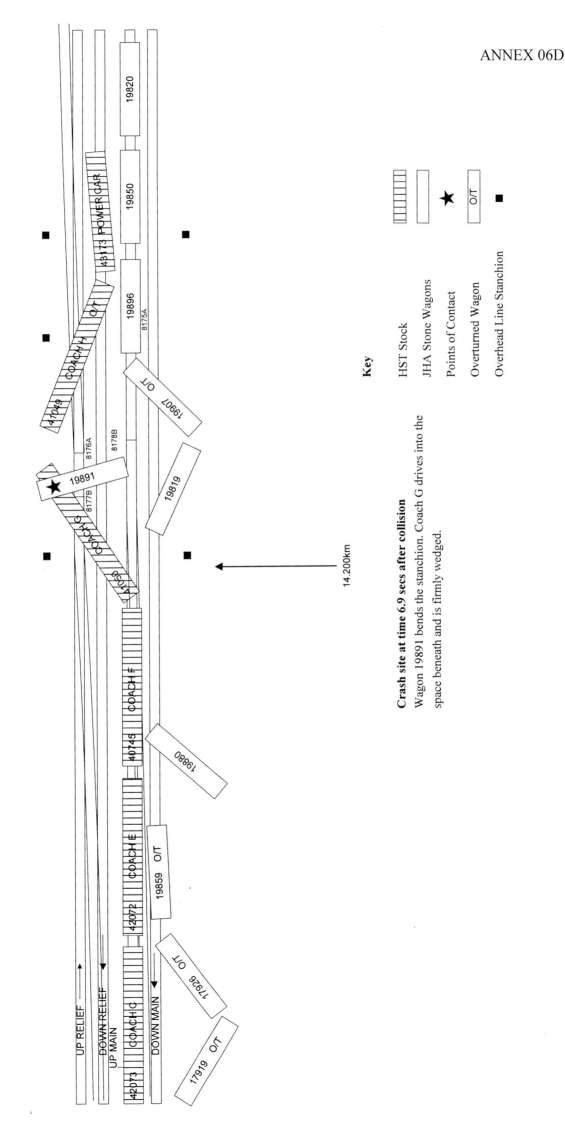

TO PADDINGTON

FROM READING

UP RELIEF →

DOWN RELIEF ↓

UP MAIN

DOWN MAIN ↓

19820

19850

4B173 POWER CAR

O/T

41049 COACH H

19896

8175A

COACH G

19891

8176A

8178B

8177B

19907 O/T

19819

14.200km

40745 COACH F

19880

42072 COACH E

19859 O/T

42073 COACH C

17926 O/T

17919 O/T

Crash site at time 6.9 secs after collision
Wagon 19891 bends the stanchion. Coach G drives into the space beneath and is firmly wedged.

Key

HST Stock

JHA Stone Wagons

★ Points of Contact

O/T Overturned Wagon

■ Overhead Line Stanchion

ANNEX 06E

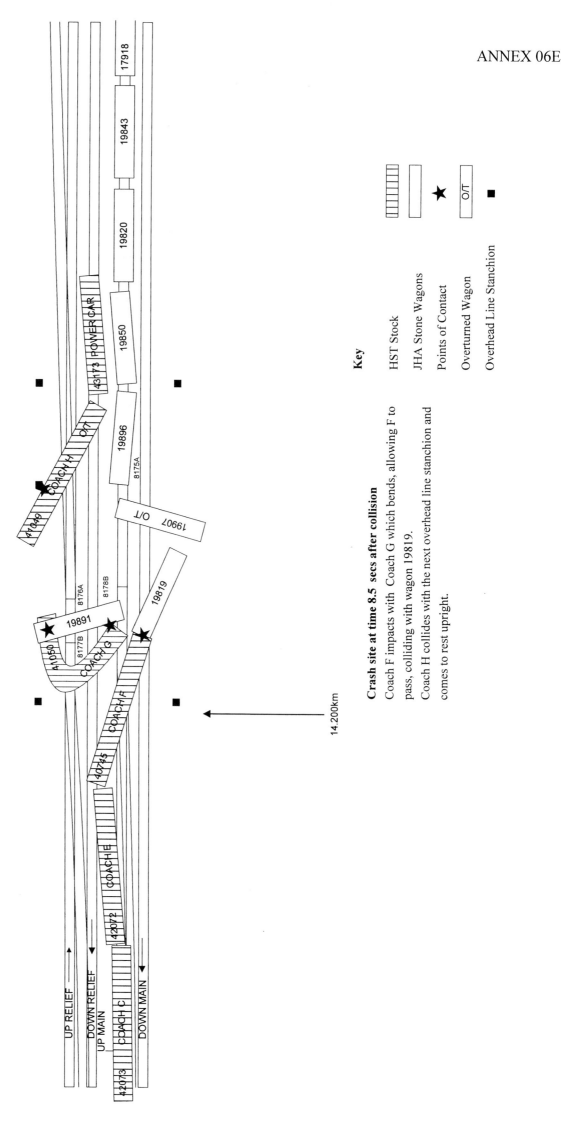

TO PADDINGTON

FROM READING

UP RELIEF

DOWN RELIEF

UP MAIN

DOWN MAIN

14.200km

Crash site at time 8.5 secs after collision

Coach F impacts with Coach G which bends, allowing F to pass, colliding with wagon 19819.

Coach H collides with the next overhead line stanchion and comes to rest upright.

Key

HST Stock

JHA Stone Wagons

Points of Contact

Overturned Wagon

Overhead Line Stanchion

Damage to Power Car 43173 (Right Hand Side)

Damage to Coach G (main picture) and to Coach F (RHS)

Damage to Coach G with Freight Wagon Coupler to left of picture / Coach F to the right

AWS ISolation Switch with lead seal in place

Driver's cab from Power Car 43173 Post Accident

RECORDING OF DRIVER'S CONVERSATION WITH THE SIGNALMAN

Hello there, 316 received

Driver This is the driver of the, the HST requesting into the er

Driver, can you hold on there a minute please? Keep quiet guys, I've got a driver on the phone Right, can you repeat all that please

Driver Er, yeah, I'm, I'm, I'm ringing from SN251 at the moment, that's the first signal, er, telephone I could get to.

What train were you driving?

Driver The HST.

You were driving the HST?

Driver Yeah I've got the head code Hang on, I've got to go in my pocket hang on, hang on that s One Alpha Forty-Seven

One Alpha Forty-Seven. Right, and your at a stand, and your ringing in from SN251, Driver are you okay?

Driver I'm okay, yeah, I was just putting me stuff away in the bag the A, the A, the, the AWS has been isolated because some, some brake problem, I believe, so, I had no AWS so, I put me stuff away in the bag and the next thing I knew, I was coming up against red, up, such coming through, through

Through Southall Station?

Driver Through Southall, yeah

Right, I see, Driver, can you bear with us one moment That's the driver of the train, have a word with him.

Yeah S251, is the nearest signal he could get to I thought the (inaudible) Dead Man you know that. (background noise inaudible)
 Hello, driver

Hello

Hello, Driver

Driver Hello there

Hello mate. Are you, where you the driver on One A Forty-Seven?

Driver One Alpha Forty-Seven, yes

Right, er,

Driver AWS is isolated.

Right

Driver And I was just putting me stuff away in the bag, like I would normally do, you see

Right

Driver And er, all of a sudden I was whizzing through Hayes with a red at Southall.

Right.

Driver I see the slow train crossing over then

Right.

Driver And I went back into the engine room

Uh-huh

Driver And this is the first time, I've been able, I've I've put (inaudible)

Is your train off the track, driver?

Driver Er, yes, it's blocking all lines

It's blocking all lines.

Driver Yes I need electricity turned off

Right We have turned of the electricity driver, it is safe to approach but don't touch.

Driver Yeah, alright

Okay. All the electricity has been switched of but as I say, you can approach it but don t touch the electrics.

Driver There's, there a police officer that would like to have a word with you mate

Yeah okay

Police Hello to you, I'm a police officer from Southall

Yes, mate

Police Are you aware what's happened, are you?

We are aware what's happened, we don't know the full details, we just know there s been a collision that's all.

Police Right, we've got um, as he said it's fully blocked we've got a train on its side

Right.

Police We've got several fatalities

Oh Christ

Police A few walking-wounded, we've got all the emergency services responding but we need everything turned off and that coming through on this line.

Yeah, yeah. I'll tell you this officer, we have switched off the power

Police Right

At Southall

Police Yep

Now its safe to approach but do not touch the wires.

Police Okay, I can

Until you get, if your around that area, make sure no one touches the wires

Police No one touches the wires.

Until someone from the electricity part of it is there

Police Okay

They will then test it and give you the authority to make sure

Police Right, okay

Okay

Police You know there's been a train approaching from the east that's stopped about two hundred yards away

Yeah, yeah, we've got all trains at a stand, no trains will be moving

Police Okay, magic.

Okay

Police Okay

Cheers.

Police Right-e-ho cheers

Passengers who died as a result of the accident

Name of Passenger	Travelling in
Allen, Peter Dobson, Mr	Coach G
Brain, Clive Mr	Coach H
Eustace, David Waring, Mr	Coach G
Kavanagh, Peter Patrick, Mr	Coach G/H
Olander, Marcus, Mr	Coach G
Petch, Anthony Richard, Mr	Coach G
Traynor, Gerard Martin, Mr.	Coach G

Passengers & Staff believed to have sustained injury as a result of the accident

Name of Passenger	Travelling in
Akbar, Sylvia, Mrs	Coach B
Albelushi, Mohamed H, Mr	Coach E
Allen, Janet, Mrs	Coach G
Alshammari, Mohamed S	Coach E
Anderson, Alexander, Mr	Coach C
Ashurst, Philip Roy, Mr	Coach A
Atkins, Mel Lucian, Mr	Coach E
Atyeo, Linda Jane	Coach C
Baker, Nicholas Charles, Mr	Coach F
Banfield, Tim, Augutus, Mr	Coach H
Bell, Alan Edward, Mr	Coach E
Bell, Alma Joyce	Coach E
Bell, Carol Ann	Coach E
Bell, George Edward, Mr	Coach E
Berlak, Harold, Mr	Coach B
Bertram, Joanne	Coach C
Boddy, John, Dr.	Coach H
Bowers, Deborah, Miss	Coach C
Brown, David, Andrew, Mr	Coach G
Buchanan, Fraser Stuart, Mr	Coach E
Burgess, Matthew David, Mr	Coach C
Bush, William, Mr	Coach A
Bye, Stella Shang Hwa, Mrs	Coach F
Carter, Marilyn Morgan	Coach C
Cleevely, Helen Louise, Miss	Coach E
Coles, John Mark Shepton, Mr	Coach E
Corey, Arthur Kenneth, Mr	Coach C
Corey, Elizabeth Marjorie, Mrs	Coach C
Coulson, Martin Geoffrey, Mr	Coach E
Davies, Marjorie, Miss	Coach A
Dean, J, W, Mr	Coach H
Dempster, Frances Diana, Dr	Coach E
Diaz, Victor, Gonzalez, Mr	Coach G
Dixey, Christopher Roger, Mr	Coach E
Doyle, Justina, Elaina, Mrs	Coach F
Duffis, Angela Yolander	Coach F
Easton, Michael Moore, Mr	Coach A
Eggen,P,C, Mr	Coach G
Eldridge, Rebecca Sian, Miss	Coach E
Ellacott, Celia Frances, Mrs	Coach E
Farrell, David, Mr	Coach B
Flaherty, Maeve Marie, Miss	Coach C
Fletcher, Marcus	Coach E
Funge, Ann	Coach C
Garnell, Jane, Mrs	Coach F
Garvey, Jane Susan,	Coach F
George, Richard Thomas Glandon	Coach F
Godfrey, Rachel	Coach F
Griffiths, K, A, Miss	Coach E
Grove, Elizbeth Susan, Mrs	Coach C
Haddow, Kenneth Harley, Mr	Coach F
Harrhy, A, D, Mr	Coach C
Harrhy, N, L, Mrs	Coach C
Harris, R, J, Miss	Coach E

Passengers & Staff believed to have sustained injury as a result of the accident

Name of Passenger	Travelling in
Harrison, L, J, Mr	PC/43173
Harte, K, Ms	Coach E
Hellier, M, D, Mr	Coach G
Henry, Patricia Bernadette	Coach B
Hepburn, J, Mrs	Coach E
Hepburn, Richard David, Mr	Coach E
Hills, Patricia Margaret	Coach C
Hollingsworth, Judith Ann, Mrs	Coach F
Jenkins, Arthur Brian, Mr	Coach E
Jenkins, Binnie A. Diane, Mrs	Coach E
Johnston, Ian Grahame, Mr	Coach F
Johnstone, Lucy, Clare	Coach C
Jones, Gaynor Maria, Mrs	Coach C
Jones, Huw, Mr	Coach E
Jones, Lynda Elizabeth, Mrs	Coach E
Jones, Stanely, Mr	Coach E
Jones,Gwyneth Alwena, Mrs	Coach E
Keefe, Terry John, Mr	Coach C
Kelly, Heather May	Coach C
Khanghauri, M, B, Mr	Coach A
Kirkpatrick, Stephanie Kathryn	Coach C
Lawrenson, H, Mr	Coach H
Lobeck, Charles Stanley	Coach E
Lockyear, Alan, Mr	Coach G
Marcus, Helen, Mrs	Coach C
Mcglinchy, Bryan David	Coach C
Mcglinchy, Shelly Yvonne, Mrs	Coach C
McGuiness, Hazel Kay, Mrs	Coach B
McGunigall, Stuart Douglas, Mr	Coach B
Mcmorrin, Anna Rhiannon, Miss	Coach E
Millidge, Jonathan Varley	Coach C
Morris, Beverly Marion, Mrs	Coach C
Morris, Robert Edward Thomas, Mr	Coach C
Moss, Albert Henry, Mr	Coach A
Moss, Jean Eleanor	Coach A
Murphy, Ciara, Bernadette, Miss	Coach E
Napier,Alan, Mr	Coach G
Nash, Shereen, Mrs	Coach E
Newsam, Anne Josephine	Coach C
O'leary, Aileen, Mrs	Coach E
O'Leary, Lorraine, Mrs'	Coach C
O'leary, Robert	Coach E
Orr, Susan Assunda Mrs	Coach B
Palmer, Barbara Veronica	Coach B
Patterson, Marcia Obrien, Mrs	Coach F
Power, Dawn Sandra	Coach E
Poyner, Marion Clara	Coach A
Price, Eileen, Mrs	Coach B
Price, Kenneth John, Mr	Coach B
Pritchard, Doreen Kathleen	Coach C
Ramsdale, Roland Hansom, Mr	Coach E
Rees, Hayden William	Coach C
Rees, Linda Janice, Mrs	Coach C
Revolta, David Charles Wishart, Mr	Coach F
Rhys, Maragret, Mrs	Coach C
Robinson, Susan, Mrs	Coach C

Passengers & Staff believed to have sustained injury as a result of the accident

Name of Passenger	Travelling in
Sanders, Barry Gerald, Mr	Coach E
Sheriff, Behanz, Mrs	Coach E
Shuttleworth, Mary	Coach F
Stevens, Mark Edwin, Mr	Coach A
Stothart, Chloe Helen, Miss	Coach C
Sutherland, George Moir, Mr	Coach A
Sutton, Nicholas George Bell	Coach A
Tawn, Peter Michael, Mr	Coach B
Tew, Jessie Maud, Mrs	Coach C
Thavasothy, Meera	Coach F
Thompson, Derek, Mr	Coach G
Thompson, Sally	Coach A
Thomson, Robin Gary, Mr	Coach B
Tomzcak, Mathin Alois Kazimerz, Mr	Coach C
Treadaway, Holly, Louise, Miss	Coach C
Tsuzuki, S, Mr	Coach H
Uemura, Y, My	Coach H
Uesaki, Y, Mrs	Coach H
Vancedaniel, Julian, Mr	Coach C
Vandermark, Adam, Mr	Coach C
Varney, Anne Felicity, Mrs	Coach G
Vicenti, Ronald, Mr	Coach B
Welfare, Ann Louise	Coach B
Welfare, Hayley Ann, Miss	Coach B
Williams, G, F, Mr	Coach H
Williams, Hywel, Mr	Coach E
Wiltshire, Joy Arminthia,	Coach F
Winslett, Lydia, Mrs	Coach C
Winslett, William Charles, Mr	Coach C

PLAN OF LOCATION OF CRASH SITE

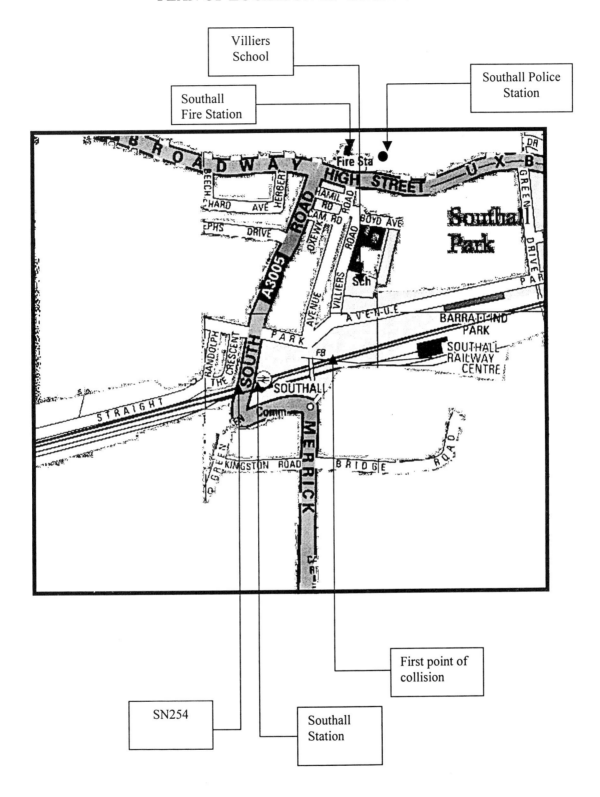

Great Western

Private and Confidential

Richard Gearge
Managing Director
Great Western Trains Company

26th September 1997

Dear Richard,

I have been involved in the recovery operation following the serious accident at Southall -that you yourself were involved, for most of the last week, my first visit to the site being on Saturday 20th September. As part of the GWTC Fleet "on call" team we rotated around the clock until Tuesday morning.

I have attended many incidents during the last several years most of which were not serious and did not involve the emergency services. Southall was my second major incident the first being the severn tunnel crash in 1991 also attended by Brian Scott and Ian Cusworth.

Following both incidnets I was left with feelings of deep concern about the immediate Post Accident liaison between the emergency services and Great Western / Railtrack (formerly British Rail for Severn tunnel).

I would like to talk firstly about Southall where for most of my time on site I was the sole Great Western Trains Company representative.

On Saturday I was primarily concerned with the recovery of the trailing power car and the three standard class vehicles that were eventually moved to Bristol.

On Sunday I arrived at the site to see most of the wreckage removed from the track and relaying was in progress. Bulldozers were at work and I watched a significant amount of vehicle debris buried in the ballast, I left site at around 02:00 on Monday and drove home.

I was back on site at 12:00 on Monday, a site meeting was in progress in bronze control. My colleague Doug Harvey had recovered some ATP modules from the "down cess" which I put into the car for safe keeping. Another colleague John Cameron had arrived on site at around 14:00 and asked if it would be possible to find any more ATP equipment, I showed the people accompanying John where they were found and as I searched around I found the ATP control cabinet and eventually the other ATP modules -purely by chance these had not been completely buried in the ballast. Later I was quizzed by the Police about ATP equipment including the Hasler unit and the "Black box" after some discussion I showed them the Hasler and handed over the modules as evidence.

On Tuesday I was approached by a railtrack official asking about AWS equipment on behalf of Nicola Pagett Railtrack Signals Engineer. Fortunately because of my detailed knowledge of the site (post accident) I was able to locate the AWS receiver which had been ripped off during the accident and bulldozed to one side.

My point is that all this possibly vital evidence could have been lost forever either by being covered with ballast or shovelled up and scrapped. I and everone else had wrongly assumed that all the relevant evidence had been removed or identified by the HSE and the Police accident investigators. This was obviously not the case and again I have become frustrated at what to me seems a fundamantal ommision in the evidence gathering process, that is to say that GWTC people were not allowed to be involved.

During the severn tunnel crash it was hours before Fleet staff were allowed near the train, during which time the emergency services tended the injured. When the train was finally moved it was getting dark. Although the train could have been driven out much earlier had there been better communication between emergency services and the railway companies.

The emergency services seem to ignore us (I suspect distrust) even though we are by profession the most knowledgeable and experienced people where our vehicles are concerned. It is my belief that in both of these incidents swift action to make contact with the appropriate people in GWTC would make sure that everything that can be done to assist, both the accident investigators and the emergency services in a technical rather than a hands on way would be done and hopefully effect a more efficient recovery.

Yours sincerely

Paul Ardiff
Production Manager SPM Depot

530975

52·000/0005

THE TREASURY SOLICITOR

Southall Inquiry Secretariat. New Connaught Rooms. Great Queen St. London WC2B 5DA

Direct Fax: 0171 405 0098   Tele 0171 430 2010
Direct Line: 0171 430 2010

Richard Crockford
Railtrack
Connaught Rooms   Our ref.: R1/51/1/105/97/8.GC.
LONDON WC2
                                   Your

16 November 1999

Dear Mr Crockford

RE SOUTHALL RAIL ACCIDENT INQUIRY

Mr Burnett has mentioned in public on a number of occasions that the Inquiry expects to hear evidence to deal with outstanding signalling issues in the middle of next week. The issue is one which can be resolved only by evidence from Railtrack and AMEY Rail.

The questions are as follows:

(i)   What arrangements were in place for maintaining and repairing the Southall signals (with SN 270 as the focus of attention) in the months leading up to the accident?
(ii)   What maintenance and repair was in fact carried out before the accident and by whom?
(iii)   Was the alignment of SN 270 checked or adjusted before the accident and is so when and by whom? If not, why not?
(iv)   Since.the accident precisely what work has been done on the relevant signals, when and by whom?
(v)   What steps were taken in response to the information provided by Mr Wilkins to various Railtrack staff (as to which see his oral evidence) that SN 270 was misaligned? If no steps were taken, why not?
(vi)   When was SN 270 realigned, by whom and why?
(vii)   What steps were taken by Railtrack to realign SN 270 is response to correspondence from the Inspectorate and the BTP?
(viii) If, as appears to be the case, the question of realignment fell into contractual interstices, how did that occur and what has been done to correct any omission?

The Inquiry is grateful to AMEY Rail for providing written explanations of some of the problems together with various maintenance records. Nonetheless, this is an important issue which must be dealt with fully by both relevant parties.

The Inquiry would like a statement dealing with all these issues from both Railtrack and AMEY Rail. It would be convenient if the relevant documents could be attached to the

Group Leader - B McKay
Team Leader - L John-Charles

statements. We request that Railtrack and AMEY Rail agree the documents which are necessary to resolve the outstanding issues and collate them into a paginated bundle. Each statement can then refer to the bundle when appropriate. I would like to be able to circulate the statements and the supporting documents in as a separate core bundle. The issue can then be virtually self-contained.

The timetable provides for this evidence to be taken next Wednesday. Therefore, I must have the statements and supporting documents in a fit state to circulate by close of play on Monday 22nd November.

The Inquiry is grateful for your help on this matter. I am copying this letter to Tom Custance for AMEY Rail with whom I would invite you to make contact to ensure that both parties . work together on the bundle.

Yours sincerely

Laurance O'Dea

cc AMEY Rail. Connaught Rooms

Railtrack Train Regulation Policy

Level 1 Statement

Scope

These Instructions relate to Railtrack–controlled infrastructure. These offer guidance to Signallers in the regulation of trains when they are not operating to the planned schedule (eg WTT, Weekly or Daily Special Notice). Where these instructions conflict with SGI 3, these instructions take precedence. Second and Third level statements, where they exist, take precedence over these instructions.

Regulating Instruction

[1]   Trains running earlier than planned and Control-arranged specials must not be allowed to proceed from a regulatory point, if this is likely to cause delay to other trains.

[2]   When one or more late-running trains approach a regulating point so that one will delay another, the Signaller must regulate trains with the aim of minimising overall delay. In reaching a judgement on the likely overall delay, account should be taken of:

   (a) The performance of the train in terms of acceleration and maximum speed

   (b) The stopping pattern of the train

   (c) Local circumstances applicable on the day - for example, temporary speed restrictions; traction on reduced power and inferior traction vice booked traction (where advised)

   (d) Regulating points (and their capacity) further along the route of the train

[3]   Zonal Controls have the authority to issue specific instructions to change priorities as laid down in [1] & [2]. In these circumstances, the Signaller must record any such instruction issued.

| Authorised : **R. Owen** | Railtrack Head of Production | June 2nd 1996 |

REGINA
-V-

GREAT WESTERN TRAINS COMPANY LIMITED
Sentencing Remarks
Before
The Hon Mr Justice Scott Baker

Those who travel on high speed trains are entitled to expect the highest standard of care from those who run them. Great Western Trains Limited failed to meet that standard and in my judgement they failed to meet it by a greater extent than they have been prepared to admit. Their failure was a significant cause of a disaster that killed seven people, injured 150 others and caused millions of pounds worth of damage. The lives of many families have been devastated.

The immediate cause of the accident was the passing of a red signal by the driver. But a substantial contributory cause was the fact that the defendant company permitted the train to run from Swansea to Paddington at speeds of up to 125 mph with the automatic warning system (AWS) isolated.

The simple solution would have been to turn the at Swansea so that the leading locomotive had an effective AWS and the defective.
The defence say the company did not do so because:

1. It was not required by the rules.
2. It was never suggested by either Railtrack or th Railway Inspectorate.
3. It was not the practice of train operating companies to do so.
4. AWS isolation was a category B failure (as opposed to category A) and it was therefore permissible for the train to continue on its journey.

Mr Caplan argued that the Defendants error should be looked at in the context of the procedures and approach of the industry as a whole and that railway safety is a matter of partnership between Railtrack, the Railway Inspectorate and the train companies; and in one sense so it is. I bear in mind Mr. Caplan's arguments, but the primary obligation to run their trains safely lies on Great Western Trains itself. The Company should have applied its mind to the risk created by allowing a high speed train to travel a journey of this length and this speed without the AWS operating. It may be that the likelihood of a driver passing a red signal at speed was relatively small. But if the event occurred the consequences were going to be, as in the event they were, appalling.

The Prosecution say that there are various other things the Company should or could have done such as adding another power car or double manning the cab.

Defence submit, with some force, that each suggestion was either impossible or impracticable. 1 do not regard these matters as relevant since the Company admits the simple solution would have been to turn the train.

There is however one matter that requires mention and that is Automatic Train Protection (ATP). At the time of the enquiry into the Clapham disaster it was envisaged that ATP would be introduced across the rail network within 5 years. Indeed an undertaking was given to that effect. There is every reason to believe that had ATP been operating on this train on this journey the accident would not have happened. The introduction of ATP was not a matter for GWT alone but for the whole rail network. ATP has been beset with technical difficulties which has been the reason for its non introduction across the board. GWT broke no obligation or undertaking by not having ATP in operation on this train. They were, however, at the time of the accident operating a pilot ATP scheme albeit with little enthusiasm. It is to be noted however that the pilot scheme was increased dramatically in extent immediately following the accident.

Had someone at Great Western Trains had the drive to do so this could have been achieved before the accident. It is ironic that Electrowatt Engineering reported in the very month of albeit after the accident:

--In the absence of ATP there is predicted to be a 26% chance of an ATP preventable accident involving a GWT train during the next 10 years. The political considerations, and the very real requirement for senior management effort that such an accident would bring, cannot be disregarded."

The fine I impose has to reflect the following:

1. The extent to which Great Western Trains fell short of the standard required of them and the risk that was thereby created. In my view it was a serious failure.

2. The extent of the disaster and in particular the number of people killed and injured.

3. The need to bring home the message to Great Western Trains and others x~ ho run substantial transport undertakings that eternal vigilance is required to ensure that accidents of this nature do not occur. In my judgement a substantial fine is required to emphasise this to a large and profitable enterprise such as the Defendant.

It has not been suggested that the accident in this case was the result of a deliberate risk taken in pursuit of profit. Rather the thrust of the complaint is that Great Western Trains did not have in place a system for preventing a high speed train operating with the AWS isolated and no alternative in place. That in my judgement is a serious fault of senior management. More time and energy should have been devoted to should have appreciating the risk of what occurred and taking steps to avoid it.

In mitigation I take into account:

1. The Defendants plea of guilty, tendered not at the first opportunity but at what Counsel considered to be the first practicable opportunity. For the avoidance of any doubt I give full credit for the plea.

2. The fact that the Defendants have a good safety record and have never before been prosecuted for an offence under the Health and safety legislation.

3. The fact that prompt action was taken after the accident to ensure that there was no further breach of the Health and Safety Act.

4. The fact that they did not break any requirement imposed on them by either railtrack or the Railway Inspectorate.

I am surprised that neither Mr. George (who it is said is in personal charge of safety at Great Western Trains) nor any other director of the company came to Court to express personally remorse for Great Western Trains breach of the Health and Safety Act and to allay any impression of complacency that may have been conveyed to the victims, their families and the public.

That said I accept Mr Caplan's submission that Great Western Trains does very much regret its responsibility for this disaster.

The fine that I impose is not intended to, nor can it, reflect the value of the lives lost or the injuries sustained in this disaster. It is however intended to reflect public concern at the offence committed.

There will be a fine of £1.5 million.

The Defendant will pay the Prosecution costs of the Health and Safety offence. There will be a Defendants costs order in respect of the manslaughter offences. Those orders will be in the terms I have already mentioned.

Tuesday 27 July, 1999

Nick Pollard
Head of News

September 16th, 1999

Professor John Uff, PhD, FEng, FICE, FCIArb, QC.,
Chairman of the Southall Rail Inquiry
C/o Peter O'Conner Esq.,

Dear Professor Uff,

I am writing on behalf of the three main UK television news broadcasters, the
BBC, ITN and Sky News, about the terms under which you have proposed that
television cameras are allowed to cover the Southall rail crash public inquiry.

We are pleased that you have allowed cameras into the inquiry. However we
have agreed only very reluctantly, to your condition that no video or audio
material from the inquiry proceedings should be transmitted before sixty
minutes have elapsed. It seems to us that this is an unnecessary condition bearing
in mind the very wide range of public proceedings and statements that are now
open to be shown live or without such restrictions. Nevertheless it would appear
that if we do not accept this condition you will not allow cameras in at all.

We are also concerned that the sixty minute delay could well lead to you, as
inquiry chairman, effectively exercising editorial control over the content of the
news reports about the inquiry by ordering that cameras should be turned off at
particular moments or that material once recorded should not be transmitted.

British Sky Broadcasting Ltd
Grant Way, Isleworth, Middlesex TW7 5QD, England
Telephone 0171 705 3949   Facsimile 0171 705 3948
e mail nick.pollard@bskyb.com
Web site http://www.sky.co.uk
Registered in England Number 2206901 VAT Registered Number 440 6274 67

- 2 -

It is our view that the decision to allow cameras to cover proceedings is the right one but also that broadcasters should be left to do their job without unnecessary hindrance.

We also believe that the restrictions you have insisted on should not in any way set a precedent for future coverage of such inquiries.

Yours sincerely,

Nick Pollard

Nick Pollard
CC: BBC, ITN

SC 1680

PROTOCOL FOR PROVISION OF BROADCAST SOUND AND VISION
FEED OF PUBLIC HEARINGS OF THE SOUTHALL RAIL ACCIDENT INQUIRY

Introduction

1.   There will be a broadcast sound and vision feed of the public hearings of evidence of the inquiry provided that this can be achieved with the minimum of disruption.

Provision of pictures and sound

2.   All arrangements for the provision of pictures and sound to broadcasters will be made by the broadcasters on a pool basis at no cost to the HSC. The pool feed will be provided on behalf of the broadcasters by an independent production company experienced in this field and will be made available to all bona fide broadcasters who wish to receive this output. The chosen provider is subject to approval of the Inquiry Chairman

3.   The HSC will permit broadcaster(s) or a production company to:

   (i) use three cameras in the inquiry room at fixed positions approved by the Chairman. The number of cameras may be reviewed by the Chairman.

   (ii) obtain a sound feed from the firm employed to provide microphones and sound recording of the proceedings;

   (iii) dependent upon the venue, have space available for their use, e.g. technical support room/edit suite, but at no cost to the inquiry;

   (iv) Take a direct feed from any computer projection, if available.

4.   The equipment used must be unobtrusive. All equipment and filming will be subject to the overall powers of the Chairman to control the procedure at the hearing. This protocol may be varied if the interests of the Inquiry so require.

Recording

5.   Cameras will remain in fixed positions throughout any half-day session.

6.   Access to the technical support room, lighting and cameras should normally be restricted to before and after each session. Exceptionally, it is recognised that access may be needed at other times; in such cases this should take place during the changeover of witnesses. Subject to the agreement of the chosen venue, the broadcasters may have access for technical purposes from 0800 on each hearing day.

7.   No equipment should be moved in or out of the inquiry room during the course of a hearing session (i.e. half-day).

8. All personnel who have access to the inquiry room during the course of a session should be suitably dressed.

9. Additional lighting, if any, must be the minimum required for filming. The Chairman will direct that lighting is dimmed or switched off if the Inquiry proceedings are adversely affected or for any other reason.

10. Subject to 10 above, lighting will not be switched on or off during the course of any individual witnesses evidence.

11. The microphones must not be operated in such a way as to pick up words that do not form part of the proceedings and must be so arranged that they pick up only words that are intended to form part of the Inquiry.

12. The Chairman will ensure that witnesses are treated sensitively, and has the power to instruct that the cameras are turned off if not satisfied that this is being achieved.

13. Passengers and relatives of deceased passengers will not be filmed if they object. The Chairman may also direct that the whole or any part of the evidence of other witnesses should not be filmed.

Coverage

14. While the HSC does not wish to make unreasonable impositions on broadcasters or a production company, some rules are necessary to take account of the special position of television cameras. The general principle is that the cameras should be able to cover questions and answers between witnesses and the Chairman, and others who are allowed to question witnesses. The following specific rules will apply:

15. No close-up shots will be permitted of: inquiry support staff, those accompanying witnesses, members of the public, or any detail of the surroundings.

16. Similarly, the confidential nature of inquiry and parties' documents should be preserved and no shots should be taken in a way that they can be read.

17. Reaction shots are permitted but these should be confined to the witness, Chairman, assessor, or the person who has asked a question. No other general reaction shots will be permitted.

18 A general wide-angle shot of the hearing room may be taken at the start and end of each hearing session but otherwise cameras should concentrate on the individuals listed in 17 above. The wide-angle camera may be used for editing purposes in a responsible way.

Broadcasting

In the event of a disturbance, cameras should not give prominence to that disturbance but continue to concentrate on the Chairman and witness; if the distur

20. While recognising the editorial independence of the broadcasters, the HSC expects that material will be used in such a way as to give a fair reflection of the nature of the proceedings and the issues under discussion.

21. Live broadcasting will not be permitted. There will be a time delay of at least 60 minutes between recording and broadcast.

22. The Chairman, of his own initiative or in response to a request from a witness or their representative, may instruct that recorded material may not be broadcast.

It is a condition of the entitlement to record material that no material recorded during the course of the hearings should be used in humorous or satirical programmes, for the purposes of advertising, or with any sound other than that recorded at the time (other than a simultaneous translation into a foreign language). A similar condition should be placed on those to whom material is passed under the pooling arrangements.

Material subsequently used in documentary format must be submitted to the Chairman who reserves the right to request any material to be withdrawn.

Thank you for your co-operation.

Media enquiries on this protocol should be directed to Peter O'Connor, HSC/Southall Rail Accident Inquiry Press Office. Tel: 07957 557057 or 07623 755426.

30 September 1997

CIRCULAR LETTER TO TRAIN OPERATING COMPANIES

AUTOMATIC WARNING SYSTEM OF TRAIN CONTROL (AWS)

Without prejudice to the outcome of any investigation or Inquiry into any specific accident, HMRI has been undertaking some general enquiries in relation to the use of the automatic warning system generally across the British Railway network. We have discovered some overly liberal interpretation of rules and this prompts me to write to all train operating companies on the network.

You will already be aware of Railway Group Standard GO/OT0013, Railway Group Standard GK/RT 0016 and Appendix 8 of the General Appendix to the Rule Book.

Clause 6.1 of Appendix 8 states that:-

"A traction unit must not enter service if the AWS is isolated, or the seal is broken on an AWS isolating handle, in any driving cab which is required to be used".

Our understanding of this is that a train should not begin a journey with the AWS in the driving cab isolated. We do not believe that this should be interpreted as simply referring to a train entering service for the day, or for a series of journeys between visits to maintenance depots.

Clause 6.3 of Appendix 8 states:

"If it is necessary to isolate the AWS, the diver must inform the Signalman at the first convenient opportunity. The train must be taken out of service at the first suitable location without causing delay or cancellation..." (my underlining)

Clause 7.4 of Appendix 8 says:-

"If there are successive failures indicating that the AWS equipment on the traction unit is defective, it must be taken out of service at the first suitable location, without causing delay or cancellation".

Railway Group Standard GO/OT 0013 provides appropriate guidance for the words "take out of service at the first suitable location, without causing delay or cancellation". I refer to clause 6.4 of that Railway Group Standard:-

> "The emphasis must be to provide a replacement traction unit/vehicle or some alternative means as soon as possible. The traction unit/vehicle must be removed from service at the destination of the train, unless replacement can be arranged before that point. Where replacement cannot be arranged at the destination (ie. the end of a branch line or similar) it may be appropriate, when all factors are taken into account, to allow the train to return from the destination to a location where replacement can be arranged".

Clause 6.5 of the same Standards says:-

> "It is not the intention to allow a traction unit/vehicle to continue in service with multiple journeys until arriving at the next stabling point".

We believe that "local guidelines" do not always follow the logic of the guidance in this Railway Group Standard.

I do not accept that there can be any other reasonable interpretation of the above, other than that a train should not commence a journey without the AWS working in the driving cab and additionally that every effort should be made to either repair or replace the defective locomotive or unit or otherwise provide effective AWS, (for example, by turning a double-ended train or attaching an additional unit) should a defect arise during a journey.

In any case use should be restricted to the completion of a single journey that has already commenced. There may be justification for certain exceptions to be put forward such as the case of a failure at the end of a branch line where it would be difficult to arrange alternative provision. In all cases the requirements of health and safety legislation would still apply and suitable additional safeguards should be put in place to ensure safety.

You will, of course, wish to undertake an urgent review of your arrangements with respect to failure and isolation of AWS equipment.

It is the case that the system of railway safety cases ensures that Railway Group Standards are to be regarded as mandatory on the railway network. In addition all railway companies are under an obligation to comply, in particular, with section 3 of the Health and Safety at Work etc. Act 1974, in that an employer is required to:-

> "conduct his undertaking in such a way as to ensure, so far as is reasonably practicable, that persons not in his employment who may be affected thereby are not thereby exposed to risk to their health or safety".

HMRI regard the AWS as an extremely important safety system and we expect all train companies to ensure that it is available for use to the maximum extent possible. Any decision to keep a traction unit in service with AWS (where fitted) defective must be fully justifiable in the context of Railway Group Standard and general legal requirements. In this context I should draw to your attention Section 40 of the above-mentioned 1974 Act which puts the onus on the duty-holder to prove (if challenged) that something was not reasonably practicable, in all the circumstances of any particular case.

You should also note that I am writing to all other TOCs and Railtrack PLC on this matter. I am also writing to work people's representatives in order to satisfy the obligations imposed upon myself under Section 28(8) of the above mentioned 1974 Act.

Finally I should advise you that I will be alerting all HMRI's Field Inspectors to this matter.

Yours sincerely

V P COLEMAN
HM Deputy Chief Inspector of Railways

RAILTRACK
Great Western

CONCLUSION

The accident occurred because train 1A47, 10.32 Swansea to Paddington, passed signal SN254 on the Up Main at Southall at danger and collided with wagons on 6V17 09.58 Allington to Southall, which was making a signalled crossing movement from the Down Relief to Southall Yard at the time. On the evidence considered by the Panel, it believes the immediate cause of the accident was that the driver did not respond to the two preceding cautionary signals and was unable to stop the train at SN254.

The Panel has not been able to establish the reasons for his failure, as he was advised not to give evidence beyond his written statement. However, other evidence shows that the driver stated, immediately after the crash, that he had bent down to put items in a bag and had looked up to see SN254 at danger.

In the absence of evidence from the driver, the Panel has not been able to ascertain whether there were any personal factors contributing to the accident, but noted that Driver Harrison had taken adequate breaks before and during his turn of duty and had not been working long hours.

The Panel notes that Driver Harrison did not have the aid of AWS which had been isolated in the cab of Power Car 47173 before the set started from Paddington on its preceding journey.

The Panel considers that the response to rules and standards regarding isolation of AWS, and the associated communication processes, may have been an underlying contributory factor to the circumstances of the accident.

The Panel also notes that, although 1A47 is designated to operate with ATP in unsupervised service running, ATP was not used.

John Ellis

John Ellis
Chairman of the Inquiry

Alison Forster

Alison Forster
Operations & Safety Manager, GW Trains

Les Wilkinson

Les Wilkinson
Production Manager, Railtrack GW

Tom Birch

Tom Birch
Operations Safety & Standards Manager, EWS

RAILTRACK
Great Western

RECOMMENDATIONS

The Panel have no recommendations to make on track or signalling systems.

1. *Human Factors*

1 1 Railtrack S&SD should review human factors or alternative control measures when Driver support systems are isolated, including the proposed Train Protection Warning System.

2. *Communication*

2.1 GWTC and other operators should review arrangements for the communication of AWS faults and other safety-related issues to ensure that verbal messages are dealt with and recorded.

2.2 GWTC, Train Operators and Railtrack should review the adequacy of training and competence of controllers and supervisors in transmitting, receiving, recording and acting upon safety-related messages.

Railtrack S&SD with members of the Railway Group should consider whether a communication system similar to GM\RT\2250 should be instituted for operational safety matters.

3. *Automatic Warning System (AWS)*

3.1 Railtrack S&SD should review the contents of Appendix 8 to the Rule Book and Railway Group Standard GO/OT0013 in particular to avoid ambiguity and to ensure that the reporting chains for failures and required actions are clarified to reflect fully the responsibilities of Railtrack, as Infrastructure Controller, and Train Operating Companies. The review should incorporate risk assessments of any proposals for change.

Train operators should urgently review their application of the requirements of GO\OT\0013, in particular, in respect of AWS.

Railtrack S&SD to undertake a national review of SPADs in respect of those involving AWS isolations or AWS non-fitted areas to determine any rail industry lessons.

3.4 Railtrack S&SD to audit compliance of TOC's with GO\OT\0013 and Appendix 8 to the Rule Book.

3.5 GWTC and other operators should review their instructions and check procedures to ensure compliance with Appendix 8 to the Rule Book requirements for the provision of the isolating handle seal.

RAILTRACK
Great Western

3.6   GWTC and other train operators should review the nature
        and level of AWS failures to determine whether present testing arrangements
        are appropriate to reduce risk to a level as low as reasonably practicable.

4.   *Regulation Policy*

4.1.   Railtrack S&SD should consider the safety implications of changes of
        substance to regulation policy, train timetabling and increases in numbers of
        trains, and give guidance to Railtrack Line and Train Operators.

5.   *Automatic Train Protection (ATP)*

5.1   All parties involved in the BR-ATP pilot scheme for GW Main Line should
        urgently review the effectiveness of the project to ensure its full conclusion.

6.   *Post incident arrangements*

6.1   As a matter of urgency, Railtrack S&SD, HMRI & BTP should seek to establish
        arrangements for the gathering of evidence, the commissioning of further
        testing and investigation to ensure that all appropriate evidence is preserved,
        gathered and assessed, including that from witnesses, and appropriate results
        made available to the various inquiry processes.

6.2   Railtrack S.&S.D. should consider whether in circumstances requiring the
        appointment of a Rail Incident Commander, GO\RT3434\2 should be
        amended to place on the R.I.C. specific responsibility for agreeing and
        commissioning expert testing arrangements, and for co-ordinating
        arrangements for the recovery and preservation of all appropriate evidence.

6.3   Railtrack Great Western should review its arrangements for the application of
        GO\RT\3434\2 in respect of the appointment of an appropriately senior RIO
        in the event of a major accident, and for the provision of suitable Bronze level
        support and communication.

6.4   Railtrack Director Operations should review the arrangements for post-
        incident liaison to ensure that emergency authorities involve the RIO in all
        Silver meetings.

RAILTRACK
Great Western

7. *Crashworthiness of Mk3 Vehicles*

7.1 The Panel did not take evidence on the crashworthiness of Mk3 vehicles, but recommends that Railtrack S&SD should review this, together with the contributory crash damage implications of lineside structures, particularly OHLE.

46 115·3

RAILTRACK

Follow-up Audit

Southall Formal Inquiry
Recommendations - AWS
Final

November 1999

Page: 3 of 12

1.0 INTRODUCTION

.1 On the 22nd September 1999, the Controller, Safety Management Systems (SMS) initiated a formal follow-up audit of the recommendations made by the internal Southall Formal Inquiry. Train operating companies were requested to respond to a detailed questionnaire to enable Railtrack S&SD to establish the current industry position on the delivery of the inquiry recommendations. A total of 36 companies responded of which 15 were verified through audit.

.2 This summary report provides the findings relating to AWS issues, as of 29 October 1999.

2.0 MANAGEMENT SUMMARY – Train Operating Companies

2.1 Contingency plans for taking trains out of service as a result of defective on-train equipment, as mandated by RGS GO/RT3437, have been developed by 30 of the 36 companies responding to the follow-up audit. At the time of audit 12 of the 30 companies were awaiting formal agreement of their plans with the respective Railtrack Lead Zone. Of the remaining six companies three have provided insufficient detail to assess progress in developing contingency plans. Contingency plans for the remaining three companies are not required as they only operate road rail vehicles within Tiii possessions.

2.2 The recommendation regarding the integrity of AWS isolating handle seals is applicable to 25 of the 36 companies and have been adequately addressed within 22 of these companies. The remaining three companies have not adequately detailed the action taken within their questionnaire response.

2.3 Processes for the review of the nature and level of AWS failures to determine whether present testing arrangements are appropriate were established in 28 of the 36 companies. Three companies had not provided the detail of their processes. Two companies are relatively new operators of on-track machines, and as such have not experienced AWS failures, with the remainder not applicable.

2.4 S&SD is actively monitoring the delivery of agreed contingency plans with Railtrack Line. Further follow-up and, where appropriate, verification audits with train operators we be actioned.

Å

LADBROKE GROVE TRAIN ACCIDENT – OPERATION BRODIE

PROTOCOL FOR INFORMATION SHARING – B.T. POLICE/RAILTRACK

The intention of this document is to set out a protocol that will facilitate the authorised sharing of information with Railtrack, in particular its Safety and Standards Directorate and thus with the Railway Group, in connection with the Ladbroke Grove Train Accident that took place on 5 October 1999.

More specifically, it provides for evidence and technical reports that have been or are obtained by British Transport Police from Messrs WS Atkins, AEA (Technology) and AMEY Rail to be disclosed to Railtrack for the purpose of enabling them to carry out an urgent and continuing internal investigation into the cause or causes of the accident. Such disclosure is subject to:

(a) consultation between British Transport Police and the Crown Prosecution Service;

(b) confirmation to British Transport Police by Her Majesty's Railway Inspectorate;

(c) the disclosure to Railtrack having no significant prejudicial effect on the ongoing police investigation or upon any interviews with persons that may be required to be carried out;

(d) the decision on disclosure will rest with the Assistant Chief Constable (Operations) or other Chief Officer as appropriate.

The standing presumption shall be, that evidence and technical reports (including written 'interim' reports) provided by the above-named organisations to British Transport Police, shall be disclosed promptly to Railtrack for the purpose stated in this document unless any of the conditions set out above prevent this.

If the Officer-in-Charge of this investigation considers that disclosure would have a prejudicial effect as in (c) above he will be required to satisfy the Assistant Chief Constable (Operations) or other Chief Officer, as to the reasons why this presumption of release should not be applied in any particular circumstances.

An overriding principle in this protocol is the recognition of the needs of safety for the travelling public and railway staff and the disclosure of matters permitting immediate learning of safety lessons for both the present and the future.

Where other evidence, reports or information are requested, it will be necessary for a written request to be made to the Assistant Chief Constable (Operations), or in his absence to another Chief Officer as other criteria may need to be taken into account before that information etc., can be released, e.g. consultation with H.M. Coroner. In these cases it will be necessary for reasons for requiring such information to be stated. British Transport Police will use its best endeavours to make or secure a prompt response to such requests.

Reasonable access for inspection of rolling stock or other physical evidence upon which technical reports have been based on reasonable notice will be permissible, with attendance by a representative of British Transport Police and/or HMRI if necessary.

There should be no direct approaches to anyone for the provision of information other than via those designated within this document.

P.W. Nicholas
Assistant Chief Constable
Date: 22 November 1999

R.J. Muttram
Director of Safety & Standards
Date: 23 November 1999

Simon Osborne
Company Secretary & Solicitor
Railtrack PLC
Railtrack House
Euston Square, London NW1

Persons designated:-

For the purposes of this protocol in addition to those persons designated by British Transport Police the designated persons from Railtrack from whom requests for information shall be made or sent to shall be Simon Osborne, Company Secretary & Solicitor, Rod Muttram, Director Safety & Standards and Garth Ratcliffe, Inquiries Officer. Such persons may after close consultation between Mr Muttram and the Assistant Chief Constable or other Chief Officer be designated in writing by either of them.

HN HL

Our ref: RI/51/1/105/1997/7 gc431

19 February 1999

Dear

Southall Rail Accident Inquiry

I set out below a list of the issues arising from the Southall Rail Accident which the inquiry is minded to investigate. It should not be regarded as a definitive statement of the scope of the Inquiry but is designed to provide a framework for the Inquiry's preparation for the public hearings later this year and for the interested parties to make their own preparation. There is inevitably some overlap between issues. A request for documents from all of the interested parties directed to the issues accompanies this letter.

1. The Incident

a) factual evidence of the immediate events preceding the accident with a view to discovering its immediate causes.

b) Background factual evidence touching on the events of the day.

c) Immediate disaster response including the response of the emergency services, rail specialists and recovery teams.

(These issues to cover signalling and train equipment.)

d) Post accident investigation

    i) whether the systems for conducting testing were thorough

    ii) whether testing was in accordance with industry standards

    iii) whether competent staff did the work

    iv) whether recording equipment is sufficient and effective.

2. The Driver (this relates to the HST driver only)

a) Initial and continuation training, including training re: AWS, ATP and fault reporting.
b) Management of standards of driver competence in accordance with Standards and Safety Case.
c) Driver's knowledge of procedures for fault reporting etc.

3. Operating Roles and Responsibilities (these encompass Railtrack and GWTC systems)

a) Driver competence.
b) Driver training.
c) Driver management and monitoring of driver competence.
d) Control responsibilities and management.
e) Train borne fault reporting and management.
f) Running of train without AWS.
g) Rule book.

4. Fleet Management and Maintenance

a) Defect reporting and management.
b) Maintenance and repair management.
c) Quality control and assurance.
d) Train maintenance both routine and 'en route'.

5. Train Protection and Safety Systems

(a) AWS
   i)   Technical description and reliability statistics up to date of accident.
   ii) Rules applicable to operation of trains with faulty AWS.
   iii) Driver's instructions before and after accident, in relation to faulty AWS.
   iv) Isolation reporting and checks on taking over.
   v)   Rules applicable to track equipment faults.
   vi) Compliance with rules regarding faults.

(b) ATP
   i)   Technical description.
   ii)   History of ATP, consideration given to its installation across the railway, reasons for deferring installation.
   iii) At time of accident at Southall at what status was ATP, on trial or operational.
   iv)   Timetable/plan for bringing ATP into use with progress against plan.
   v)   Responsibility for introduction of ATP nationally.
   vi)   Condition of ATP equipment on train and track at the time of the accident.
   vii) Maintenance and repair arrangements for track and train equipment including fault reporting and recording.
   viii) Training of drivers in the use of ATP and allocation to ATP equipped trains and services.

(c) Train Control
   i) TPWS.
   ii) ARS. (Are the principles correct)
   iii) Removal of second driver from cab.
   iv) SPAD prevention measures.
   v) Routing of trains - freight across path of passenger train.

6. Railway Safety

a) Safety cases and industry standards.   }   Applicability to the Railtrack/GWTC
b) Procedures for developing safety cases. }   relationship and to
c) Adequacy of safety cases.   }   Railtrack and their Contractors.
d) Monitoring and auditing of safety case. }
e) Safety management structures including contractual framework.
f) Reports into previous accidents with similarities to the Southall accident and the responses thereto. Have relevant recommendations from the past been acted upon? If not, why not.
g) Communication of safety related information.
h) The use of recording equipment for trains, signalling and radio/telephone.

7. Track and Signalling

a) Description of track and signalling equipment and systems in place (also of recording systems).
b) Condition of track and signalling and its impact on the accident.
c) Actions of signallers affecting the Southall accident.
d) Signalling rules and policy.
e) Maintenance of track and signalling equipment.
f) Safety management re: signal sighting. track layout, signal spacing and the effect of supports and other structures.
g) Impact of Heathrow Express Project.

8. Crashworthiness

a) Ability of carriages to withstand impact.
b) Improvement in internal design to protect passengers in crash. Lessons of previous accidents.
c) Research on crash worthiness.
d) Reasons for severe damage to coach G.
e) Freight wagon design.

9. Post-accident action over safety

a) Steps taken by the railway industry and HM Railway Inspectorate to act upon the apparent causes of the Southall accident.
b) Details of safety measures introduced as a result of the Southall Accident.
c) The delay in the start of the Inquiry.

HSC
Health & Safety Commission
From the Chair
Bill Callaghan

The Rt Hon Lord Cullen PC
Ladbroke Grove Rail Inquiry
Romney House
Marsham Street
London
SW1P 3RA

Professor John Uff QC
Southall Rail Accident Inquiry
New Connaught Rooms
61-65 Great Queen Street
London
WC2

5 November 1999

Dear Professor Uff,

Ladbroke Grove Rail Inquiry
Southall Rail Accident Inquiry

The Health and Safety Commission has considered the inter-relation of these inquiries which were established under section 14(2)(b) of the Health and Safety at Work etc Act 1974.

In his letter of 19 February 1999, Professor Uff set out a list of issues arising from the Southall Rail Accident to which he was minded to direct his inquiry. Following the tragic accident at Ladbroke Grove Junction, which will clearly give rise to further evidence on a number of these issues, Professor Uff informed parties in his letters of 12 and 19 October how he was minded to proceed. In particular he stated that he did not propose to deal with certain of the matters which he had listed earlier.

The Commission supports the determination expressed in Professor Uff's letter of 19 October that the Southall Inquiry should not be held up by the investigation into the accident at Ladbroke Grove Junction. At the same time, the Commission is anxious that all the issues which were originally identified by Professor Uff should be properly and comprehensively considered, and that victims of the Southall accident should have the opportunity to be heard in an inquiry into them.

The Commission therefore supports the view taken by Professor Uff, as set out in his letters of 12 and 19 October 1999, that the Southall Rail Accident Inquiry should not deal with the subjects set out in the letter of 19 February which are detailed below. However, it considers that in view of the interest of Southall victims in these subjects, they should be the subject of a joint inquiry chaired by both of you. The Commission is therefore, with the consent of the Deputy Prime Minister, appointing you jointly for this purpose under Section 14(2)(b) of the 1974 Act.

Rose Court, 2 Southwark Bridge, London SE1 9HS
Direct Line: 0207 717 6610 Fax: 0207 717 6644
e-mail: chairmans.office.hsc@hse.gov.uk

Reducing risks - protecting people

The Commission expects that you will each deal separately with whatever you consider it appropriate to investigate within each of your existing terms of reference, subject to the exception in each case of matters which you are to deal with jointly. You will sit together to consider the following subjects, namely

    (i)   Train Protection and Warning Systems
    (ii) the future application of Automatic Train Protection systems
    (iii) SPAD prevention measures

taking account in particular of

    the Southall rail accident on 19 September 1997;
    the rail accident at Ladbroke Grove Junction on 5 October 1999;
    the technical assessment for the Deputy Prime Minister of rail safety systems by Sir David Davies

with a view to making general recommendations in regard thereto.

Having regard to the wide ranging remit of Lord Cullen, the Commission considers it appropriate that wider matters within issue 6 of Professor Uff's letter of 19 February 1999 to the Southall Parties should be dealt with by Lord Cullen; and that the Southall Inquiry should consider issue 6 matters only in the direct context of the Southall accident.

No doubt Professor Uff will draw to the attention of Lord Cullen any matters arising in Professor Uff's own inquiry which would be more appropriately taken forward by Lord Cullen.

Yours sincerely

Bill Callaghan
Chair
Agreed by the Chair and signed in his absence
Sarah Gawley
Acting Commission Secretary

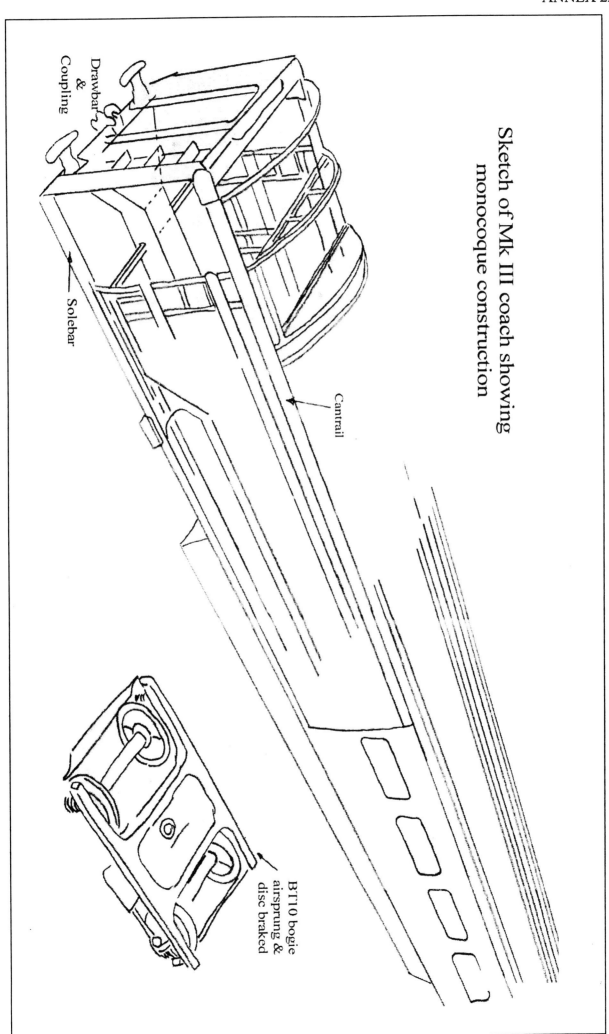

Sketch of Mk III coach showing monocoque construction

Drawbar & Coupling

Solebar

Cantrail

BT10 bogie airsprung & disc braked

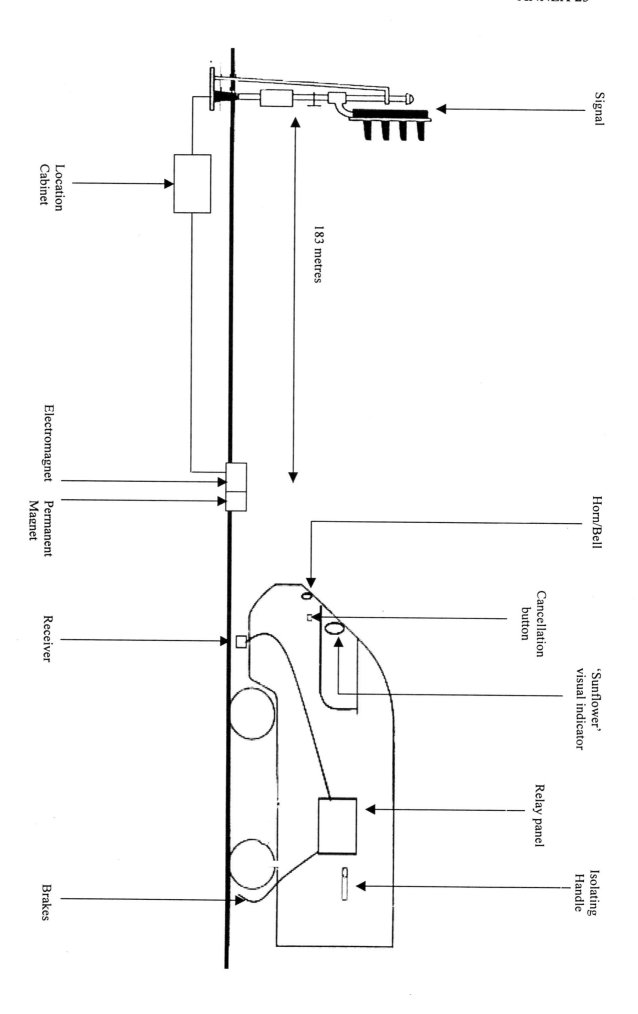

Signal

Location
Cabinet

183 metres

Electromagnet

Permanent
Magnet

Receiver

Brakes

Horn/Bell

Cancellation
button

'Sunflower'
visual indicator

Relay panel

Isolating
Handle

ANALYSIS OF GWT AWS IN SERVICE ISOLATIONS OVER THE PERIOD 01/01/97 TO 19/09/97 BY INDIVIDUAL EQUIPMENT

EQUIPMENT	NUMBER OF FAULTS
RECEIVER	24
RELAY PANEL	04
WIRING	5
CONVERTER	04
RESET BUTTON	01
NO FAULT FOUND	45
TOTAL	83

DIAGRAM OF ATP

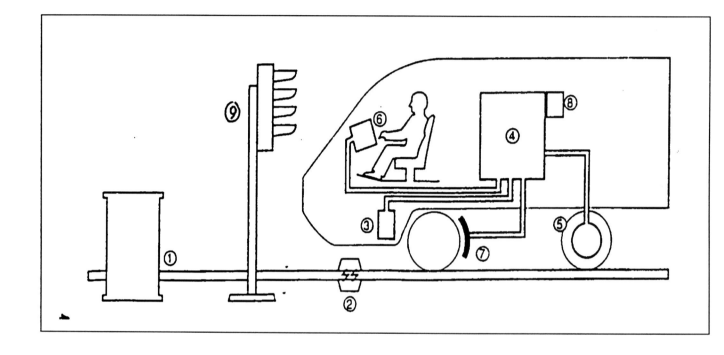

1. Lineside equipment supplies information on speed limits, gradients and the signal(9) aspect to:-
2. A track transmitter which transmits data telegrams to:-
3. An antenna on the train from which they are passed to:-
4. An onboard computer. This has details of train length, weight, formation and braking characteristics entered by the drivers at the start of the journey along with his identification (6).
5. The tachometer, which provides train speed and distance travelled to the computer, which has triplicated channels. The computer calculates a speed distance curve for the train.
6. The terminal and display showing safe speed and signal aspect. If the driver fails to respond correctly to the information displayed in the cab, the computer causes:-
7. A brake application.
8. A data recorder, which records all the relevant information.
9. Signal.

British Railways Board
Sir Bob Reid
Chairman

31st March, 1994

The Rt. Hon. John MacGregor, O.B.E., M.P.
Secretary of State for Transport,
2 Marsham Street,
London, SW1P 3EB.

I have pleasure in enclosing the Report on Automatic Train Protection (ATP). There has been a comprehensive programme of work supporting this report and there are a number of documents which your officials may wish to call on when reviewing the report with my staff. Our co-operation in this regard is assured.

You will know that the Board committed itself to evaluating ATP as long ago as November 1988. Following the Purley and Belgrove accidents, Sir Anthony Hidden, in his Clapham Report, urged the Board to develop the system and install it across the network with the minimum of delay. He also recommended the Board take steps to improve its methods of appraising safety expenditure and integrate them into its business appraisal processes.

The Report now presented to you represents the outcome of the work. It confirms the successful development of two ATP systems which are now in full operation on two separate routes and which have proved technically fit for B.R. purpose. Designing, developing and implementing these systems over 450 miles of track and in 140 traction units has taken much of the five years since the original decision was taken to evaluate automatic train protection.

The Report appraises the costs and benefits of a comprehensive installation. It deals with a range of issues concerning appraisal methodology, installation options and alternative protection measures. It also describes the evolution of the processes by which safety expenditure is now evaluated within British Rail. The current risk assessment approach towards safety expenditure and safety benefits from operational enhancements fully meet, I believe, Hidden's concerns on appraisal of expenditure. Safety assessment is now an integral part of investment appraisal.

Cont'd.....

-3-

The Board believes this Report tackles issues which have serious implications. With the changes in the industry about to be implemented, the future of ATP will not be for British Rail alone. But if responsibility was entirely with the Board it would adopt the following specification programme:

1. Completion of the Chiltern Line pilot installation to cover normal service operation.

2. Completion of the Great Western London-Bristol route and HST fleet pilot for normal service operation including, in due course, the Heathrow Express new link and consideration of extension of ATP to other fleets using the route, and extension of track coverage through the Severn Tunnel.

   (Extensions to the pilot subject to cost/benefit appraisal, and on the basis:

   > extension beyond Bristol through the Severn tunnel to be examined in the light of the HMRI Report on the 1991 collision;

   > extension to other fleets, because without this the safety benefits will not be fully realised.)

3. Adoption of either ATP or Automatic Train Control (ATC) as standard for new high speed lines - including Channel Tunnel rail link - in line with European practice.

4. Inclusion of ATP/ATC in the study of the case for renewal of the West Coast Main Line.

   (The commitment is to study only, and fitment would take place only if benefits exceeded costs.)

5. Inclusion of provision for ATP in the assessment of all new rolling stock, signalling and related investment schemes.

   (There are useful economies when ATP is part of resignalling schemes, which close study might increase from the 30% level currently visible. As with 4. the commitment is to study only; fitment would be subject to benefits exceeding costs.)

6. Investigation of the scope for significant improvement in the cost/benefit relation of ATP through development of both the technology and its selective application.

Cont'd.

-4-

(Particularly in mind here is (a) the real scope for
cost reduction through better development of the
technology and (b) the question whether ATP fitment
to a relatively small number of vulnerable locations
would offer significant improvement in the
cost/benefit relation.)

7. Work on reducing SPADs and overspeeding errors
    through other technical and non technical processes.

    (The technical possibilities in mind here are the
    investigation of SPAD mitigation devices. The
    non-technical ones are the driver supervision,
    selection, training and motivation programmes already
    underway, plus actions such as the Alcohol and Drugs
    Policy.)

    In addition to these specific action points, the
Board will now, with your support and with Railtrack and
the HSE, sponsor and participate in a seminar discussing
risk assessment and investment decision making in the
area of safety expenditure. Following that the British
Rail and Railtrack Boards will meet to review what action
should be taken in the light of that seminar.

    Should your or your officials require any further
information or interpretation of the Report, please do
not hesitate to contact me. Meantime, I shall look
forward to having your reaction to this important piece
of work.

Yours sincerely,

BOB REID

Copy to:
  R. Horton, Esq.
  D. Rayner, Esq.

HSC
Health & Safety Commission
From the Chairman
Frank J Davies CBE OStJ

The Rt Hon Brian Mawhinney
Secretary of State for Transport
Department of Transport,
2, Marsham Street
London SW1P 3EB

23 December 19

Dear Secretary of State,

AUTOMATIC TRAIN PROTECTION

John MacGregor wrote to me last May requesting the Commission's advice, by the Autumn, on the report by British Rail (BR) on Automatic Train Protection (ATP) and on the issue of the values to be placed on a statistical life for safety investment purposes. I am pleased to respond.

In its consideration of the report, the Commission had very much in mind the need to introduce systems to prevent accidents from signals passed at danger, overspeeding or buffer stop collisions. These situations have the potential to cause catastrophic accidents. The recommendations of the Hidden Inquiry recognised this need. It is now five years since the report of the Hidden Inquiry was published and the Commission is concerned that action is seen to be taken on its recommendations.

We are aware that, concurrently with our consideration of the BR report, the Railway Inspectorate (RI) have been engaged in technical discussions with Railtrack (who, as national infrastructure controller, now has the prime responsibility for deciding on action to improve the safety of track and signalling). These discussions have not so far produced any firm indication from Railtrack of their intentions as regards reducing or preventing the incidence of signals passed at danger, overspeeding and buffer stop collisions.

RI for their part have been independently considering what criteria they might apply to identifying parts of the network where measures to prevent these accidents are especially desirable and could be expected to yield value for money. We have asked HSE to report back by June 1995, on the progress that has been made in reaching agreement with Railtrack on such criteria, with an expectation of receiving a proposed strategy by that time.

Turning to the BR report, we are impressed by its openness and transparency, particularly the full statement of the data used; the clarity of the exposition, and the recognition of the important uncertainties. These have made it easier for us to assess the validity of the methodology used by BR and the

robustness of the conclusions. We note that the report relates
to a specific system of ATP ie that piloted on the Chiltern and
Great Western Lines. The conclusions reached in the report
therefore apply only to that specific system and its associated
costs. They do not necessarily apply to the generic concept of
automatic train protection by technological means to complement
the vigilance of the driver. Our views that follow must be seen
in that light.

HSE experts have examined the report and believe that BR's
approach is basically sound. However, they have questioned some
of the assumptions made and would have carried out some of the
cost calculations in a different way. Experts from HSE, British
Rail (BR), and Railtrack have met to discuss and resolve
technical issues. The main outcomes are set out in the Annex.
As you will see, there are no substantial differences of view on
the technical issues raised by the report. However, the issue of
alternatives to the piloted ATP systems, to which we have
referred above, remains unresolved.

HSE has made it clear in those discussions that any conclusions
based on the assessment of the costs and benefits presented in
the report are without prejudice to the Commission's views on the
need to introduce some system or systems for preventing the kind
of accidents that ATP are designed to avert. It is, in our view,
a case of horses for courses and decisions should be made on a
judgement of whether ATP as piloted or some variant, or
alternative measures are, in given situations, reasonably
practicable. Sir Bob Reid's letter of 31 March 1994 to John
MacGregor made clear that if responsibility lay entirely with the
British Railways Board ATP or Automatic Train Control would be
adopted as standard on new high speed lines including the Channel
Tunnel rail link and will be given full consideration when
Railtrack undertakes major resignalling works. The Commission
regard this as the minimum response to the need and expect
Railtrack to carry forward that undertaking by the British
Railways Board.

The judgement on what is reasonably practicable can take as its
starting point the philosophical framework (known as TOR)
published by HSE for deciding which risks are unacceptable,
tolerable and broadly acceptable. This has gained considerable
acceptance within industry (including the railway industry) and
has helped to provide the basis for justifying decisions whereby
risks are judged to be worth the benefits.

The framework involves acceptance of an upper limit above which
particular risk is regarded as unacceptable to HSE as a
regulator. This upper limit is taken to be a chance of death of
1 in 1,000 per annum for workers and 1 in 10,000 per annum for
members of the public.

Below the upper limit is a region where a balance has to be
struck between the costs and demonstrated benefits of any

The Tolerability of Risk from Nuclear Power Stations. HMSO
1992. ISBN 0 11 886368 1.

increment to the existing level of safety, ie, of risk reduction.
There must of course be confidence that a risk is actually being
controlled at the relevant level, known as ALARP (as low as
reasonably practicable). The lowest point at which it would be
considered sensible to address any risk would be where the chance
of death was about one in a million per year.

The BR target of 1 in 100,000 per year for the overall risk of
death to regular commuters, one of the most exposed group of
passengers, is already being achieved. The global application of
ATP would therefore address degrees of risk which are in the
lower portion of the "ALARP" region. On the principles which HSE
usually applies, this has two implications:-

(a)   the value of life which has to be assumed in any
        balancing of cost and risk would not be enhanced by the
        factor of "gross disproportion" which is applied to
        risks further up the tolerability scale, or where the
        chance is particularly hard to estimate.

(b)   it becomes reasonable to take into account the
        availability and value for money of alternative ways of
        making risk reducing investments.

An overall judgement as to the cost effectiveness of
comprehensive application of any particular safety improvement
will often mask situations where investment at particular
locations may be cost effective while full application is not.
In the case of ATP cost effectiveness at a particular location
will depend on such factors as the frequency of services, the
complexity of the system, and differing costs for more limited
application.

Taking all these factors into account, HSE have told us that the
introduction of ATP as piloted on a network-wide basis could not
be regarded as reasonably practicable by the criteria they
usually apply, and that there are alternative safety investments
which would be likely to yield greater effectiveness in terms of
lives saved, and better value for money. We endorse these
judgements. However it would in our view be unreasonable to rule
out the possibility that particular applications of ATP or indeed
other automatic devices or other measures giving protection
against ATP preventable accidents (ATPPAs) on parts of the
network might yield good value in terms of reduced loss of life.
We have taken into account, moreover, that there is a public
expectation that automatic means of protection will be introduced
at least on a partial basis, following the information given by
British Rail to the Hidden Inquiry and the latter's
recommendations five years ago and in view of developments on
some foreign railways. The European Commission's intention to
introduce a directive on the interoperability of the high speed
network in Europe, and the indications that the need to reduce
accidents from signals passed at danger will figure in their
calculations is also a relevant factor.

The report refers to the prospects offered by alternative more
advanced technology. The timescale for its possible introduction

is very uncertain and could be long especially bearing in mind
the need to test and demonstrate any new system. At the same
time, the emergence of modified and possibly cheaper versions of
ATP than those so far tested by British Rail could lead to
favourable outcomes in value for money terms, and should be
pursued on an urgent basis.

Although Mr MacGregor invited us to do so, we would prefer not to
pronounce on the vexed question of the value of life to be
applied in such calculations. HSE have suggested that where
catastrophic risk is concerned, the value cannot reasonably be
less than three times the estimate which we understand your
Department applies to situations of risk to individuals, and this
conclusion was endorsed by Sir John Cullen in a letter to Mr
MacGregor dated 9 November 1992. The BR report mentions for such
applications a value of £3.5 million as a possibility. What does
seem clear is that in any catastrophic accident, the damage in
terms of public confidence, additional costs, and harms and risks
to people quite aside from the number of deaths is substantially
greater than damage connected with the generality of risks to
individuals. While there may be two views about the rightness of
factoring added costs to reflect this extra damage into the
"value for life", and we would prefer not to enter into this
essentially technical argument, it seems obvious that they need
to be taken into account in some way; and it is clear to us also
that whatever balance is struck, it needs to be firmly on the
side of safety where doubt arises.

In this respect, chapters 8 and 9 of the report seem relevant.
These place the risks of ATP preventable accidents in context
with other risks and examine the effects that investing in ATP
would have on overall safety on the railways if its introduction
were to displace other safety investments. In the time
available, it has not been possible for HSE to evaluate the
conclusions reached in these chapters. The Executive has,
however, asked HMRI to take these factors into account, as well
as the balance of costs and risks - in relation particularly to
new investments - when they explore with Railtrack the possible
options available for tackling ATP preventable accidents and
possible criteria for identifying parts of the network where
measures to prevent such accidents could yield value for money.

As I said at the outset, we have asked for a report on the
outcome of these discussions by June 1995. The report from BR
has acted most usefully as a catalyst. We now need to move
towards achieving a solution to what we regard as an issue of
serious concern.

Yours sincerely

Frank J Davies CBE OStJ
Chairman

THE DEPARTMENT OF TRANSPORT

PRESS NOTICE NO: 98

DATE: 30 March 1995

EXHIBIT No. 451   A

NOT FOR PUBLICATION, BROADCAST OR
USE ON CLUB TAPES BEFORE:

30 MAR 1995 15-30

This document is issued in advance on the
strict understanding that no approach is
made to any organisation or person about
its contents before the time of publication.

MAWHINNEY ENDORSES HSC VIEW ON FUTURE OF AUTOMATIC TRAIN PROTECTION

Dr Brian Mawhinney, the Secretary of State for Transport, today endorsed the view of the Health and Safety Commission (HSC) that automatic train protection (ATP) measures may be justified on parts of the rail network.

However, he said that he also agreed with the advice of British Rail and Railtrack, endorsed by the HSC, that the fitment of ATP throughout the network could not be justified because the costs far outweigh the benefits. Replying to a Parliamentary Question from Bob Dunn MP (Dartford), Dr Mawhinney said:

"Serious railway accidents are relatively rare and there has been a significant improvement in railway safety in recent years. Accidents involving signals passed at danger (SPADs), overspeeding and buffer stop collisions, which ATP would prevent, are infrequent and account for about 3% of fatalities and injuries (excluding trespassers and suicides). But there is no room for complacency about the need to pursue cost effective measures to reduce the risk of accidents to the lowest reasonably practicable level.

"On the basis of advice I have received from the HSC, I have concluded that applications of ATP, other automatic devices or measures giving protection against ATP-preventable accidents may be justified on parts of the network.

"British Rail and Railtrack have advised me that network-wide fitment of ATP as piloted is not justifiable because the costs far outweigh the benefits. The HSC has endorsed this view and, furthermore, considers that there are alternative safety investments which would be likely to yield greater effectiveness in terms of lives saved, and better value for money."

Dr Mawhinney stressed that British Rail and Railtrack remain committed to a co-ordinated programme to reduce the risks associated with signals passed at danger, overspeeding and buffer stop collisions. He explained that Railtrack is giving high priority to the development of appropriate techniques for analysing the costs and benefits of all safety projects addressing these risks and their application at individual locations and confirmed that he has asked the HSC for an overall progress report in July.

In addition he said that the HSC has advised that ATP or Automatic Train Control (ATC) should be adopted as standard on new high speed lines including the Channel Tunnel Rail Link and that full consideration should be given to installing ATP within future major resignalling works, such as modernisation of the West Coast Main Line.

HOUSE OF COMMONS

( ) :

To ask the Secretary of State for Transport, what advice he has received from the Health and Safety Commission (HSC) and Railtrack on train protection strategy, and if he will make a statement.

SIR GEORGE YOUNG

The Health and Safety Commission has considered Railtrack's strategy for reducing the incidence of signals passed at danger, buffer stop collisions and overspeeding. Historically, such risks have accounted for less than one third of all casualties in collisions and derailments, and about 3% of total casualties on the railway, excluding trespassers and suicides.

The Health and Safety Executive (HSE) is pursuing, as a matter of priority, discussions with Railtrack, British Rail, and others as required, about action to develop and implement the wide range of measures to which they are committed in the train protection strategy. Objectives for reducing the risks in question will again be included in the annual Railway Group Safety Plan.

Railtrack and BR are pursuing five initiatives to reduce the incidence of signals passed at danger.

Firstly, nine tenders were received by Railtrack for the development and pilot installation of a new Train Protection and Warning System (TPWS), and tender evaluation is proceeding to plan. This system is potentially capable of reducing risks arising from signals passed at danger, overspeeding and buffer stop collisions. TPWS would enhance the existing Automatic Warning System (AWS) by adding functions which would, if necessary, apply the brakes automatically on the approach to, or at, certain signals, and which could not be overridden by the driver. Trials of TPWS will take place in 1996, and the aim is to start wider installation in 1997. The pilot trials and initial operational use will demonstrate the extent to which it is practicable to install TPWS.

Secondly, the current trial of a Driver Reminder Appliance, to reduce the risk of starting against a red signal, is expected to be completed by the end of this year. Subject to the outcome of the trial, the intention is to assess the fitting of the device to all traction units operating on Railtrack's infrastructure, with a target for complete installation of the end of 1997.

Thirdly, the existing Automatic Train Protection installations on the Great Western and Chiltern Lines should be brought into full service next year. Meanwhile, those passenger trains with ATP fitted are being run with a supervisor in support of the driver.

Fourthly, measures to improve braking performance and driver and systems performance continue. The pilot trials of an emergency

.anding device to improve rail adhesion are encouraging.

Finally, and in the longer term, the reduction of risk arising
from signals passed at danger and overspeeding is expected to
come from a new primary control system consisting of radio-based
cab signalling. Railtrack has invited tenders for a development
contract for such a system as part of the project to modernise
the West Coast Main Line.

Copies of the full advice from the HSC and Railtrack, and my
response, have been placed in the Library of the House.

Printed and published by the Health and Safety Executive
C40   2/00